THE COLOURED COUNTIES

THE COLOURED COUNTIES
Poems of Place in England and Wales

Selected and with an introduction by

John Arlott

'We have lived this landscape.'
EDMUND BLUNDEN

'Here of a Sunday morning
My love and I would lie,
And see the coloured counties,
And hear the larks so high
About us in the sky'
A. E. HOUSMAN
(from Bredon Hill)

J M Dent & Sons Ltd
London

First published in Great Britain 1988

Introduction and Selection © John Arlott 1943, 1988
All rights reserved. No part of this publication may be reproduced,
stored in a retrieval system, or transmitted in any form or by any
means, electronic, mechanical, photocopying, recording or otherwise,
without prior permission of J M Dent & Sons Ltd.

Photoset by Deltatype Ltd, Ellesmere Port
Printed and made in Great Britain by
Butler & Tanner Ltd, Frome and London
for J M Dent & Sons Ltd
91, Clapham High Street, London SW4 7TA

British Library Cataloguing in Publication Data

The Coloured Counties: poems of place in England and Wales.
1. Poetry in English. Special subjects.
England. Anthologies
I. Arlott, John, *1914–*
821'.008'03242

ISBN 0-460-07005-3

Contents

To the memory of my kindly friend and mentor,
GEORGE ROSTREVOR HAMILTON

ORIGINAL PREFACE TO *LANDMARKS*

(1943)

The aim of this anthology is to present a picture of England and Wales—in the particular town, village, landscape—seen through the eyes of many writers of English verse. Our general rule has been to confine ourselves to verse which is truly topographical, that is to say, which is strictly concerned with the spirit or appearance of a particular place or district.

This rule has limited our scope in various ways, of which two may be mentioned at once. First, it has meant the exclusion of scenes which the poet has not identified by place-names or otherwise. Often the scene, though it may be very English, is yet essentially ideal, no more related to one definite place than the characters of a novelist are related to the several men and women of his acquaintance. Often again, although the poet may have a single place in his mind's eye, he avoids revealing its whereabouts as carefully as the nature-lover who will not betray his favourite bit of country. In this matter we have thought it right to respect the reticence of the poet; moreover, if we were to yield to the temptation of following up any clues he may give, we should not seldom be led to wrong, or at least doubtful, attributions. And so—clue or no clue—we have passed by *L'Allegro* and *Il Penseroso*, and have had to be content with their distant reflection in, for example, the charm, mild but real, of Dyer's *Grongar Hill*. We have passed by Collins' *Ode to Evening*, and we have taken nothing from the lovely nature-verse of Robert Bridges, who vowed that he would keep secret his 'bower beside the silver Thames'.

Secondly, we have omitted verse in which natural scene is so dominated by human mood or interest that the attention of the reader, instead of being directed—as it constantly is in Wordsworth—to a landscape enhanced or transfigured, is perforce diverted to the human figure in the foreground or to the passionate mind of the poet himself. The presence of place-name is not enough, even when combined with exquisite appreciation of country. Thus in Housman there is so much of the 'lad' to 'Shropshire' that few of his poems pass our test; while in Thomas Hardy the faithfully observed pictures of Wessex are so deeply withdrawn into the brooding on human affairs and chances that, in all his work, it is difficult to find poems in which the spirit of place rises to independence or sufficiently prevails.

Along with the spirit of place goes the spirit of time. We may see it at work changing the bias of the poet from curiosity about Nature and her marvels to a mood of cultured appraisement; or, at a later stage, from enthusiasm about building development to the note of cynicism or distaste. In its more subtle movement it is easier to feel than to define, for it commonly acts below the surface, like a changing undercurrent in the flow of tradition.

The first important figure we meet is that of Drayton, who in his vast *Polyolbion* undertakes to cover single-handed the same map as our other contributors. He has a deep affection for his native soil, and an eye devoted to its rich and changing contours. But like any one of his river-nymphs, Severn or Trent, he is prone to wander in Classical fancy-dress through mazes of distracting myth, matter of fact, history and allegory. It is an astonishing pageant, tedious enough in its slow course, yet with a wealth of observation now and again catching the gleam of poetry. The influence of the Latin Classics, here so evident, was to persist through centuries in varying form and degree, and was long to encourage fancies and conceits which veil or distort the English scene. Generally speaking, the seventeenth-century writers, for all their curious pursuit of ideas, have a good perception of the actual, as in Marvell's gem-like picture of the woodpecker. Usually, however, it is the lesser verse-writers who are content to fix their attention on details of the town and countryside. Their talent is well illustrated by a number of journey-poems, then much in vogue, from which we have taken a few extracts. If Horace was their model, he did not prevent them from displaying, in their unpolished imitations, a very English zest, humour and objective interest.

A new turn was given to topographical verse by Sir John Denham, whose once-famous *Cooper's Hill*, though written so early as 1642, had a far reaching effect on eighteenth-century modes. Here we may quote Dr Johnson on Denham:—

'He seems to have been, at least among us, the author of a species of composition that may be denominated *local poetry*, of which the fundamental subject is some particular landscape, to be poetically described, with the addition of such embellishments as may be supplied by historical retrospection or incidental mediation.'[1]

It will be evident that 'topographical verse', as we understand it, is narrower than 'local poetry', for we have sought to cut out all

[1] *Lives of the English Poets.*

'embellishments', except where intimately related to the presiding atmosphere of place. It often happens that witty or moral reflection, together, it may be, with digression into narrative, imposes its character on a whole poem, so that the topographical interest is in fact slight and subordinate. This is so with *Cooper's Hill* itself, which does not appear in our collection, despite its influence on many compositions with a better topographical claim.

Other strong influences, direct or indirect, were those of Milton, already noted; of Thomson who, except for the prospect from Hagley, does not profess to paint any particular scene; of Pope, who cares little for the country, enforcing rather the study of man; and, later, of Gray the romantic. The 'local poetry' in spate during the eighteenth century has often a large element of local landscape, followed sooner or later by that 'incidental meditation' on the nobler subject of man which was thought necessary to dignify the verse. As one writer put it:

> 'Here let description cease; but still prolong
> Thy task, O Muse, and moralize the song.'[1]

The poets have as a rule, little appreciation of the actual or the distinctive; their scenery with its pleasing prospects, rustic cots and gentlemen's seats, is generalized and can be exceedingly wearisome. But it can also exercise a civilized charm like that of elegant tapestry, while occasionally even so dull a poem as Jago's *Edge-hill* can provide entertainment which was not intended. We do not suggest that all the poets of landscape conformed. To name no others, Cowper with his delicate power of delineation and Crabbe with his stark veracity stand out as individuals.

By the latter poet we are carried over into the nineteenth century, with its greater richness and diversity. It is fortunate in two modest poets, John Clare and William Barnes, who differ as widely as East Anglia from Dorset, yet are alike in pure genius for the country. The major poets, with the one towering exception of Wordsworth, contribute little to topographical verse, but their influence, itself drawing new life from the fountain-head of Greece, is beyond all calculation. That of Keats is particularly felt in the great elegies of Matthew Arnold, *The Scholar-Gipsy* and *Thyrsis*, where Classical feeling is transfused into an English landscape sensitively loved. As for Wordsworth, who has so immortalized the Lake District, he may truly be said, working with the spirit of time, to have put man on new terms with Nature. Instead of the urbane condescension, typical (though not universal) in the eighteenth century, there enters a new sympathy and reverence. The poet is no longer

[1] *Weekly Magazine; or, Edinburgh Amusement*, III, 370 (1769).

constrained to elevate his descriptions by tacking on to them a human theme. In the measure that he feels with the spirit as well as the senses, he passes from the natural to the human by unforced transition, without any jolt or change of gear.

It would be untrue, however, even in the briefest summary, to ignore the forces that made for lower vitality. If man's vision of the universe was enlarged, so also, with the progress of science, was the area of his self-esteem. If his language was enriched, so also, under pressure of the claim to noble utterance, did it grow more conscious and ceremonial. In the result much dry, solemn, portentous verse was written, and the academic landscape can rival that of any other period for dullness.

At the end of the century the flow of topographical verse continued steadily, John Davidson and Lionel Johnson both producing work of distinction, and the latter keeping alive the Classical tradition which had already begun to wane. In the age which is now in the making, man's self-esteem has been shattered: the loss of that doubtful asset was needed for his health, but much else has gone with it. The poet has weakened both in his attachment to the past and in his sense of great values. He has become shy of claiming a high vocation, and often speaks with the accent of one who is ready to abdicate his honours. But while he has lost in the apprehension of relative value as between one kind of poetry and another, at least he has gained in the recognition that every kind is to be valued for itself. He has got rid of pretentiousness, not altogether, but in one of its forms. For example, he does not scorn 'mere' nature-poetry or 'mere' topography, but is ready to subdue himself to the landscape seen and felt, rightly judging that it is worth while. And so the time has been rich in both these kinds. Some of the best poets have been chary of attaching their work to any particular place; yet never before perhaps have so many short and purely topographical poems been written, nor, in proportion to the inevitable dead matter, so many with a keen eye for the object and a happy precision of phrase. It is significant that in our selections from the work of the last forty or fifty years the ratio of complete poems to passages from poems is far higher than in any other period.[1] As indicating the diversity of achievement, we may instance two poets so original and different as Mr Andrew Young and Mr John Betjeman. Mr Young writes with great economy, matching a crystal-clear perception with an exact felicity of word and image. Mr Betjeman's avowed aim is topographical; with an insight which often strikes one as clever or impish, he yet has real feeling, and excels in conveying a local atmosphere. This gift, essential as it is to the ideal topographical poem, is far from common. The Genius Loci is easily scared, whether by a voice overloud in praise, or by thoughts which would burden him with an alien humanity.

It will be obvious to the reader that in all periods we have included verse of very different quality. Beyond adding a reminder of our topographical aim, we cannot indicate in detail the varied considerations which have determined our choice. Some parts of England and Wales had been favoured by poetry more than others, and this fact has, we think, more to do with the local distribution of the verse than our own idiosyncrasies: the 'landmarks' are, in the first instance, those made by the poets. In any case we do not propose a county championship. While some counties are more generously treated than others, none, in England or Wales, is entirely unrepresented; as regards Wales, it must be remembered that there is a long and fine tradition, still alive to-day, of native verse, which, being in Welsh, is outside our scope. Starting with London, we have gone round the whole country more or less clockwise, ending up with the Midlands. Our hope has been to get together a company from which may emerge a fairly representative picture of the country as a whole, a levy

Collected choicely, from each county some.[2]

We dedicate the result, if we may, to all whose affection for that country has been quickened by the experience of the past years.

G.R.H.
J.A.

1943

[1] Complete poems are subscribed only by the author's name; passages from poems both by the author's name and by the title of the poem from which the extract is taken.
[2] 2*Henry VI*, iii, 1.

PREFACE TO THE COLOURED COUNTIES

When the original *Landmarks* edited with George Rostrevor Hamilton, appeared in 1943 it was a considerable experience for me. For, though it is an ordinary enough matter to edit a book, it is different when it is a first book. This new edition, retitled *The Coloured Counties*, is therefore dedicated to Sir George Rostrevor Hamilton, in still deeply felt gratitude for his kindness in befriending, guiding and helping a young writer who was much out of his depth in the world of writing and publishing. Sir George was generous, too, to push the young man into writing verse: and to correct that work for its errors of scansion without seeming in any way condescending.

For the junior member of the collaboration, it was a matter of raking happily, almost headily, through all those solid works of verse to be found on the shelves of Southampton University—from whose staff members, also, came immense generosity. The reviews that *Landmarks* received provided a considerable encouragement and to turn back to it now is to relive many literary excitements. That search, too, often swung into separate reading and enjoyment, which proved an education in itself.

The fresh searching for *The Coloured Counties* compels a realization of the extent to which topographical verse has changed over the last forty or so years. Then there was, of course, the two-volume collection, *Poems of Place*, edited by Longfellow and published in 1877; and importantly, too, the critical work *Topographical Poetry in XCIII-century England*, by the American Robert Arnold Aubin. On the whole, though, the subject had received remarkably little attention until John Betjeman became the voice of topography in Britain. A year after *Landmarks* was published, he and Geoffrey Taylor produced their *English, Scottish and Welsh Landscape*—an anthology in the 'New Excursions into English Poetry' series, edited by W. J. Turner and Sheila Shannon—with lithographs by John Piper. Betjeman and Taylor were already engaged on that collection before *Landmarks* was published. Since his days on *The Architectural Review*, John Betjeman had himself written sensitive prose on topography as well as architecture. It was he who set the fashion for topographical poetry in Britain, often with a dash of humour which he consciously introduced to remove any suggestion of pomposity.

Anyone who doubts John Betjeman's influence in this direction should turn to his personal collections of poetry from his earliest, *Mount Zion*, published in 1931, through to *Continual Dew, Old Lights for New Chancels, New Bats in Old Belfries, High and Low, Nip in the Air* and *Uncollected Poems* : while it is implicit in virtually all his prose volumes and in the autobiographical poem *Summoned by Bells*. There the reader will find the influence that has played a marked part in the general poetic scene in Britain since—but unconnected with—the first publication of *Landmarks*. It has been the wit, and even the irony in Betjeman's work, linked to immense topographical perception, that has united many different poets in a precise and essentially clear-sighted approach to this form of verse.

There are, of course, many additions in *The Coloured Counties*— notably the anonymous introductory 'Properties of the Shires of England' (a most happy discovery of Geoffrey Grigson), items by Gerard Manley Hopkins, Coventry Patmore, and previously overlooked pieces by S. T. Coleridge, Thomas Hardy, Lionel Johnson, Richard le Gallienne, Alfred Tennyson, John Clare, William Wordsworth, John Keats, and many others, notably Dylan Thomas. Most of the fresh material here, however, has been written in the intervening years and it is extremely interesting to notice the varying influences of John Betjeman and his topographical interests on these recent poets.

It has also been helpful to look through *The Faber Book of Poems and Places* edited by Geoffrey Grigson, and the District Series published by Messrs Secker and Warburg. Above all, it has been a delight to return after so many years to a collection of verse, the attitude to which has been changed by one's own change of life as well as by access to new material. *Landmarks* came about, in a way, as an escape—from police duty in the hazards of war—to books. *The Coloured Counties*, landmarks revisited one might say, has gathered together many poets who were released from the constraints of that war to savour cherished places with a blend of triumph and nostalgia. From Drayton's *Polyolbion*, and even earlier, down to this new collection, our real subject is the rich and varied, urban and rural, rustic and sophisticated, country of the many, and chequered, counties of England and Wales. It remains eternally fresh and enchanting.

JOHN ARLOTT, 1988

A Prologue

The Properties of the Shires of England

The properte of every shire
I shall you tell, and ye will hear.
  Herefordshire shield and spear:
  Worsetshire wring pear.
  Gloucetershire shoe and nail:
  Bristowe ship and sail.
  Oxenfordshire gird the mare:
  Warwykshire bind bere.
  London resortere:
  Sowtherey great bragere.
  Esex full of good hoswifes:
  Middlesex full of strives.
  Kentshire hot as fire:
  Sowseke full of dirt and mire.
  Hertfordshire full of wood:
  Huntingdonshire corn full good.
  Bedfordshire is nought to lack:
  Bokinghamshire is his make.
  Northamptonshire full of love
  Beneath the girdle and not above.
  Lancastreshire fair archere:
  Chestreshire thwakkere.
  Northumbreland hasty and hot:
  Westmorland [tot for sote!]
  Yorkshire full of knights:
  Lincolnshire men full of mightes.
  Cambridgeshire full of pikes:

Holond full of great dykes.
Norfolk full of wiles:
Southfolk full of stiles.
I am of *Shropshire* my shins be sharp:
Lay wood to the fire, and dress me my harp.
Notinghamshire full of hogs:
Derbyshire full of dogs.
Leicetershire full of beans:
Staffordshire full of queans.
Wiltshire fair and plain:
Barkshire fill the wain.
Hampshire dry and wete.
Somersetshire good for wheat.
Devenshire mighty and strong:
Dorseteshire will have no wrong.
Pinnokshire is not to praise:
A man may go it in two days.
Cornewaile full of tin:
Walis full of goote and kene.
That Lord that for us all did die
Save all these shires. *Amen* say I.

ANON

LONDON

To the City of London

London, thou art of townes A *per se.*
  Soveraign of cities, semeliest in sight,
Of high renoun, riches, and royaltie;
  Of lordis, barons, and many a goodly knyght;
  Of most delectable lusty ladies bright;
Of famous prelatis in habitis clericall;
  Of merchauntis full of substaunce and of myght:
London, thou art the flour of Cities all.

Gladdith anon thou lusty Troy novaunt,
  Citie that some tyme cleped was New Troy,
In all the erth, imperiall as thou stant,
  Pryncesse of townes, of pleasure, and of joy,
  A richer restith under no Christen roy;
For manly power, with craftis naturall,
  Fourmeth none fairer sith the flood of Noy:
London, thou art the flour of Cities all.

Gemme of all joy, jasper of jocunditie,
  Most myghty carbuncle of vertue and valour;
Strong Troy in vigour and in strenuytie;
  Of royall cities rose and geraflour;
  Empresse of townes, exalt in honour;
In beawtie beryng the crone imperiall;
  Swete paradise precelling in pleasure:
London, thou art the flour of Cities all.

Above all ryvers thy Ryver hath renowne,
  Whose beryall stremys, pleasaunt and preclare,
Under thy lusty walls renneth down,
  Where many a swanne doth swymme with wyngis fair;

Where many a barge doth saile, and row with are,
Where many a ship doth rest with toppe-royall.
   O! towne of townes, patrone and not compare:
London, thou art the flour of Cities all.

Upon thy lusty Brigge of pylers white
   Been merchauntis full royall to behold;
Upon thy stretis goth many a semely knyght
   In velvet gownes and in cheynes of gold.
   By Julyus Cesar the Tour founded of old
May be the hous of Mars victoryall,
   Whose artillary with tonge may not be told:
London, thou art the flour of Cities all.

Strong be thy wallis that about the standis;
   Wise be the people that within the dwellis;
Fresh is thy ryver with his lusty strandis;
   Blith by thy chirches, wele sownyng be thy bellis;
   Rich be thy merchauntis in substance that excellis;
Fair be their wives, right lovesom, white and small;
   Clere by thy virgins, lusty under kellis:
London, thou art the flour of Cities all.

Thy famous Maire, by pryncely governaunce,
   With swerd of justice the rulith prudently.
No Lord of Parys, Venyce, or Floraunce
   In dignytie or honoure goeth to hym nye.
   His is exempler, loode-ster, and guye;
Pryncipall patrone and roose orygynalle,
   Above all Maires as maister moost worthy:
London, thou art the flour of Cities all.

WILLIAM DUNBAR

A Ballad of London

Ah, London! London! our delight,
Great flower that opens but at night,
Great City of the Midnight Sun,
Whose day begins when day is done.

Lamp after lamp against the sky
Opens a sudden beaming eye,

Leaping alight on either hand,
The iron lilies of the Strand.

Like dragonflies, the hansoms hover,
With jewelled eyes, to catch the lover;
The streets are full of lights and loves,
Soft gowns, and flutter of soiled doves.

The human moths about the light
Dash and cling close in dazed delight,
And burn and laugh, the world and wife,
For this is London, this is life!

Upon thy petals butterflies,
But at thy root, some say, there lies
A world of weeping trodden things,
Poor worms that have not eyes or wings.

From out corruption of their woe
Springs this bright flower that charms us so,
Men die and rot deep out of sight
To keep this jungle-flower bright.

Paris and London, World-Flowers twain
Wherewith the World-Tree blooms again,
Since Time hath gathered Babylon,
And withered Rome still withers on.

Sidon and Tyre were such as ye,
How bright they shone upon the Tree!
But Time hath gathered, both are gone,
And no man sails to Babylon.

Ah, London! London! our delight,
For thee, too, the eternal night,
And Circe Paris hath no charm
To stay Time's unrelenting arm.

Time and his moths shall eat up all.
You chiming towers proud and tall
He shall most utterly abase,
And set a desert in their place.

RICHARD LE GALLIENNE

The Thames

Then *Westminster* next great *Tames* doth entertaine;
That vaunts her Palace large, and her most sumptuous Fane:
The Land's tribunall seate that challenge for hers,
The crowning of our Kings, their famous sepulchers.
Then goes he on along by that more beauteous Strand,
Expressing both the wealth and bravery of the Land.
(So many sumptuous Bowres, within so little space,
The All-beholding Sun scarse sees in all his race.)
And on by *London* leads, which like a Crescent lies,
Whose windowes seem to mock the Star-befreckled skies;
Besides her rising Spyres, so thick themselves that show,
As doe the bristling reeds, within his Banks that growe.
There sees his crouded Wharfes, and people-pestred shores,
His Bosome over-spread, with shoales of labouring ores:
With that most costly Bridge that doth him most renowne,
By which he cleerely puts all other Rivers downe.

MICHAEL DRAYTON, *Polyolbion*

His Teares to Thamasis

I send, I send here my supremest kiss
To thee, my silver-footed Thamasis.
No more shall I reiterate thy Strand,
Whereon so many Stately Structures stand:
Nor in the summers sweeter evenings go
To bath in thee (as thousand others doe,)
No more shall I along thy christall glide,
In Barge (with boughes and rushes beautifi'd)
With soft-smooth Virgins (for our chaste disport)
To Richmond, Kingstone, and to Hampton-Court:
Never againe shall I with Finnie-Ore
Put from, or draw unto the faithfull shore:
And Landing here, or safely Landing there,
Make way to my Belovèd Westminster:
Or to the Golden-cheap-side, where the earth
Of Julia Herrick gave to me my Birth.
May all clean Nimphs and curious water Dames,
With Swan-like-state flote up and down thy streams:
No drought upon thy wanton waters fall

4

To make them Leane, and languishing at all.
No ruffling winds come hither to discease
Thy pure, and Silver-wristed Naides.
Keep up your state, ye streams; and as ye spring,
Never make sick your Banks by surfeiting.
Grow young with Tydes, and though I see ye never,
Receive this vow, so fare-ye-well for ever.

ROBERT HERRICK

The Thames of Commerce

Then Commerce brought into the public Walk
The busy Merchant; the big Warehouse built;
Rais'd the strong Crane; choak'd up the loaded Street
With foreign Plenty; and thy Stream, O THAMES,
Large, gentle, deep, majestic, King of Floods!
Chose for his grand Resort. On either hand,
Like a long wintry Forest, Groves of Masts
Shot up their Spires; the bellying Sheet between
Possess'd the breezy Void; the sooty Hulk
Steer'd sluggish on; the splendid Barge along
Row'd regular, to Harmony; around,
The Boat, light-skimming, stretch'd its oary Wings;
While deep the various Voice of fervent Toil
From Bank to Bank increased.

JAMES THOMSON, *The Seasons*

Queen Victoria Goes Boating

What sight was that which loyal eyes
Beheld with horror—not surprise—
    On Thames's filthy tide,
Which bore Victoria, England's Queen
Who, down the River having been,
And the *Leviathan* ship seen,
    Back to her palace hied?

Familiar with the River's smell
Who cannot fancy, all too well,
    The odour which prevailed,

Which rose from the polluted stream
As thick, but not so white, as cream,
And in a suffocating steam,
    The Royal sense assailed?

How shall I state what thousands saw,
Indignant, yet oppressed with awe,
    Their blood which well nigh froze?
The River's perfume was so vile,
The Sovereign, as she neared Dogs' Isle,
Was fain to hold—nay do not smile—
    A bouquet to her nose.

Where shall the Constitution go,
If sewage shall much longer flow,
    The banks, old Thames, between?
The Lords and Commons, by thy breath,
Which both their Houses poisoneth,
Thou sickenest almost to death,
    And hast not spared the Queen!

ANON

By Millwall Dock

While the water-wagon's ringing showers
Sweetened the dust with a woodland smell,
'Past noon, past noon, two sultry hours',
Drowsily fell
From the schoolhouse clock
In the Isle of Dogs by Millwall Dock.

Mirrored in shadowy windows draped
With ragged net or half-drawn blind
Bowsprits, masts, exactly shaped
To woo or fight the wind,
Like monitors of guilt
By strength and beauty sent,
Disgraced the shameful houses built
To furnish rent.

From the pavements and the roofs
In shimmering volumes wound
The wrinkled heat;

Distant hammers, wheels and hoofs,
A turbulent pulse of sound,
Southward obscurely beat,
The only utterance of the afternoon,
Till on a sudden in the silent street
An organ man drew up and ground
The Old Hundredth tune.

JOHN DAVIDSON, *In the Isle of Dogs*

Shadwell Stair

I am the ghost of Shadwell Stair.
   Along the wharves by the water-house,
   And through the dripping slaughter-house,
I am the shadow that walks there.

Yet I have flesh both firm and cool,
   And eyes tumultuous as the gems
   Of moons and lamps in the lapping Thames
When dusk sails wavering down the pool.

Shuddering the purple street-arc burns
   Where I watch always; from the banks
   Dolorously the shipping clanks,
And after me a strange tide turns.

I walk till the stars of London wane
   And dawn creeps up the Shadwell Stair.
   But when the crowing syrens blare
I with another ghost am lain.

WILFRED OWEN

Blackfriars

By the shot tower near the chimneys,
   Off the road to Waterloo,
Stands the cottage of 'The Ancient'
   As in eighteen-forty-two.
Over brickwork, brownish brickwork,
   Lilac hangs in London sun

And by light fantastic clockwork
   Moves the drawbridge, sounds the gun.
When the sunset in the side streets
   Brought the breezes up the tide,
Floated bits of daily journals,
   Stable smells and silverside.
And the gaslight, yellow gaslight,
   Flaring in its wiry cage,
Like the Prison Scene in *Norval*
   On the old Olympic stage,
Lit the archway as the thunder,
   And the rumble and the roll,
Heralded a little handcart,
   And 'The Ancient' selling coal.

JOHN BETJEMAN

Composed Upon Westminster Bridge
(Early Morning)

Earth has not anything to show more fair:
Dull would he be of soul who could pass by
A sight so touching in its majesty:
This City now doth, like a garment, wear
The beauty of the morning; silent, bare,
Ships, towers, domes, theatres, and temples lie
Open upon the fields, and to the sky:
All bright and glittering in the smokeless air.
   Never did sun more beautifully steep
In his first splendour, valley, rock, or hill;
Ne'er saw I, never felt, a calm so deep!
The river glideth at his own sweet will:
Dear God! the very houses seem asleep;
And all that mighty heart is lying still!

WILLIAM WORDSWORTH

London Town

A mighty mass of brick, and smoke, and shipping,
  Dirty and dusky, but as wide as eye
Could reach, with here and there a sail just skipping.
  In sight, then lost amidst the forestry
Of masts; a wilderness of steeples peeping
  On tiptoe through their sea-coal canopy;
A huge, dun cupola, like a foolscap crown
On a fool's head,—and there is London Town!

LORD BYRON, *Don Juan*

The Sleepers

As I walked down the waterside
  This silent morning, wet and dark;
Before the cocks in farmyards crowed,
  Before the dogs began to bark;
Before the hour of five was struck
By old Westminster's mighty clock:

As I walked down the waterside
  This morning, in the cold damp air,
I saw a hundred women and men
  Huddled in rags and sleeping there:
These people have no work, thought I,
And long before their time they die.

That moment, on the waterside,
  A lighted car came at a bound:
I looked inside, and saw a score
  Of pale and weary men that frowned;
Each man sat in a huddled heap,
Carried to work while fast asleep.

Ten cars rushed down the waterside,
  Like lighted coffins in the dark;
With twenty dead men in each car,
  That must be brought alive by work:
These people work too hard, thought I,
And long before their time they die.

W. H. DAVIES

Fleet Street

Wisps and rags of cloud in a withered sky,
A strip of pallid azure, at either end,
Above the Ludgate obelisk, above
The Temple griffin, widening with the width
Below, and parallel with the street that counts
Seven hundred paces of tesselated road
From Ludgate Circus west to Chancery Lane:
By concrete pavement flanked and precipice
Of windowed fronts on this side and on that,
A thoroughfare of everything that hastes,
The sullen tavern-loafers notwithstanding
And hawkers in the channel hunger-bit.

Interfluent night and day the tides of trade,
Labour and pleasure, law and crime, are sucked
From every urban quarter: through this strait
All business London pours.

JOHN DAVIDSON, *Fleet Street*

London Voluntary

Down through the ancient Strand
The spirit of October, mild and boon
And sauntering, takes his way
This golden end of afternoon,
As though the corn stood yellow in all the land
And the ripe apples dropped to the harvest-moon.

Lo! the round sun, half-down to the western slope—
Seen as along an unglazed telescope—
Lingers and lolls, loth to be done with day:
Gifting the long, lean, lanky street
And its abounding confluences of being
With aspects generous and bland;
Making a thousand harnesses to shine
As with new ore from some enchanted mine,
And every horse's coat so full of sheen
He looks new-tailored, and every 'bus feels clean,
And never a hansom but is worth the feeing;

And every jeweller within the pale
Offers a real Arabian Night for sale;
And even the roar
Of the strong streams of toil, that pause and pour
Eastward and westward, sounds suffused—
Seems as it were bemused
And blurred, and like the speech
Of lazy seas on a lotus-haunted beach—
With this enchanted lustrousness,
This mellow magic, that (as a man's caress
Brings back to some faded face, beloved before,
A heavenly shadow of the grace it wore
Ere the poor eyes were minded to beseech)
Old things transfigures, and you hail and bless
Their looks of long-lapsed loveliness once more:
Till Clement's, angular and cold and staid,
Gleams forth in glamour's very stuffs arrayed;
And Bride's her aëry, unsubstantial charm
Through flight on flight of springing, soaring stone
Grown flushed and warm,
Laughs into life full-mooded and fresh-blown;
And the high majesty of Paul's
Uplifts a voice of living light, and calls—
Calls to his millions to behold and see
How goodly this his London Town can be!

For earth and sky and air
Are golden everywhere,
And golden with a gold so suave and fine
That looking on its lifts the heart like wine.
Trafalgar Square
(The fountains volleying golden glaze)
Shines like an angel-market. High aloft
Over his couchant Lions, in a haze
Shimmering and bland and soft,
A dust of chrysoprase,
Our Sailor takes the golden gaze
Of the saluting sun, and his flames superb,
As once he flamed it on his ocean round.
The dingy dreariness of the picture-place,
Turned very nearly bright,
Takes on a luminous transiency of grace,
And shows no more a scandal to the ground.

The very blind man pottering on the kerb,
Among the posies and the ostrich feathers
And the rude voices touched with all the weathers
Of the long, varying year,
Shares in the universal alms of light.

The windows, with their fleeting, flickering fires,
The height and spread of frontage shining sheer,
The quiring signs, the rejoicing roofs and spires—
'Tis El Dorado—El Dorado plain,
The Golden City! And when a girl goes by,
Look! as she turns her glancing head,
A call of gold is floated from her ear!
Golden, all golden! In a golden glory,
Long-lapsing down a golden coasted sky,
The day not dies but seems
Dispersed in wafts and drifts of gold, and shed
Upon a past of golden song and story
And memories of gold and golden dreams.

W. E. HENLEY

Narcissus

By white St Martin's, where the fountain shone
And plashed unheard in the busy morning air,
March, with rippling shadow and sudden sun,
Laughing riotous round the gusty square,
From frail narcissus heaped in baskets there
Blew to me, as I passed, its odour keen,
Keen and strange, subtle and sweet;
And lo! all new and green,
Spring for me had entered the stony street.

LAURENCE BINYON

The Coster Market

A storm of voices, fetid air,
    Blind stir and stress for places,
A screaming sky of naphtha flare,
    A surging sea of faces;

The coster market's molten dirt
Smoulders on the evening's skirt.

The barrows sway and swear and sweat;
The pavement seethes and hustles;
Bananas, spuds and mignonette,
Trousers, tripe and mussels,
All gross needings of the world,
Heaped and to the scramble hurled.

The greasy radiance, ablare
With still contending riot.
Blurs below; the upper air,
Immensely black and quiet,
Bends like pity and afar
Draws the uncorrupted star.

F. O. MANN

After the Great Fire

The Muse, visiting London's Remains, sees the ruins of Old St Paul's, and of St Faith's in whose crypt the booksellers had placed their stocks.

This was, said some, PAUL's *Reverend Edifice*;
The World did not its like comprise:
A *Carved Roof* its *Marble Pillars* crown'd,
And *these* to *that* vast Arches bound.

* * *

But, so *intense* was the *surrounding Flame*,
The *Marble gap'd*, and *loss'd* the *Frame*.
The *Roof*, fail'd by its *Propps, forc'd* into th' *Earth*,
To seek the *Place* that gave it *Birth*.
Now nought remains but *Ruines* rudely *torn*,
Like *Cliffs*, which fretting *Waves* have worn.
Chipp'd, like *rough-hew'd Oak*, when th' *Axe* doth *pare*
Its *Trunk* to an *uneven Square*.

These *Vaults* (said others) do St *Faith* comprise:
False Faith! write on her, Here *she lies*.
Rich pawns the *Letter'd Tribe* did there *depose*,
But a *deceitful Guardian* chose.
Like *Sybyll's Leaves*, the *scorched Learning* fell,
Scatter'd by *Winds* too *farre* to *tell*.

SIMON FORD, *Londons Remains*

Westminster Abbey and St Paul's

—Length'ning ayles, and windows that impart
A gloomy steady light to chear the heart,
Such as affects the soul, and which I see
With joy, celestial *Westminster*! in thee.
Not like Saint PAUL'S, beneath whose ample dome
No thought arises of the life to come.
For, tho' superb, not solemn is the place,
The mind but wanders o'er the distant space,
Where, 'stead of thinking on their God, most men
Forget his presence to remember *Wren*.

WILLIAM WOTY, *Church-Langton*

Street Dangers

Who would of *Watling-street* the Dangers share,
When the broad Pavement of *Cheap-side* is near?
Or who that rugged Street would traverse o'er,
That stretches, O *Fleet-ditch*, from thy black Shore
To the *Tow'rs* moated Walls? Here Streams ascend
That, in mix'd Fumes, the wrinkled Nose offend.
Where Chandlers Cauldrons boil; where fishy Prey
Hide the wet Stall, long absent from the Sea;
And where the Cleaver chops the Heifer's Spoil,
And where huge Hogsheads sweat with trainy Oil,
The breathing Nostril hold; but how shall I
Pass, where in Piles *Carnavian* Cheeses lye;
Cheese, that the Table's closing Rites denies,
And bids me with th' unwilling Chaplain rise.

O bear me to the Paths of fair Pell-Mell,
Safe are thy pavements, grateful is thy Smell!
At distance, rolls along the gilded Coach,
No sturdy Carmen on thy Walks encroach;
No Lets would bar thy Ways, were Chairs deny'd,
The soft Supports of Laziness and Pride;
Shops breathe Perfumes, thro' Sashes Ribbons glow,
The mutual Arms of Ladies, and the Beau.
Yet still ev'n Here, when Rains the Passage hide,

oft' the loose Stone spirts up a muddy Tide
Beneath thy careless Foot; and from on high,
Where Masons mount the Ladder, Fragments fly;
Mortar, and crumbled Lime in Show'rs descend,
And o'er thy Head destructive Tiles impend.

JOHN GAY, *Trivia*

Macadam's Road

Thy first great trial in this mighty town
Was, if I rightly recollect, upon
   That gentle hill which goeth
Down from 'The County' to the Palace gate,
   And, like a river, thanks to thee, now floweth
Past the Old Horticultural Society—
The chemist Cobb's, the house of Howell and James,
Where ladies play high shawl and satin games—
    A little *Hell* of lace!
And past in the Athenaeum, made of late,
    Severs a sweet variety
Of milliners and booksellers who grace
    Waterloo Place,
Making division, the Muse fears and guesses,
'Twixt Mr Rivington's and Mr Hessey's.
Thou stood'st thy trial Mac! and shaved the road
From Barber Beaumont's to the King's abode
So well, that paviours threw their rammers by,
Let down their tuck'd shirt sleeves, and with a sigh
Prepared themselves, poor souls, to chip or die!

THOMAS HOOD, *Ode to Mr McAdam*

Life-Guardsman

Joy of the Milliner, Envy of the Line,
Star of the Parks, jack-booted, sworded, helmed,
He sits between his holsters, solid of spine;
Nor, as it seems, though Westminster were whelmed,
With the great globe, in earthquake and eclipse,
Would he and his charger cease from mounting guard,

15

This Private in the Blues, nor would his lips
Move, though his gorge with throttled oaths were charred!
He wears his inches weightily, as he wears
His old-world armours; and with his port and pride,
His sturdy graces and enormous airs,
He towers in speech his Colonel countrified,
   A triumph, waxing statelier year by year,
   Of British blood, and bone, and beef, and beer.

W. E. HENLEY

Holy Thursday

'Twas on a holy Thursday, their innocent faces clean,
The children walking two and two, in red, and blue, and green:
Grey-headed beadles walked before, with wands as white as snow,
Till into the high dome of St Paul's they like Thames waters flow.

O what a multitude they seemed, these flowers of London town!
Seated in companies they sit, with radiance all their own.
The hum of multitudes were there, but multitudes of lambs,
Thousands of little boys and girls raising their innocent hands.

Now like a mighty wind they raise to heaven the voice of song,
Or like harmonious thunderings the seats of heaven among:
Beneath them sit the aged men, wise guardians of the poor.
Then cherish pity, lest you drive an angel from your door.

WILLIAM BLAKE

St James's Prayers

Last Sunday at St James's prayers,
   The prince and princess by,
I, drest in all my whale-bone airs,
   Sat in a closet nigh.
I bow'd my knees, I held my book,
   Read all the answers o'er;
But was perverted by a look,
   Which pierced me from the door.
High thoughts of Heaven I came to use,

With the devoutest care,
Which gay young Strephon made me lose,
    And all the raptures there.
He stood to hand me to my chair,
    And bow'd with courtly grace;
But whisper'd love into my ear,
    Too warm for that grave place.
'Love, love,' said he, 'by all adored,
    My tender heart has won.'
But I grew peevish at the word,
    And bade he would be gone.
He went quite out of sight, while I
    A kinder answer meant;
Nor did I for my sins that day
    By half so much repent.

TOM D'URFEY

Piccadilly

Piccadilly! Shops, palaces, bustle, and breeze,
The whirring of wheels, and the murmur of trees;
By night or by day, whether noisy or stilly,
Whatever my mood is, I love Piccadilly.

Wet nights, when the gas on the pavement is streaming,
And young Love is watching, and old Love is dreaming,
And Beauty is whirling to conquest, where shrilly
Cremona makes nimble thy toes, Piccadilly.

FREDERICK LOCKER, *Piccadilly*

Kensington Gardens

Where *Kensington* high o'er the neighb'ring lands
'Midst greens and sweets, a Regal fabrick, stands,
And sees each spring, luxuriant in her bowers,
A snow of blossoms, and a wilde of flowers,
The Dames of *Britain* oft in crowds repair
To gravel walks, and unpolluted air.
Here, while the Town in damps and darkness lies,

They breathe in sun-shine, and see azure skies;
Each walk, with robes of various dyes bespread,
Seems from afar a moving Tulip-bed,
Where rich Brocades and glossy Damasks glow,
And Chints, the rival of the show'ry Bow.

THOMAS TICKELL, *Kensington Gardens*

Kensington Gardens
The Tramps

The tramps slink in at half past four
in the sweet summer weather,
and stretch upon the grass and snore
peaceably all together.

They look like litter on the grass,
(and not like sleeping men)
that life—the feaster—dropped, and has
not tidied up again.

HUMBERT WOLFE

On the Albert Memorial

Immortal Albert, why this mortal strife
On thy Memorial 'twixt Death and Life—
That all too deathless tinsel round thy head,
And round thy feet those all too lifeless dead?

G. ROSTREVOR HAMILTON

The London Sunday

The seventh day this—the Jubilee of man!
London! right well thou know'st the day of prayer:
Then thy spruce citizen, washed artisan,
And smug apprentice gulp their weekly air:

Thy coach of hackney, whiskey,[1] one-horse chair,
And humblest gig through sundry suburbs whirl,
To Hampstead, Brentford, Harrow make repair;
Till the tired jade the wheel forgets to hurl,
Provoking envious jibe from each pedestrian churl.

Some o'er the Thamis row the ribboned fair,
Others along the safer turnpike fly;
Some Richmond-hill ascend, some scud to Ware,
And many to the steep of Highgate hie.
And ye, Boeotian Shades! the reason why?
'Tis to the worship of the solemn Horn,
Grasped in the holy hand of Mystery,
In whose dread name both men and maids are sworn,
And consecrate the oath[2] with draught, and dance till mourn.

LORD BYRON, *Childe Harold*

New Cross
Suburban Landscape

Pallid with heat, a stark metallic sky
    Is looped above the siding, drably scarred
    With rails that flank a sooty engine-yard,
Ash-heaps and sheds and roofing all awry.

Derelict mouse-grey trucks are mirrored by
    The sepia of a mute canal, where charred
    Gasometers squat sullenly on guard,
And barges drowse and boilers faintly sigh.

To-night the arc-lamps, poised from slender stems,
    Will bloom like silvery fruits. Signals will gleam
With shifting specks of jade and crimson gems.

Then: music: hiss and gasp of throttled steam,
    Staccato gamut of the shunted trains,
    And murmurous diapason of the cranes.

PAUL SELVER

---

[1] A light carriage.
[2] 'Swearing on the horns' at Highgate. For the 'tedious foolery' of this custom the curious may be referred to Hone's *Everyday Book* (1827, ii, 80–87).

Business Girls

From the geyser ventilators
    Autumn winds are blowing down
On a thousand business women
    Having baths in Camden Town.

Waste pipes chuckle into runnels,
    Steam's escaping here and there,
Morning trains through Camden cutting
    Shake the Crescent and the Square.

Early nip of changeful autumn,
    Dahlias glimpsed through garden doors,
At the back precarious bathrooms
    Jutting out from upper floors.

And behind their frail partitions
    Business women lie and soak.
Seeing through the draughty skylight
    Flying clouds and railway smoke.

Rest you there, poor unbelov'd ones,
    Lap your loneliness in heat.
All too soon the tiny breakfast,
    Trolley-bus and windy street!

JOHN BETJEMAN

In Praise of London

City of beauty, flower of cities all—
Where 'Themmes' runs swiftly, and the 'buses roar
(Even down the stately reaches of Whitehall)
While chocolate trams invade the Surrey shore—
Yours is a glamour which the years enhance
And in your grimy streets lives all romance!

When I go out into the world
To see the wonders there unfurl'd,
Though marvelling much, when I lie down
My thoughts fly back to my own town.
Memories of familiar streets

Comfort me under foreign sheets
And Cockney humour brings the laugh
When *bocks* of foreign beer I quaff.

My thoughts fly home. I see again
Remembered houses, roads and men.
The great town grows before my eyes,
I hear its murmurs and its sighs,
Travel, in dreams, the streets I knew
And roam from Greenwich Park to Kew.

I love to think of bland Pall Mall
(Where Charles made love to pretty Nell)
And rich South Audley Street, and Wapping,
And Bond Street and the Christmas shopping,
Knightsbridge, the Inner Circle train,
And Piccadilly and Park Lane;
Kensington, where 'nice' people live ·
Who give you tea (top-hat) at five;
And Church Street, and that little path
Which leads to the Broad Walk and the Pond
Where boys sail boats and sparrows bath—
And the dear woodland slope beyond. . .

I love Hyde Park, the Serpentine,
And Marble Arch at half-past nine,
The graceful curve of Regent Street,
The Queen Anne charm of Cheyne Walk
(Its church, with Polyphemus' eye,
And those great chimneys, climbing the sky!)—
The Inns of Court and that discreet
Tavern where Johnson used to talk;
The bustle of Fleet Street and the blare
Of Oxford Circus, Leicester Square;
Charing Cross Road, with books for all
In shop and window, case and stall;

Imperial Westminster, the Stores,
Where Colonel Tompkins buys cigars;
The Athenaeum where he snores;
The 'Troc', and several other bars;
The hall where Marie makes us roar
With jokes our consciences deplore
And where dear Vesta Tilley sings

—Our 'London Idol', bless her heart!—
Where Robey leaps on from the wings,
And good old X forgets her part.

Then who can think of Richmond Hill
In summertime, without a thrill?—
Remembering days with Rose or Nan
When friendship ended, love began,
And glamorous evenings in the park
Under the beech trees hush'd and dark—
The deer that gaze with glistening eyes
The London lights aglow in the skies
(But far away) and no sound there
Save the caught breath and little sighs
That come from joy too great to bear.

Richmond, all London lovers know
Your upland glades, and how, below,
The bright Thames twines about your knees
Through the green tracery of your trees. . .
And just as I, on Whitsunday,
Have brought my girl to spend the day,
So to your hill my father came
And sure, my son will do the same.

DOUGLAS GOLDRING, *In Praise of London*

Suburbia

Peace to each swain, who rural rapture owns,
As soon as past a toll and off the stones!
Whose joy, if buildings solid bliss bestow,
Cannot, for miles, an interruption know:
Save when a gap, of some half-dozen feet,
Just breaks the continuity of street;
Where the prig architect, with *style* in view,
Has doled his houses forth, in two by two;
And rear'd a row upon the plan, no doubt,
Of old men's jaws, with every third tooth out.
Or where, still greater lengths in taste to go,
He warps his tenements into a bow;
Nails a scant canvass, propt on slight deal sticks,

Nick-named *veranda*, to the first-floor bricks;
Before the whole, in one snug segment drawn,
Claps half a road of turf he calls a lawn;
Then, chuckling at his lath-and-plaster bubble,
Dubs it the CRESCENT,—and the rents are double

* * *

And here and there, thrown back a few yards deep
Some *staring* coxcombry pretends to *peep*;
Low paled in front, and shrubb'd with laurels in,
That sometimes flourish higher than your chin.
Here modest Ostentation sticks a plate,
Or daubs Egyptian letters on the gate,
Informing passengers 'tis '*Cowslip Cot*'
Or '*Woodbine Lodge*' or 'Mr Pummock's *Grot*'.
Oh! why not, Vanity! since debts bestow
Such names on dog-holes, squeezed out from a row,
The title of *Horn Hermitage* entail
Upon the habitation of a snail?
Why not inscribe ('twould answer quite as well)
'Marine Pavillion' on an oyster-shell?

GEORGE COLMAN (THE YOUNGER), *London Rurality*

The Fields from Islington

The fields from Islington to Marybone,
To Primrose Hill and Saint John's Wood,
Were builded over with pillars of gold;
And there Jerusalem's pillars stood.

Her little-ones ran on the fields,
The Lamb of God among them seen,
And fair Jerusalem, his Bride,
Among the little meadows green.

Pancrass and Kentish-town repose
Among her golden pillars high,
Among her golden arches which
Shine upon the starry sky.

The Jew's-harp-house and the Green Man,
The Ponds where Boys to bathe delight,
The fields of Cows by William's farm,
Shine in Jerusalem's pleasant sight.

WILLIAM BLAKE, *Jerusalem*

OUT FROM LONDON: TO ALL QUARTERS

Farewell

I

Go where we may, rest where we will,
Eternal London haunts us still.

THOMAS MOORE, *Rhymes on the Road*

II

Needless it were to say how willingly
I bade the huge Metropolis farewell,
Its din, and dust and dirt, and smoke and smut,
Thames' water, paviour's ground, and London sky:
Wearied of hurried days and restless nights,
Watchmen, whose office is to murder sleep
When sleep might else have weighed one's eyelids
    down. . . .
Escaping from all this, the very whirl
Of mail-coach wheels bound outward from Lad-lane
Was peace and quietness.

ROBERT SOUTHEY, *Epistle to Allan Cunningham*

Road to Canterbury

I

Bifil that in that seson on a day,
In Southwerk at the Tabard as I lay

Redy to wenden on my pilgrymage
To Caunterbury with ful devout corage,
At nyght was come into that hostelrye
Wel nyne and twenty in a compaignye,
Of sondry folk, by adventure yfalle
In felaweshipe, and pilgrimes were they alle,
That toward Caunterbury wolden ryde.
The chambres and the stables weren wyde,
And wel we weren esed atte beste.
And shortly, whan the sonne was to reste,
So hadde I spoken with hem everichon
That I was of hir felaweshipe anon,
And made forward erly for to ryse,
To take oure wey ther as I yow devyse.

GEOFFREY CHAUCER, *The Prologue*

II *(c. 1907)*

But now, behold! the southern roads along,
Pours from the city's heart the pilgrim throng.
To Canterbury still their way they wend
Through Southwark streets—but with what different end.
With mien how different, from the Tabard's door
Rode forth that joyous pilgrimage of yore!
Though scarce less various seems each motley kind,
For these no bridles jingle in the wind;
No hospitable Host, with converse gay,
No Miller's bagpipe cheers them on their way;
But Hunger with his sunken cheek is there,
To-day's Resourcelessness, To-morrow's Care;
From many a dreary haunt of dwindled Trade,
Of seated Labour and of Crafts decayed,
They quit their alleys, and, with fitful joy,
In Kent's fair gardens snatch a month's employ.

W. J. COURTHOPE, *Hop-Picking*

Flight from the Pestilence
(1625)

Those, who in all their lifetyme, never went
So farr as is, the neerest part of *Kent*:

Those, who did never travaile till of late,
Half way to *Pancrage* from their Citie gate;
Those, who might thinke, the *Sunne* did rise at *Bowe*
And Sett at *Acton*, for ought they did knowe
And dreame young *Partridge* suck not, but are fedd,
As *Lambes* and *Rabbetts*, wch of Eggs are bredd.
Ev'n some of these, have Iorneyes ventred on
ffive myles by land, (as farr as *Edmonton*).
Some hazzarded themselves, from *Lyon-kea*,
Almost as far as *Erith*, downe by Sea.
Some were by misadventure cast on Shore
Att *Cockolds Hauen*, and will come no more,
Some row'd against ye Streame, and stragled out
As farr as *Hounslow Heath*, or thereabout;
Some clymed *Highgate Hill*, and there they see
The world soe large, that they amazed bee.
Yea some, are gone so farr, that they doe knowe
Ere this, how wheate is made, and Mault doth growe.
 Oh! how some trudgd, and bustled vp and downe,
To gett themselves a furlong out of Towne.
And, how they were becumbred to provide,
That had, about a Mile or twoe to ride,
But when whole *households*, farther off were sent,
You would haue thought, the Muster of it, meant
To furnishe forth some *Nauy*, and that hee
Had gott his neighbours *Venturers*[1] to bee,
ffor all the neere acquaintance thereabout,
By lending somewhat, healp to set them out.

* * *

 And had you heard, how lowd the Coaches rumbled
Beheld how *Carrs*, and *Carts*, together iumbled:
Seene how the wayes, wth people thronged were;
The *Bandes* of ffoote, the *Troopes* of Horsemen there
What multitudes away by land were sent;
How many thousands forth by water went;
And how the wealth of *London* thence was borne,
You would have wondred: And almost haue sworne,
The *Citie* had beene leaving her foundation,
And seeking out another Scituation:
Or that some Enimye, wth dreadful powre,
Was coming to besiege, and to devoure.

GEORGE WITHER, *History of the Pestilence*

[1] i.e to venture money for a voyage of trade or discovery.

London to Folkestone

A constant keeping-past of shaken trees,
And a bewildered glitter of loose road;
Banks of bright growth, with single blades atop
Against white sky: and wires—a constant chain—
That seem to draw the clouds along with them
(Things which one stoops against the light to see
Through the low window; shaking by at rest,
Or fierce like water as the swiftness grows);
And, seen through fences or a bridge far off,
Trees that in moving keep their intervals
Still one 'twixt bar and bar; and then at times
Long stretches of green level, where one cow,
Feeding among her fellows that feed on,
Lifts her slow neck, and gazes for the sound.

Fields mown in ridges; and close garden-crops
Of the earth's increase; and a constant sky
Still with clear trees that let you see the wind;
And snatches of the engine-smoke, by fits
Tossed to the wind against the landscape, where
Rooks stooping heave their wings upon the day.

Brick walls we pass between, passed so at once
That for the suddenness I cannot know
Or what, or where begun, or where at end.
Sometimes a station in grey quiet; whence,
With a short gathered champing of pent sound,
We are let out upon the air again.
Pauses of water soon, at intervals,
That has the sky in it;—the reflexes
Of the trees move towards the bank as we go by,
Leaving the water's surface plain. I now
Lie back and close my eyes a space; for they
Smart from the open forwardness of thought
Fronting the wind.

*   *   *

I did not scribble more,
Be certain, after this; but yawned, and read,
And nearly dozed a little, I believe;
Till, stretching up against the carriage-back,

I was roused altogether, and looked out
To where the pale sea brooded murmuring.

D. G. ROSSETTI, *A Trip to Paris and Belgium*

Journey Home to the North

Know then with Horses twain, one sound, one lame,
On *Sunday's* Eve I to St *Alban's* came,
Where, finding by my Body's lusty state,
I could not hold out home at that slow rate,
I found a Coach-man, who, my case bemoaning,
With three stout Geldings, and one able Stoning,
For eight good Pounds did bravely undertake,
Or for my own, or for my Money's sake,
Through thick and thin, fall out what could befall,
To bring me safe and sound to *Basford-hall*.
Which having drunk upon, he bid good-night,
And (Heaven forgive us) with the Morning's light,
Not fearing God, nor his Vice-gerent Constable,
We roundly rowling were the Road to *Dunstable*,
Which, as they chim'd to Prayers, we trotted through,
And 'fore elev'n ten minutes came unto
The town that *Brickhill* height, where we did rest,
And din'd indifferent well both man and beast.
'Twixt two and four to *Stratford*, 'twas well driven,
And came to *Tocester* to lodge at Even.
Next day we din'd at *Dunchurch*, and did lie
That night four miles on our side *Coventry*.
Tuesday at Noon at *Lichfield* Town we baited,
But there some Friends, who long that hour had waited,
So long detain'd me, that my Charioteer
Could drive that night but to *Uttoxeter*.
And where the *Wedn'sday*, being Market-day,
I was constrain'd with some kind Lads to stay
Tippling till afternoon, which made it night
When from my Hero's Tow'r[1] I saw the light
Of her Flambeaux, and fanci'd as we drave
Each rising Hillock was a swelling wave,
And that I swimming was in *Neptune's* spight,
To my long long'd for Harbour of delight.

And now I'm here set down again in peace,
After my troubles, business, Voyages,
The same dull Northern clod I was before,
Gravely enquiring how ewes are a Score,
How the Hay-harvest, and the Corn was got,
And if or no there's like to be a rot;
Just the same Sot I was e'er I remov'd,
Nor by my travel, nor the Court improv'd;
The same old-fashion'd Squire, no whit refin'd,
And shall be wiser when the Devil's blind;
But find all here too in the self-same state,
And now begin to live at the old rate,
To bub old Ale, which nonsense does create,
Write lewd epistles, and sometimes translate
Old Tales of Tubs, of *Guyenne*, and *Provence*,
And keep a clutter with th' old Blades of *France*,
As *D'Avenant* did with those of *Lombardy*,
Which any will receive, but none will buy
And that has set *H. B.*[2] and me awry.
My River still through the same Chanel glides,
Clear from the Tumult, Salt and dirt of Tides,
And my poor fishing-house,[3] my Seat's best grace,
Stands firm and faithful in the self-same place
I left it four months since, and ten to one
I go a Fishing e'er two days are gone:
So that (my Friend) I nothing want but thee
To make me happy as I'd wish to be;
And sure a day will come I shall be bless'd
In his enjoyment whom my heart loves best;
Which when it comes will raise me above men
Greater than crowned Monarchs are, and then
I'll not exchange my Cottage for *White-hall*,
Windsor, *the Louvre*, or th' *Escurial*.

CHARLES COTTON, *Epistle to John Bradshaw, Esq.*

[1] The Beacon Tower on the hill-top in the grounds of Basford (Beresford) Hall.
[2] Henry Brome, Cotton's publisher.
[3] Erected by Cotton, 'Piscatoribus Sacrum 1674'.

The Tributaries of the Thames

Around his throne the sea-born brothers stood,
Who swell with tributary urns his flood:
First the fam'd authors of his ancient name,
The winding *Isis*, and the fruitful *Tame*:
The *Kennet* swift, for silver eels renown'd;
The *Loddon* slow, with verdant alders crown'd;
Cole, whose dark streams his flow'ry islands lave;
And chalky *Wey*, that rolls a milky wave:
The blue transparent *Vandalis* appears;
The gulphy *Lee* his sedgy tresses rears;
And sullen *Mole*, that hides his diving flood;
And silent *Darent*, stain'd with *Danish* blood.

ALEXANDER POPE, *Windsor Forest*

Rivers Arise

Rivers arise; whether thou be the son,
Of utmost *Tweed*, or *Oose*, or gulphie *Dun*,
Or *Trent*, who like some earth-born Giant spreads
His thirty Armes along the indented Meads,
Or sullen *Mole* that runneth underneath,
Or *Severn* swift, guilty of Maidens death,
Or rockie *Avon*, or of Sedgie *Lee*,
Or Coaly *Tine*, or antient hallowed *Dee*,
Or *Humber* loud that keeps the *Scythians* Name,
Or *Medway* smooth, or Royal Towred *Thame*.

JOHN MILTON, *At a Vacation Exercise*

Counties Compared

Cantabrian hills the purple saffron show;
Blue fields of flax in Lincoln's fenland blow;
On Kent's rich plains, green hop-grounds scent the gales;
And apple-groves deck Hereford's golden vales.

Shelter'd by woods the weald of Sussex lies;
Her smooth green downs sublime from Ocean rise:
That, fittest soil supplies for growth of grain;
These, yield best pasture for the fleecy train.

Say, friends! whoe'er his residence might chuse,
Would these sweet scenes of sylvan shade refuse,
And seek the black waste of the barren wold,
That yields no shelter from the heat or cold?

Dull are slow Ousa's mist-exhaling plains,
Where long rank grass the morning dew retains;
Who pastures there in Autumn's humid reign,
His flock from sickness hopes to save in vain.

The bleak, flat, sedgy shores of Essex shun,
Where fog perpetual veils the winter sun;
Though flattering Fortune there invite thy stay,
Thy health the purchase of her smiles must pay.

JOHN SCOTT, *Eclogue II*

The South Country

When I am living in the Midlands
    That are sodden and unkind,
I light my lamp in the evening:
    My work is left behind;
And the great hills of the South country
    Come back into my mind.

The great hills of the South Country
    They stand along the sea;
And it's there walking in the high woods
    That I could wish to be,
And the men that were boys when I was a boy
    Walking along with me.

The men that live in North England
    I saw them for a day:
Their hearts are set upon the waste fells,
    Their skies are fast and grey;
From their castle-walls a man may see
    The mountains far away.

The men that live in West England
   They see the Severn strong,
A-rolling on rough water brown
   Light aspen leaves along.
They have the secret of the rocks,
   And the oldest kind of song.

But the men that live in the South Country
   Are the kindest and most wise,
They get their laughter from the loud surf,
   And the faith in their happy eyes
Comes surely from our Sister the Spring
   When over the sea she flies;
The violets suddenly bloom at her feet,
   She blesses us with surprise.

I never get between the pines
   But I smell the Sussex air;
Nor I never come on a belt of sand
   But my home is there.
And along the sky the line of the Downs
   So noble and so bare.

A lost thing could I never find,
   Nor a broken thing mend:
And I fear I shall be all alone
   When I get towards the end.
Who will there be to comfort me
   Or who will be my friend?

I will gather and carefully make my friends
   Of the men of the Sussex Weald,
They watch the stars from silent folds,
   They stiffly plough the field.
By them and the God of the South Country
   My poor soul shall be healed.

If I ever become a rich man,
   Or if ever I grow to be old,
I will build a house with deep thatch
   To shelter me from the cold,
And there shall the Sussex songs be sung
   And the story of Sussex told.

I will hold my house in the high wood
   Within a walk of the sea,

And the men that were boys when I was a boy
  Shall sit and drink with me.

HILAIRE BELLOC

The West Country
Rivers in Devon

Those rivers in that lost country,
They were clear as a clear brown bead is
Or red with the earth that rain washed down
    Or white with china clay;
And some tossed foaming over boulders,
And some curved mild and tranquil,
In wooded vales securely set
    Under the fond warm day.

Okement and Erme and Avon,
Exe and his ruffled shallows,
I could cry as I think of those rivers
    That knew my morning dreams;
The weir by Tavistock at evening
When the circling woods were purple,
And the Lowman in spring with the lent-lilies,
    And the little moorland streams.

For many a hillside streamlet
There falls with a broken tinkle,
Falling and dying, falling and dying,
    In little cascades and pools,
Where the world is furze and heather
And flashing plovers and fixed larks
And an empty sky, whitish blue,
    That small world rules.

There, there, where the high waste bog-lands
And the drooping slopes and the spreading valleys,
The orchards and the cattle-sprinkled pastures
    Those travelling musics fill,
There is my lost Abana,
And there is my nameless Pharpar
That mixed with my heart when I was a boy,
    And time stood still.

SIR JOHN SQUIRE, *Rivers*

34

Wales

Mother of holy fire! Mother of holy dew!
Thy children of the mist, the moor, the mountain side,
These change not from thine heart, these to thine heart allied:
These, that rely on thee, as blossoms on the blue.
O passionate, dark faces, melancholy's hue!
O deep, gray eyes, so tragic with the fires they hide!
Sweet Mother, in whose light these live! thou dost abide,
Star of the West, pale to the world: these know thee true.

No alien hearts may know that magic, which acquaints
Thy soul with splendid passion, a great fire of dreams;
Thine heart with lovelier sorrow, than the wistful sea.
Voices of Celtic singers and of Celtic Saints
Live on the ancient air; their royal sunlight gleams
On moorland Merioneth and on sacred Dee.

LIONEL JOHNSON

Welsh Landscape

To live in Wales is to be conscious
At dusk of the spilled blood
That went to the making of the wild sky,
Dyeing the immaculate rivers
In all their courses.
It is to be aware,
Above the noisy tractor
And hum of the machine
Of strife in the strung woods,
Vibrant with sped arrows.
You cannot live in the present,
At least not in Wales.
There is the language for instances,
The soft consonants
Strange to the ear.
There are cries in the dark at night
As owls answer the moon,
And thick ambush of shadows,
Hushed at the fields' corners.
There is no present in Wales,

35

And no future;
There is only the past,
Brittle with relics,
Wind-bitten towers and castles
With sham ghosts;
Mouldering quarries and mines;
And an impotent people,
Sick with inbreeding,
Worrying the carcase of an old song.

R. S. THOMAS

In Wild Wales
At the Eisteddfod

The close-ranked faces rise,
With their watching, eager eyes,
And the banners and the mottoes blaze above;
And without, on either hand,
The eternal mountains stand,
And the salt sea river ebbs and flows again,
And through the thin-drawn bridge the wandering winds complain.

*   *   *

The Menai ebbs and flows,
And the song-tide wanes and goes,
And the singers and the harp-players are dumb;
The eternal mountains rise
Like a cloud upon the skies,
And my heart is full of joy for the songs that are still,
The deep sea and the soaring hills, and the steadfast Omnipotent Will.

SIR LEWIS MORRIS, *At the Eisteddfod*

The North Country

In another country, black poplars shake themselves over a pond,
And rooks and the rising smoke-waves scatter and wheel from the works
  beyond:

The air is dark with north and with sulphur, the grass is a darker green,
And people darkly invested with purple move palpable through the scene.

Soundlessly down across the counties, out of the resonant gloom
That wraps the north in stupor and purple travels the deep, slow boom
Of the man-life north imprisoned, shut in the hum of the purpled steel
As it spins to sleep on its motion, drugged dense in the sleep of the wheel.

Out of the sleep, from the gloom of motion, soundlessly, somnambule
Moans and booms the soul of a people imprisoned, asleep in the rule
Of the strong machine that runs mesmeric, booming the spell of its word
Upon them and moving them helpless, mechanic, their will to its will
   deferred.

Yet all the while comes the droning inaudible, out of the violet air,
The moaning of sleep-bound beings in travail that toil and are will-less
   there.
In the spellbound north, convulsive now with a dream near morning,
   strong
With violent achings heaving to burst the sleep that is now not long.

D. H. LAWRENCE

The East Country
Reconquest

Once a year the East country
Remembers its ancient master:
The fluid corn,
The grey-green swirling oats and luminous barley
Brim up between banked hedges—
The strong tides join and sweep irresistibly over
Houses and telegraph poles
Till only the towered poplars and islanded cathedrals,
Lincoln, Ely,
Look to the Pennines and High Germany.

R. N. CURREY

Living in the Midlands

When men offer thanks for the bounties
That they in their boyhood have known,
When poets are praising their counties,
What ought I to say of my own?

Its highways are crowded with lorries
And buses encumber its lanes;
Its hills are used chiefly as quarries,
Its rivers used chiefly as drains.

The country is all over-ridden
By townsmen, ill-mannered and proud,
And Beauty, unless it is hidden,
Is trampled to death by the crowd.

Disforested, featureless, faded—
Describe me a place if you can
Where Man was by Nature less aided
Or Nature less aided by Man.

And yet though I keep in subjection
My heart, as a rule, to my head,
I still feel a sneaking affection
For ————,[1] where I was bred.

For still, here and there, is a village
Where factories have not been planned,
There still are some acres of tillage,
Some old men still work on the land.

And how can I help but remember
The Midsummer meadows of hay,
The stubbles dew-drenched in September,
The buttercups golden in May?

For we who seek out and discover
The charms of my county can be
As proud as a plain woman's lover
Of beauties the world does not see.

COLIN ELLIS

[1] Shall we say 'Middleshire'?

The People of the Counties
(Hodge Speaks)

Now therefore you shall understand
My folk yet people every shire
From Lizard to Northumberland.
They till the levels of the east,
Where blow grass borders the sea-strand,
And in the dunes for man and beast
They win their fodder. They make fat
The lean, themselves they profit least;
But this is not to wonder at.
Where Ouse and Trent and Humber coil
'Twixt reedy marsh and meadow-flat,
Where Thames grows turbid with the moil
Of London's pool and London's mart,
They bank the water into soil,
And spread the dung and lead the cart.
Find you them in the stormy west
Where from long Cleator to the Start
The land meets ocean, crest with crest,
Throwing her rocky bastions up:
There is my kindred's upland nest
Who lead their sheep for bite and sup
By mountain path and waterfall
To where the grass grows in a cup
Of rearing cliff and craggy wall.
And thence the upland rivers race
A nobler course; thence best of all
Flings Severn down, to earn her grace
There where she broadens to the main
And giveth Bristol pride of place.
Go seek my kith on hill and plain,
Whether in Cumberland's deep dales,
In York's dark moors or Lincoln's fen,
In Westmorland's hill-shadowed vales;
From the scarred Peak and Splintry Edge,
By Salop's stony march with Wales,
To grassy boss and grassy ledge,
To pastoral Wilts, to Somerset,
To Dartmoor holding up her ridge
Against the west wind and the wet;

In billowy breadths of open down
   Where the bright rivers ripple and fret,
And each hill wears a beechen crown,
   And every village hides in trees;
   And on the heath, by market town,
By holt and brake, from Axe to Tees—
   Seek there, for there my root is thrown
   Between the Eastern and Western seas.

MAURICE HEWLETT, *The Song of the Plow*

❦ 3 ❦

THE HOME COUNTIES AND THE SOUTH COUNTRY

MIDDLESEX   *Strawberry Hill*

> Some cry up Gunnersbury,
>   For Sion some declare,
> Some say, that with Chiswick House
>   No villa can compare;
> But ask the beaux of Middlesex,
>   Who know the country well,
> If Strawberry-hill, if Strawberry-hill,
>   Don't bear away the bell.
>
> Some love to roll down Greenwich-hill,
>   For this thing and for that,
> And some prefer sweet Marble-hill,
>   Though sure 'tis somewhat flat;
> Yet Marble-hill and Greenwich-hill,
>   If Kitty Clive can tell,
> From Strawberry-hill, from Strawberry-hill,
>   Will never bear the bell.
>
> Though Surrey boasts its Oatlands,
>   And Clermont kept so jim,
> And some prefer sweet Southcoats,
>   'Tis but a dainty whim;
> But ask the gallant Bristol,
>   Who doth in taste excel,
> If Strawberry-hill, if Strawberry-hill,
>   Don't bear away the bell.

Since Denham sung of Cooper's,
  There's scarce a hill around,
But what in song or ditty,
  Is turn'd to fairy ground.
Ah! peace be with their memory,
  I wish them wondrous well,
But Strawberry-hill, but Strawberry-hill,
  Will ever bear the bell.

Great William dwells at Windsor,
  As Edward did of old,
And many a Gaul and many a Scot
  Have found him full as bold.
On lofty hills like Windsor
  Such heroes ought to dwell;
Yet the little folks on Strawberry-hill
  Like Strawberry-hill as well.

WILLIAM PULTENEY, Earl of Bath

Description of Hampstead
(1815)

A steeple issuing from a leafy rise,
  With farmy fields in front and sloping green,
  Dear Hampstead, is thy southern face serene,
Silently smiling on approaching eyes,
Within, thine-ever shifting looks surprise,
  Streets, hills and dells, trees overhead now seen,
  Now down below, with smoking roofs between,—
A village, revelling in varieties.
Then northward what a range—with heath and pond!
  Nature's own ground; woods that let mansions through
And cottaged vales with billowy fields beyond,
  And clump of darkening pines and prospects blue,
And that clear path through all, where daily meet
Cool cheeks, and brilliant eyes, and morn-elastic feet!

LEIGH HUNT

Islington
(1827)

Thy fields; fair Islington! begin to bear
Unwelcome buldings, and unseemly piles;
The streets are spreading, and the Lord knows where
Improvement's hand will spare the neighb'ring stiles:
The rural blandishments of Maiden Lane
Are ev'ry day becoming less and less,
While kilns and lime roads force us to complain
Of nuisances time only can suppress.
A few more years, and Copenhagen House
Shall cease to charm the tailor and the snob;
And where attornies' clerks in smoke carouse,
Regardless wholly of to-morrow's job,
Some Claremont Row, or Prospect Place shall rise,
Or terrace, p'rhaps, misnomered Paradise.

J. G. (Hone's *Table Book*)

Highgate to St Albans
(January 1733)

Descending hence my heart went pit a pat,
Whilst viewing *Finchley's* dreadful plain I sat.
There luckily I join'd a coach and four,
One skip behind with arms, and one before.
Thus proud in pocket, and in heart elate,
I paid a turnpike, and improve my gait.
Two miles from hence began fam'd *Barnet* town;
From hence a mile the battle of *King John*.
Here where a vale to *Enfield* points the eye,
In furious battle furious *Monks* did die.

And now the sun had thaw'd with friendly ray
The sliding danger of th'obdurate way.
No *Cockney* I, but with *Newmarket* haste
The straggling town of *Mimms* is quickly past.
Another mile, *Saint Alban's* was in view,
And the broad road of gravel I pursue.
Three bottoms here with danger I descend,
And every bottom gives a pistol'd fiend.

But luck this once attends the Martyr's shrine,
He sav'd me now, and now with him I dine.

Here, *Britain*, with due reverence repair,
And own the mother of thy Churches here,
Which ages past a monument has stood
Of *British* truth, first seal'd by *Alban's* blood.

KENRICK PRESCOT, *To Levet Blackborne, Esq.*

Swans' Journey

From *Stansted* unto *Hodsdon* goes these Swannes,
From thence to *Broxborne*, and to *Wormley* wood
And to salute the holy house of Nunnes,
That late belong'd to captaine *Edward Dennie*,
A knight in Ireland of the best accompt
Who late made execution on our foes,
I meane of Spanyardes, that with open armes
Attempted both against our Queene and us:
There now Lord *Talbot* keepes a noble house.
Now see these Swannes the new and worthie seate
Of famous *Cicill*, treasoror of the land,
Whose wisedome, counsell, skill of Princes state
The world admires, then Swannes may doe the same:
The house it selfe doth shewe the owners wit,
And my for bewtie, state, and everything,
Compared be with most within the land.
Downe all along through Waltham street they passe,
And wonder at the ruins of the Abbay,
Late supprest, the walles, the walkes, the monumentes,
And everiething that there is to be seen.
Among them all a rare devise they see,
But newly made, a waterworke: the locke
through which the boates of *Ware* doe pass with malt.
This locke contains two double doores of wood,
Within the same a Cesterne all of Plancke,
Which only fils when boates come there to passe
By opening of these mightie dores with sleight,
And strange devise, but now decayed sore.
And as they stayed here, they chaunst to see
The stately crosse of *Elnor*, *Henries* wife.

Then *Enfield* house, that longes unto our Queene,
They all behold, and with due reverence
Salute the same.
    From hence by *Hackney*, *Leyton*, and old-Foord,
They come to *Stratford*, cal'd also the *Bowe*:
And underneath the bridge that thwartes the streame
And partes the shires of *Middlesex*, and *Essex* both.
At last (though long and wearie was their way)
They come unto the mouth of river *Lee*,
Where all the Swannes of that part of the *Thames*
Attend to see this royall companie:
So that from *Woolwich* to *Blackwall* was seene
Nor water, nor the medowes thereabout.
For looke how in a frostie night or day,
When Snowe hath fallen thicke upon the grounde,
Eche gasing eye is dasel'd with the sight,
So Lillie-white was land and strand beseene
With these faire Swannes, the birdes of lovely love.

W. VALLANS, *A Tale of two Swannes*

HERTFORDSHIRE *In Hertfordshire*

                My roving sight
Pursues its pleasing course o'er neighb'ring hills,
Where frequent hedge-rows intersect rich fields
Of many a different form and different hue,
Bright with ripe corn, or green with grass, or dark
With clover's purple bloom; o'er Widbury's mount
With that fair crescent crown'd of lofty elms,
Its own peculiar boast; and o'er the woods
That round immure the deep sequester'd dale
Of Langley, down whose flow'r-embroider'd meads
Swift Ash thro' pebbly shores meandering rolls,
Elysian scene! as from the living world
Secluded quite; for of that world, to him
Whose wand'rings trace thy winding length, appears
No mark, save one white solitary spire
At distance rising thro' the tufted trees.

              *   *   *

How beautiful,
How various is yon view! delicious hills
Bounding smooth vales, smooth vales by winding streams
Divided, that here glide thro' grassy banks
In open sun, there wander under shade
Of aspen tall, or ancient elm, whose boughs
O'erhang grey castles, and romantic farms,
And humble cots of happy shepherd swains.
Delightful habitations! with the song
Of birds melodious charm'd, and bleat of flocks
From upland pastures heard, and low of kine
Grazing the rushy mead, and mingled sounds
Of falling waters and of whisp'ring winds—
Delightful habitations! o'er the land
Dispers'd around, from Waltham's osier'd isles
To where bleak Nasing's lonely tower o'erlooks
Her verdant fields; from Raydon's pleasant groves
And Hunsdon's bowers on Stort's irriguous marge,
By Rhye's old walls, to Hodsdon's airy street;
From Haly's woodland to the flow'ry meads
Of willow-shaded Stansted, and the slope
Of AMWELL's Mount, that crowned with yellow corn
There from the green flat, softly swelling, shows
Like some bright vernal cloud by Zephyr's breath
Just rais'd above the horizon azure bound.

JOHN SCOTT, *Amwell*

Barnabee in Hertfordshire

Thence to Ware, where mazie Amwell
Mildly cuts the Southerne Channell;
Rivers streaming, banks resounding,
Middleton with wealth abounding:
Mightily did these delight me;
'O, I wish'd them Aqua vitæ!'
Thence to Wademill, where I rest me
For a pot, for I was thirstie;
On me cryde they and did hout me,
And like Beetles flockt about me:
'Buy a whip, Sᵣ! No, a Laddle;
'Where's your horse, Sᵣ! where your Saddle?'

*   *   *

Thence to Roiston, where grasse groweth,
Medes, flocks, fields, the plowman soweth,
Where a pious Prince frequented,
Which observing, this I vented:
'Since all flesh to Fate's a debtor,
'Retchlesse wretch, why liv'st no better?'

RICHARD BRAITHWAIT, *Barnabees Journall, His Northern Journey, Third Part*

Hoddesdon

The lanes of England never end.
In Hertfordshire I found my lane,
and followed where it ran,
content to let it be my country friend
and show to me ground-ivy in the grass,
which as I passed deceived my eyes
with glints like violets; the yellow there
that are abundant in the early year,
from brazen dandelion
to burnished lesser celandine,
and gaps in hedges opened wide
as windows in the countryside,
with sudden landscapes breaking in
upon the byway's privacy.

A team of horses, hour by hour,
drags a harrow through the heavy fields;
and larks fly up from nearer meadows, sing
to larks below, concealed.
A wood beyond the field and meadow has
a hundred greens in it;
and, stretched below, the lowlands lie
melting into distant sky.
In the ceaseless changes here
there is a constancy,
assured as every year
has buds that open into leaves,
the looked-for early sun upon the dew,
the yellow harvest piled in sheaves,
and, in small hands that gathered them,

47

wild flowers to make a diadem.
There is a deeper constancy
than continents or kingdoms ever knew.
Each cotton has a flower bed,
a patch for cabbages, and red
geraniums behind the window pane.
By open doors old people sit in wait
to watch whatever happens in the lane;
past generations, centuries dead, begin
the local history they perpetuate,
and news of it is heard of at the inn,
where Jack, the parish hedger, drinks and plays—
whose forebears hedged and ditched in Tudor days.

A. S. WILSON, *These Remain*

SURREY

Kew

(1763)

Here *Britons* view (nor wander far from Home)
The boasted Monuments of *Greece* and *Rome*.
Our wond'ring Sight what various Structures strike!
Th' *Alhambra* grotesque; or the Fane antique.
The pleas'd Spectator lifts his curious Eyes;
See's mooned *Mosques* and mimic Temples rise.
Of fabled *Phoebus* here the bright Abode;
There the proud Seat of *China's* great Pagod:
Religious Lies of ev'ry Age and Clime;
And recent Ruins nothing hurt by time.

GEORGE RITSO, *Kew Gardens*

Croydon

In a house like that
    Your Uncle Dick was born;
Satchel on back he walked to Whitgift
    Every week-day morn.

Boys together in Coulsdon woodlands,
    Bramble-berried and steep,
He and his pals would look for spadgers
    Hidden deep.

The laurels are speckled in Marchmont Avenue
    Just as they were before,
But the steps are dirty that still lead up to
    Your Uncle Dick's front door.

Pear and apple in Croydon gardens
    Bud and blossom fall
But your Uncle Dick has left his Croydon
    Once for all.

JOHN BETJEMAN

On Holmbury Hill

The narrow paths branch every way up here
And cross and tangle and are nowhere clear
And the empty sky, swept clean by a rainy breath,
Smiles on our tortuous scrambling underneath.
But here's the top, for round a sudden bend.
We stumble breathless on the unlooked for end
And stare across the misty weald. Below
The lonely trains through the wide country go,
Each with its plume of steam. And westward, see,
Past the far shoulder streams tumultuously
A black and driven storm across the air
And casts about the downs its troubled hair.
Thick at the middle, at the edges thinned,
Heeling over like a ship before the wind,
It eats the weald up with a greedy mouth.
Still, twenty miles or further to the south,
Dimly and grandly Chanctonbury stands
A moment clear above the blotted lands.
It's gone. But still the blue and empty sky
Smiles on over our heads unwittingly.

EDWARD SHANKS

Green Surrey

O, Farnham, green Farnham, what hop-rounds are there
That with Farnham's fair hop-grounds can ever compare!
And what pleasure it were once again but to lie
On Guildford's green hillsides beneath the blue sky!
O, the green hills of Surrey, the sweet hills of Surrey,
The dear hills of Surrey, I'll love till I die.

O, Dorking is pleasant, and Dorking is green,
And sweet are the woods and the walks of Deepdene,
And for Dorking's sweet meadows in vain I must sigh,
And Deepdene's green woods will no more meet my eye;
But the green woods of Surrey, the sweet woods of Surrey,
The dear woods of Surrey, I'll love till I die.

O, Kent has fair orchards; no pleasanter show
Than her apple-trees blooming in April I know,
Save the orchards round Reigate, sweet Reigate, that lie
With their red and white blossoms so fair 'neath the sky.
O, the green fields of Surrey, the sweet fields of Surrey,
The dear fields of Surrey, I'll love till I die.

WILLIAM C. BENNETT, *The Green Hills of Surrey: An Emigrant Song*

Surrey Hills

Sweet Health, I seek thee! hither bring
Thy balm that softens human ills;
Come, on the long-drawn clouds that fling
Their shadows o'er the Surry-Hills.
Yon green-topt hills, and far away
Where late as now I freedom stole,
And spent one dear delicious day
On thy wild banks, romantic *Mole.*

Ay, there's the scene![1] beyond the sweep
Of London's congregated cloud,
The dark-brow'd wood, the headlong steep,
And valley-paths without a crowd!

[1] Box Hill and the beautiful neighbourhood of Dorking, in Surrey.

Here, Thames, I watch thy flowing tides,
Thy thousand sails am proud to see;
For where the *Mole* all silent glides
Dwells Peace,—and Peace is wealth to me!

ROBERT BLOOMFIELD, *Shooter's Hill*

KENT

The Weald of Kent

The common saying goes, that on the hill
A man may lie in bed to work his farm,
Propping his elbows on his window-sill
To watch his harvest growing like a charm.
But the man who works the wet and weeping soil
Down in the Weald, must marl and delve and till
His three-horse land, fearing nor sweat nor droil.
For through the winter he must fight the flood,
The clay, that yellow enemy, that rots
His land, sucks at his horses' hooves
So that his waggon plunges in the mud,
And horses strain, but waggon never moves;
Delays his plough, and holds his spud
With yeavy spite in trenching garden-plots,
The catchy clay, that does its utmost harm,
And comes into his house, to spoil
Even his dwelling creeps into his bones
Before their time, and makes them ache,
Leaving its token in his husky tones;
And all through summer he must see the clay
Harden as brick, and bake,
And open cracks to swallow up his arm,
Where neither harrow, hoe, nor rake
Can rasp a tilth, but young and eager shoots
Pierce into blank, and whither at the roots.
Yet with his stupid loyalty he will say,
Being a wealden man of wealden land,
Holding his wealden honour as a pledge,
'In times of drought those farms up on the ridge,
Light soil, half sand,
With the first summer gale blow half away',
And lifts his eye towards the hill with scorn.

But only a bold man ploughs the Weald for corn,
Most are content with fruit or pasture, knowing
Too well both drought and winter's heavy going;
So the lush Weald to-day
Lies green in distance, and the horizon's sweep
Deepens to blue in woods, with pointed spire
Pricking the foreground by the village tiles,
And the hop-kiln's whitened chimney stares between
Paler and darker green of Kentish miles,
And rarely a patch of corn in metal fire
Burnished by sunset ruffles in the green;
But meadow, shaw, and orchard keep
The glaucous country like a hilly sea
Pure in its monotone.

V. SACKVILLE-WEST, *The Land*

Kent Hop-Garden

Around the garden the blue landscape glows:
Fair is the social scene: away, repose!
Time, Weather, Mood, Occasion, Sun, and Sky,
Bid every roof the household task lay by;
And all alike, the matron and the maid,
Join son or lover and the harvest aid.
Shrouded at first in deep pavilions green,
Proceeds the toil, not silent, though unseen;
But soon, with glimpse of flying hands revealed,
Blue skirt, red bodice, fleck the brightening field,
As the strong hinds, in each deplenished row,
Lay the stripped poles, like captive standards, low;
Then for their eager troops fresh booty win,
Measure each brimming, feed each empty bin,
Within whose bosom, thick as Danaë's shower,
Descends the golden cluster, flower by flower.
A grateful odour floats upon the breeze,
And lulls the labourer's sense with soothing ease;
Or spreads its soft narcotic influence round,
Where cradled babes lie fast in slumber bound;
Above their heads glad talk and rustic mirth resound.

Meantime, from the gay harvest throng apart,
High in the oast the drier plies his art,
To feed the kiln, and keep an even flame
In the round stove, a wight of peerless fame;
Through all the neighbouring dales renowned as much
For certain judgement as for finer touch.
The loaded wains arrived, he bids them pour
The yellow affluence on the topmost floor,
Heavy with dews of heaven. Anon, below,
He stirs the furnace to a tempered glow,
And feeds the flame with sulphur's brightening blend:
From the moist flowers the drowsy fumes ascend,
Rush through the cowl to mingle with the day,
And in blue vapour breathe their weight away.
Then, hour by hour, amid the dwindled heap,
For the last proof his feeling fingers creep;
And as the shrivelling stalks show hard and dry,.
The cooling chamber claims the rich supply.

Thus all conspire to win the common good,
With varied skill, but kindly brotherhood.
October brings the toiling garden rest;
The oast's last yield is in the canvas pressed;
The last red embers in the kiln expire;
The last tired labourer's hand receives his hire:
To Labour and to Wealth alike be given
Exchange of thanks; from both the praise to Heaven:
Then, with glad hearts, let all united come
And at the Landlord's feast sing Harvest Home.

W. J. COURTHOPE, *Hop-Picking*

Above the Medway

Hark! from yon high grey Downs the tremulous musical
    sheep-bells
Call us to come and behold all that our shepherds can show;
Who with their low-wheel'd huts abide in the field for the
    lambing,
Watching night and day over the weak of the fold.
Ah! from those high grey Downs, what a

height, what a scope, of enjoyment!
Songs of the mating birds heard in the hollows afar—
Songs of the lark in air, or the clamorous chirp of the
    starlings,
Seated aloft in crowds, talking together at eve.

You who would know what it is to rejoice in the beauty of
    England,
Come to these high grey Downs; come in an evening of
    Spring—
Come in the Autumn noons, or come in a sweet Summer
    morning—
Stand upon Darland Heights, gaze on the glories around!
Look to the east, far down, where the broad white Roman
    highway
Scores the green flank of the hills, stately and sound as of old;
Look to the east, far down, where Medway sweeps to the
    ocean,
Meeting the broader Thames, surging away to the Nore.
There, by the tall sea banks, by the low rich pastures of Essex
There go the ships, far off, bearing the wealth of the world;
Bearing it on the tide, to the port and harbour of London,
Bearing it thence in turn out to the ocean again.
Near, o'er the Medway stream, look down on an humbler
    traffic—
Fishermen's craft alone, barges and boats of the shore:
Yes, and yon giant hulks, where soldiers live as in barracks,
Learning their terrible trade, disciplined daily to war.
Ah, look away from them, look away from the forts in the
    channel
(Needed and wanting once, soon to be needed again),
Look to the smiling shores, to the villages set in the
    woodland,
Orchards and red-roof's farms, churches and castles and all.
Then to the west turn round, and see right on to the
    landward.
Fold upon fold, the hills rising like waves of the sea:
But at your feet, low down, lies the silent valley of Darland.
Winding in many a curve up to the highlands afar;
Steep are its purple sides, where folded flocks are a-slumber,
And on the further slope, warm in the depth of the vale,
Cluster'd hop-poles stand, like the tents of an army
    encamping,

Soon to be sever'd and ranged, soon to be leafy and green.
Over against us here, on the opposite height, on the summit,
Hempstead stands alone, grey with its gables and barns;
And from Hempstead farm, right on to the western horizon,
Fold upon fold, our hills rise like the waves of the sea;
Crested with high dim lawns, and tufted with copses and
     timber.
Till on the lucid sky loftier ridges appear.

A. J. MUNBY

Tunbridge Wells
(c. 1800)

No more a word I'll sing or say
Of *Turnham Green*, or *Swansea Bay*;
The Muse another story tells,
Her present love is *Tunbridge Wells*.

To Indolence, with heart serene,
Apollo dedicates the scene;
A mind that vacancy repels
Is best away from *Tunbridge Wells*.

Oblivion buries in repose
The debts and cares that Avarice knows;
The keepsake has a thousand spells
For hands and hearts in *Tunbridge Wells*.

The Goddess of the mineral spring
Has rosy health upon her wing;
Each cup the appetite impels,
No better cook for *Tunbridge Wells*.

The morning's letters, or the news,
A short and listless hour amuse:
In vain abroad the battle swells,
It's a mere *novel* at the *Wells*.

GEORGE HARDINGE, *Tunbridge Wells*

Beechwoods at Knole

How do I love you, beech-trees, in the autumn,
Your stone-grey columns a cathedral nave
Processional above the earth's brown glory!

I was a child, and loved the knurly tangle
Of roots that coiled above a scarp like serpents,
Where I might hide my treasure with the squirrels.

I was a child, and splashed my way in laughter
Through drifts of leaves, where underfoot the beech-nuts
Split with crisp crackle to my great rejoicing.

Red are the beechen slopes below Shock Tavern,
Red is the bracken on the sandy Furze-field,
Red are the stags and hinds by Bo-Pit Meadows,

The rutting stags that nightly through the beech-woods
Bell out their challenge, carrying their antlers
Proudly beneath the antlered autumn branches.

I was a child, and heard the red deer's challenge
Prowling and belling underneath my window,
Never a cry so haughty or so mournful.

V. SACKVILLE-WEST

At Rugmer

Among sequestered farms and where brown orchards
Weave in the thin and coiling wind, and where
The pale cold river ripples still as moorhens
Work their restless crossing,
Among such places, when October warnings
Sound from each kex and thorn and shifting leaf,
We well might wander, and renew some stories
Of a dim time when we were kex and thorn,
Sere leaf, ready to hear a hissing wind
Whip down and wipe us out; our season seemed
At any second closing.
So, we were wrong. But we have lived this landscape,
And have an understanding with these shades.

EDMUND BLUNDEN

Dover Cliffs

Heere's the place: stand still: how fearefull
And dizie 'tis, to cast one's eyes so low,
The Crowes and Choughes, that wing the midway ayre
Shew scarce so grosse as Beetles. Halfe way downe
Hangs one that gathers Sampire: dreadfull Trade:
Me thinkes he seemes no bigger than his head.
The Fishermen, that walke upon the beach
Appeare like Mice: and yond tall Anchoring Barke,
Diminish'd to her Cocke: her Cocke, a Buoy
Almost too small for sight. The murmuring Surge,
That on th' unnumbred idle Pebbles chafes.
Cannot be heard so high.

WILLIAM SHAKESPEARE, *King Lear*

In Romney Marsh

As I went down to Dymchurch Wall,
    I heard the South sing o'er the land;
I saw the yellow sunlight fall
    On knolls where Norman churches stand.

And ringing shrilly, taut and lithe,
    Within the wind a core of sound,
The wire from Romney town to Hythe
    Alone its airy journey wound.

A veil of purple vapour flowed
    And trailed its fringe along the Straits;
The upper air like sapphire glowed;
    And roses filled heaven's central gates.

Masts in the offing wagged their tops;
    The swinging waves pealed on the shore;
The saffron beach, all diamond drops
    And beads of surge, prolonged the roar.

As I came up from Dymchurch Wall,
    I saw above the Down's low crest
The crimson brands of sunset fall,
    Flicker and fade from out the west.

Night sank: like flakes of silver fire
　　The stars in one great shower came down;
Shrill blew the wind; and shrill the wire
　　Rang out from Hythe to Romney town.

The darkly shining salt sea drops
　　Streamed as the waves clashed on the shore;
The beach, with all its organ stops
　　Pealing again, prolonged the roar.

JOHN DAVIDSON

Dungeness

Like rowling Hills, the Billowes beate and roare
Against the melancholly Beachie shore,
That if we landed, neither strength nor wit
Could save our Boate from being sunke or split.
To keepe the Sea, sterne puffing *Eols* breath
Did threaten still to blow us all to death,
The waves amaine (unbid) oft boorded us,
Whilst we almost three hours beleaguered thus,
On every side with danger and distresse,
Resolv'd to run on shore at *Dengie Nesse*.
There stand some thirteene Cottages together,
To shelter Fishermen from winde and weather
And there some people were as I suppos'd,
Although the dores and windowes all were kept clos'd:
I neere the land, into the Sea soone leapt
To see what people those same houses kept,
I knock'd and cal'd, at each, from house to house,
But found no forme of mankinde, Man[1] or Mouse.

JOHN TAYLOR, *A Discovery by Sea*

SUSSEX　　　　　*Sussex*

God gave all men all earth to love,
　　But, since our hearts are small,
Ordained for each one spot should prove

---

[1] No dwelling within neere three miles of those Cottages.

Belovèd over all;
That, as He watched Creation's birth,
  So we, in godlike mood,
May of our love create our earth
  And see that it is good.

So one shall Baltic pines content,
  As one some Surrey glade,
Or one the palm-grove's droned lament
  Before Levuka's Trade.
Each to his choice, and I rejoice
  The lot has fallen to me.
In a fair ground—in a fair ground—
  Yea, Sussex by the sea!

No tender-hearted garden crowns,
  No bosomed woods adorn
Our blunt, bow-headed, whale-backed Downs,
  But gnarled and writhen thorn—
Bare slopes where chasing shadows skim,
  And, through the gaps revealed,
Belt upon belt, the wooded, dim,
  Blue goodness of the Weald.

Clean of officious fence or hedge,
  Half-wild and wholly tame,
The wise turf cloaks the white cliff edge
  As when the Romans came.
What sign of those that fought and died
  At shift of sword and sword?
The barrow and the camp abide,
  The sunlight and the sward.

Here leaps ashore the full Sou'west
  All heavy-winged with brine,
Here lies above the folded crest
  The Channel's leaden line;
And here the sea-fogs lap and cling,
  And here, each warning each,
The sheep-bells and the ship-bells ring
  Along the hidden beach.

We have no waters to delight
  Our broad and brookless vales—
Only the dewpond on the height

Unfed, that never fails—
  Whereby no tattered herbage tells
    Which way the season flies—
Only our close-bit thyme that smells
    Like dawn in Paradise.

Here through the strong unhampered days
    The tinkling silence thrills;
Or little, lost, Down churches praise
    The Lord who made the hills:
But here the Old Gods guard their round,
    And, in her secret heart,
The heathen kingdom Wilfrid found
    Dreams, as she dwells, apart.

Though all the rest were all my share,
    With equal soul I'd see
Her nine-and-thirty sisters fair,
    Yet none more fair than she.
Choose ye your need from Thames to Tweed,
    And I will choose instead
Such lands as lie 'twixt Rake and Rye,
    Black Down and Beachy Head.

I will go out against the sun
    Where the rolled scarp retires,
And the Long Man of Wilmington
    Looks naked toward the shires;
And east till doubling Rother crawls
    To find the fickle tide,
By dry and sea-forgotten walls,
    Our ports of stranded pride.

I will go north about the shaws
    And the deep ghylls that breed
Huge oaks and old, the which we hold
    No more than Sussex weed;
Or south where windy Piddinghoe's
    Begilded dolphin veers,
And red beside wind-bank'd Ouse
    Lie down our Sussex steers.

So to the land our hearts we give
    Till the sure magic strike,

And Memory, Use and Love make live
    Us and our fields alike—
That deeper than our speech and thought,
    Beyond our reason's sway,
Clay of the pit whence we were wrought
    Yearns to its fellow-clay.

God gives all men all earth to love,
    But since man's heart is small,
Ordains for each one spot shall prove
    Belovèd over all.
Each to his choice, and I rejoice
    The lot has fallen to me
In a fair ground—in a fair ground—
    Yea, Sussex by the sea!

RUDYARD KIPLING

Hastings

'Twas August—Hastings every day was filling—
Hastings that 'greenest spot on memory's waste'.
With crowds of idlers willing or unwilling
To be bedipped—to be noticed—or be braced,
And all things rose a penny in a shilling.
Meanwhile, from window and from door, in haste
'Accommodation bills' kept coming down,
Gladding 'the world of letters' in that town.

Each day pour'd in new coachfuls of new cits,
Flying from London smoke and dust annoying,
Unmarried Misses hoping to make hits,
And new-wed couples fresh from Tunbridge toying,
Lacemen and placemen, ministers and wits,
And Quakers of both sexes, much enjoying
A mornings reading by the ocean's rim,
That sect delighting in the sea's broad brim.

THOMAS HOOD, *A Storm at Hastings*

Far Meadow

Far Meadow is a road of villas now.
Bright pink-tiled roofs thrust up blunt wedges
into a smoke-streaked sky.
The green earth was flayed
to make those crazy-paving paths and skimpy hedges,
those sparse and trivial lawns. Where I
once lay with Amaryllis in the shade
a red door flaunts 'Killarney' on its brow;
at 'Mon Abri' a ruminating cow
sprawled, sad-eyed, as we played;
and 'Kosy Kot' competes with 'U-an-I'
where, under a languid maple bough,
fat cotton clouds crawled by
with crinkled edges
while I protested but obeyed.
Gone trees, gone maid,
gone clouds and ruminating cow.
Far Meadow is a road of villas now.

DANIEL GEORGE

Blackdown

Come, come, and climb with me to this great Down
    Where the sea-roar of pines puts care to sleep,
And 'midst the blaeberry and heather brown
    Watch far below resistless shadows sweep
The Wealden plain whose villages ray fire
From many a chanted shire—
    Walk with me now above the plains and seas
Ere in us both the springs of life expire—
    And leave with hearts flung open to the breeze
Self-muttering cities, that have lost horizons,
To sink behind the mountains and the trees!

HERBERT TRENCH, *Song on Blackdown*

Written on the Sands below Beachy Head
(1797)

With giant-port high towering o'er the main,
    BEACHY, thy cliffs in massy grandeur rise
    Like some cleft castle, which with calm disdain
    Still braves the outrage of inclement skies:
The daws that round thy chalky summit soar
    Are dimly seen, and feebly heard their cries,
    While the hoarse tide that flows with horrid roar,
    Round many a fallen crag indignant sighs,
And steeps in foam yon sable-vested chain
    Of rocky terrors; England's wide defence
    Against her foes; where oft th' invading Dane
Fell a stern victim to his bold pretence;
    Where proud Iberia's vast Armada fled,
    And with its countless wrecks th' unsated ocean fed.

THOMAS PARK

Brighton

All electric, down from London
Every hour the green trains run,
Bearing tribes of worshippers
To the doubtful Brighton sun.

Kipling has sung of the Sussex Downs
And Belloc of Wealden beer,
But I would tell a different tale,
Of a domed and garnished pier.

Of an elegant Adam fireplace
In a third-rate dancing club,
Forgotten print of the Regent
In a dusty, smoke-fumed pub.

Regency houses, row on row,
In crescent, square and street,
With pediment, pillar and portico,
'BED & BREAKFAST' all complete.

Strange-wrought Gothic street-lamps,
Churches a-gleam with tile
Jostling the chrome and marble
Of super-cinema style.

From the tomb-like cold Pavilion,
Drawing Rooms and Dome
Regency ghosts are sweeping
Through the town that was their home.

Do they see the plaster peeling,
The fly-blown fluted ceiling
Regency houses tumbled down,
Hove another, *nicer* town,
The Phaeton gone for the family car,
Electric light in the Oyster-bar,
And buses bluing the salt sea-air
Under the trees in Castle Square?

Would they sing to the swing of the dance band,
Sway to the play with the grand-stand,
Swerve in a curve at the ice-rink,
Savour the flavour of soft drink,
Find this a madder, gladder revel
Than their elegant, arrogant dance with the Devil?

And would they return to Hell by way
Of Brighton beach on a summer's day?
Would they trip with trippers up-to-date
And, Regency ghosts immaculate,
Arm in arm and devil-may-care
Past the whelk-stalls, through the profanity,
Step
    down
        the
            steep
                stone
                    stair
                        Into the huddle of hot humanity?

JOHN ARLOTT

Brighton Pier

How even, flat and similar,
These strips of plank beneath our feet,
Unconscious quite, my weary eyes
Force me to tread on every joint
Of plank to plank.
I seem to lay my road
Treading flat the boarding as I go—
And so I ponder,
Think still further, further, from me.
Then thump, thump, thump,
These leaden feet tread on my mind
And bring me back again.
Strips of white trouser
Shooting to and fro,
Jumping forward, jerking back,
Gay blazers, skirts of flimsy muslin,
Squirts of sunshine, flopping hats—
The planks re-echoing and springing to the footsteps.
Here, at the water's edge, I stop.
And lean upon the parapet:—

There are pierrots dancing in their booth
Flooded with strong draughts of sunlight;
They twist and turn beneath the rays
Like wisps of faint blue smoke.
I cannot hear their song:
But distant sounds
Like bubbles breaking
Reach my ears.—
Small waves roll gently forward,
Raise their tired heads
And slowly break to foam—
As sudden as you turn
A page over in a book.

SACHEVERELL SITWELL

Off the Sussex Coast

Then madly, gladly out to sea we thrust,
Gainst windes and stormes and many a churlish Gust:
By *Kingston* Chappell, and by *Rustington*,
By little *Hampton*, and by *Middleton*,
To *Bognores* fearefull Rockes, which hidden lie
Two miles into the Sea, some wet, some dry.

JOHN TAYLOR, *A Discovery by Sea*

The Run of the Downs

The Weald is good, the Downs are best—
I'll give you the run of 'em, East to West.
Beachy Head and Winddoor Hill,
They were once and they are still.
Firle, Mount Caburn and Mount Harry
Go back as far as sums'll carry.
Ditchling Beacon and Chanctonbury Ring,
They have looked on many a thing,
And what those two have missed between 'em,
I reckon Truleigh Hill has seen 'em.
Highden, Bignor and Duncton Down
Knew Old England before the Crown.
Linch Down, Treyford and Sunwood
Knew Old England before the Flood;
And when you end on the Hampshire side—
Butser's old as Time and Tide.
    The Downs are sheep, the Weald is corn,
    You be glad you are Sussex born!

RUDYARD KIPLING

BERKSHIRE   ## The Plough
                 A Landscape in Berkshire

Above yon sombre swell of land
    Thou see'st the dawn's grave orange hue,
With one pale streak like yellow sand,

And over that a vein of blue.

The air is cold above the woods;
All silent is the earth and sky,
Except with his own lonely moods
    The blackbird holds a colloquy.

Over the broad hill creeps a beam,
    Like hopes that gilds a good man's brow;
And now ascends the nostril-steam
    Of stalwart horses come to plough.

Ye rigid ploughmen, bear in mind—
    Your labour is for future hours:
Advance—spare not—nor look behind—
    Plough deep and straight with all your powers.

R. HENGIST HORNE

The Scholar-Gipsy

Go, for they call you, shepherd, from the hill;
    Go, shepherd, and untie the wattled cotes;
        No longer leave thy wistful flock unfed,
    Nor let thy bawling fellows rack their throats,
        Nor the cropp'd grasses shoot another head.
            But when the fields are still,
    And the tired men and dogs all gone to rest,
        And only the white sheep are sometimes seen
        Cross and recross the strips of moon-blanch'd green,
    Come, shepherd, and again begin the quest.

Here, where the reaper was at work of late—
    In this high field's dark corner, where he leaves
        His coat, his basket, and his earthen cruse,
    And in the sun all morning binds the sheaves,
        Then here, at noon, comes back his stores to use—
            Here will I sit and wait,
    While to my ear from uplands far away
        The bleating of the folded flocks is borne,
        With distant cries of reapers in the corn—
    All the live murmur of a summer's day.

Screen'd is this nook o'er the high, half-reap'd field,
 And here till sun-down, shepherd, will I be.
  Through the thick corn the scarlet poppies peep,
 And round green roots and yellowing stalks I see
  Pale pink convolvulus in tendrils creep;
   And air-swept lindens yield
 Their scent, and rustle down their perfumed showers
  Of bloom on the bent grass where I am laid,
  And bower me from the August sun with shade;
 And the eye travels down to Oxford's towers.

And near me on the grass lies Glanvil's book—
 Come, let me read the oft-read tale again:
  The story of the Oxford scholar poor,
 Of pregnant parts and quick inventive brain,
  Who, tired of knocking at preferment's door,
   One summer morn forsook
 His friends, and went to learn the gipsy lore,
  And roam'd the world with that wild brotherhood,
  And came, as most men deem'd, to little good,
 But came to Oxford and his friends no more.

But once, years after, in the country lanes,
 Two scholars, whom at college erst he knew,
  Met him, and of his way of life enquired;
 Whereat he answer'd, that the gipsy crew,
  His mates, had arts to rule as they desired
   The workings of men's brains,
 And they can bind them to what thoughts they will.
  'And I', he said, 'the secret of their art,
  When fully learn'd, will to the world impart;
 But it needs heaven-sent moments for this skill.'

This said, he left them, and return'd no more.—
 But rumours hung about the country-side,
  That the lost Scholar long was seen to stray,
 Seen by rare glimpses, pensive and tongue-tied,
  In hat of antique shape, and cloak of grey,
   The same the gipsies wore.
 Shepherds had met him on the Hurst in spring;
  At some lone alehouse in the Berkshire moors,
  On the warm ingle-bench, the smock-frock'd boors
 Had found him seated at their entering,

But, 'mid their drink and clatter, he would fly.
 And I myself seem hard to know thy looks,

68

And put the shepherds, wanderer, on thy trace;
And boys who in lone wheatfields scare the rooks
  I ask if thou hast pass'd their quiet place;
    Or in my boat I lie
Moor'd to the cool bank in the summer heats,
  'Mid wide grass meadows which the sunshine fills,
  And watch the warm, green-muffled Cumner hills,
And wonder if thou haunt'st their shy retreats.

For most, I know, thou lov'st retired ground:
  Thee, at the ferry, Oxford riders blithe,
    Returning home on summer nights, have met
Crossing the stripling Thames at Bab-lock-hithe,
    Trailing in the cool stream thy fingers wet,
      As the slow punt swings round;
  And leaning backward in a pensive dream,
    And fostering in thy lap a heap of flowers
    Pluck'd in shy fields and distant Wychwood bowers,
And thine eyes resting on the moonlit stream.

And then they land, and thou art seen no more:—
  Maidens, who from the distant hamlets come
    To dance around the Fyfield elm in May,
Oft through the darkening fields have seen thee roam,
    Or cross a stile into the public way.
      Oft thou hast given them store
Of flowers—the frail-leaf'd white anemony,
    Dark bluebells drench'd with dews of summer eves,
    And purple orchises with spotted leaves—
But none hath words she can report of thee.

And, above Godstow Bridge, when hay-time's here
  In June, and many a scythe in sunshine flames,
    Men who through those wide fields of breezy grass
Where black-wing'd swallows haunt the glittering Thames,
    To bathe in the abandon'd lasher pass,
      Have often pass'd thee near
Sitting upon the river bank o'ergrown;
    Mark'd thine outlandish garb, thy figure spare,
    Thy dark vague eyes, and soft abstracted air—
But, when they came from bathing, thou wert gone.

At some lone homestead in the Cumner hills,
  Where at her open door the housewife darns,

Thou hast been seen, or hanging on a gate
To watch the threshers in the mossy barns.
  Children, who early range these slopes and late
    For cresses from the rills,
Have known thee watching, all an April day,
  The springing pastures and the feeding kine;
    And mark'd thee, when the stars come out and shine,
Through the long dewy grass move slow away.

In autumn, on the skirts of Bagley Wood—
  Where most the gipsies by the turf-edged way
    Pitch their smoked tents, and every bush you see
With scarlet patches tagg'd and shreds of grey,
    Above the forest-ground called Thessaly—
      The blackbird, picking food,
Sees thee, nor stops his meal, nor fears at all;
  So often has he known three past him stray,
  Rapt, twirling in thy hand a wither'd spray,
And waiting for the spark from heaven to fall.

And once, in winter, on the causeway chill
  Where home through flooded fields foot-travellers go,
    Have I not pass'd thee on the wooden bridge,
Wrapt in thy cloak and battling with the snow,
    Thy face towards Hinksey and its wintry ridge?
      And thou hast climb'd the hill,
And gain'd the white brow of the Cumner range;
  Turn'd once to watch, while thick the snowflakes fall,
  The line of festal light in Christ Church hall—
Then sought thy straw in some sequester'd grange.

But what—I dream! Two hundred years are flown
  Since first thy story ran through Oxford halls,
    And the grave Glanvil did the tale inscribe
That thou wert wander'd from the studious walls
    To learn strange arts, and join a gipsy tribe;
      And thou from earth art gone
Long since, and in some quiet churchyard laid—
  Some country nook, where o'er thy unknown grave
  Tall grasses and white flowering nettles wave,
Under a dark, red-fruited yew-tree's shade.

MATTHEW ARNOLD, *The Scholar-Gipsy*

Laleham: Matthew Arnold's Grave

Beside the broad, gray Thames one lies,
With whom a spring of beauty dies:
Among the willows, the pure wind
Calls all his wistful song to mind;
And, as the calm, strong river flows,
With it his mightier music goes;
But those winds cool, those wavers lave,
The country of his chosen grave.
Go past the cottage flowers, and see,
Where Arnold held it good to be!
Half church, half cottage, comely stands
An holy house, from Norman hands:
By rustic Time well taught to wear
Some lowly, meditative air:
Long ages of a pastoral race
Have softened sternness into grace;
And many a touch of simpler use
From Norman strength hath set it loose.
Here, under old, red-fruited yews,
And summer suns, and autumn dews,
With his lost children at his side,
Sleeps Arnold: Still those waters glide,
Those winds blow softly down their breast:
But he, who loved them, is at rest.

LIONEL JOHNSON

Lollingdon Downs

Up on the downs the red-eyed kestrels hover,
Eyeing the grass.
The field-mouse flits like a shadow into cover
As their shadows pass.

Men are burning the gorse on the down's shoulder;
A drift of smoke
Glitters with fire and hangs, and the skies smoulder,
And the lungs choke.

Once the tribe did thus on the downs, on these downs, burning
Men in the frame,
Crying to the gods of the downs till their brains were turning
And the gods came.

And to-day on the downs, in the wind, the hawks, the grasses,
In blood and air,
Something passes me and cries as it passes,
On the chalk downland bare.

JOHN MASEFIELD

View from Faringdon Hill

More westward when we cast our wandering eyes
Level as oceans bed the champaign lies:
While like some promontory's rugged brow
Proud BADBURY's height o'erlooks the plain below,
Where, in yon SAXON camp, the mill its sails
Spreads to the wind, and courts the rising gales.
Beneath how open lies the spacious scene!
No lofty mountains envious intervene;
But o'er the extended lawns our fancies stray,
Till lost in hazy mists they fade away,
By faint degrees the distant prospect dies,
And the blue landscape melts into the skies.

Where gently COLE's pellucid waters glide,
Here FAIRFORD rears her tower with conscious pride;
Whose windows, with historic painting dight,
Arrest the curious traveller's wondering sight:
And there, conspicuous 'mid the lawny glade,
Fair CIRENCESTER spread her ample shade.

HENRY JAMES PYE, *Faringdon Hill*

The Shepherd

Within a wattled cote on Ridgeway Down
Tending his labouring ewes by the faint light
Of his horn-lantern, through the cloudy night

The shepherd hears high overhead a flight
Of raiders making for some Western town.

Shielding the light within his coat, he stands
For a brief troubled moment harkening
To that deep drone of death upon the wing;
Then turns to his own business, to bring
Innocent life to birth with tender hands.

WILFRID WILSON GIBSON

Upper Lambourne

Up the ash tree climbs the ivy,
    Up the ivy climbs the sun.
With a twenty thousand pattering
    Has a valley breeze begun,
Feather ash, neglected elder,
    Shift the shade and make it run—

Shift the shade toward the nettles,
    And the nettles set it free
To streak the stained Cararra headstone
    Where, in nineteen-twenty-three,
He who trained a hundred winners
    Paid the Final Entrance Fee.

Leathery limbs of Upper Lambourne,
    Leather skin from sun and wind,
Leathery breeches, spreading stables,
    Shining saddles left behind,
To the down the string of horses
    Moving out of sight and mind.

Feathery ash in leathery Lambourne
    Waves above the sarsen stone,
And Edwardian plantations
    So coniferously moan
As to make the swelling downland,
    Far surrounding, seem their own.

JOHN BETJEMAN

HAMPSHIRE　　　　　　*Silchester*

(The Roman Calleva)

For these old city-walls, a half-league round,
Are but the girdle now of rural ground;
These stones from far-off fields, toil-gathered thence
For man's protection, but a farm's ring-fence;
The fruit of all his planning and his pain
By Nature's certain hand resumed again!

Yet eyes instructed, as along they pass,
May learn from crossing lines of stunted grass,
And stunted wheat-stems that refuse to grow,
What intersecting causeways sleep below.
And ploughshare, deeplier delving on its path,
Will oft break in on pavement quaint or bath;
Or flax-haired little one, from neighbouring cot,
Will hap on rusted coin, she knows not what;
'Bout which though grave collectors make great stir,
Some pretty pebble found had more contented her.

From trees that shade thine amphitheatre,
Hoarse caws the rook, and redbreast carols clear;
All silent else! nor human foot nor call
Are heard today within its turfy wall;
Gone—many a century since—its shouts, its shows;
Here thought may now hold commune with repose.

JOHN KENYON, *Silchester*

Basingstoke

Of Basingstoke in Hampshire
The claims to fame are small:—
A derelict canal
And a cream and green Town Hall.

At each week-end the 'locals'
Line the Market Square,
And as the traffic passes,
They stand and stand and stare.

LESLIE THOMAS

Winchester

Music is the thought of thee;
Fragrance, all thy memory.
Those thy rugged Chambers old,
In their gloom and rudeness, hold
Dear remembrances of gold.
Some first blossoming of flowers
Made delight of all the hours;
Greatness, beauty, all things fair
Made the spirit of thine air:
Old years live with thee; thy sons
Walk with high companions.
Then, the natural joy of earth,
Joy of very health and birth!
Hills, upon a summer noon:
Water Meads, on eves of June:
Chamber Court, beneath the moon:
Days of spring, on Twyford Down,
Or when autumn woods grew brown;
As they looked, when here came Keats
Chaunting of autumnal sweets;
Through this city of old haunts,
Murmuring immortal chaunts;
As when Pope, art's earlier king,
Here, a child, did nought but sing;
Sang, a child, by nature's rule,
Round the trees of Twyford School:
Hours of sun beside Meads' Wall,
Ere the may began to fall;
Watching the rooks rise and soar,
High from lime and sycamore:
Wanderings by old-world ways,
Walks and streets of ancient days;
Closes, churches, arches, halls,
Vanished men's memorials.

LIONEL JOHNSON, *Winchester*

75

Selborne

I

Oft on some evening, sunny, soft, and still
The Muse shall lead thee to the beech-grown hill,
To spend in tea the cool, refreshing hour,
Where nods in air the pensile, nest-like bower;[1]
Or where the hermit hangs the straw-clad cell,[2]
Emerging gently, from the leafy dell;
By Fancy plann'd; as once th' inventive maid
Met the hoar sage amid the secret shade;
Romantic spot! from whence in prospect lies
Whate'er of landscape charms our feasting eyes;
The pointed spire, the hall, the pasture-plain,
The russet fallow, or the golden grain,
The breezy lake that sheds a gleaming light,
Till all the fading picture fail the sight.

* * *

Now climb the steep, drop now your eye below,
Where round the blooming village orchards grow;
There, like a picture, lies my lowly seat,
A rural, shelter'd, unobserv'd retreat.
Me far above the rest Selbornian scenes,
The pendent forests, and the mountain greens
Strike with delight; there spreads the distant view,
That gradual fades till sunk in misty blue:
Here Nature hangs her slopy woods to sight,
Rills purl between and dart a quivering light.

GILBERT WHITE, *The Invitation to Selborne*

II

When day declining sheds a milder gleam,
What time the may-fly haunts the pool or stream;
When the still owl skims round the grassy mead,
What time the timorous hare limps forth to feed;
Then be the time to steal adown the vale,

---

[1] A kind of arbour on the side of a hill.
[2] A grotesque building, contrived by a young gentleman, who used on occasion to appear in the
character of a hermit.

And listen to the vagrant cuckoo's tale;
To hear the clamorous curlew call his mate,
Or the soft quail his tender pain relate;
To see the swallow sweep the dark'ning plain
Belated, to support her infant train;
To mark the swift in rapid giddy ring
Dash round the steeple, unsubdued of wing;
Amusive birds!—say where your hid retreat
When the frost rages and the tempests beat;
Whence your return by such nice instinct led,
When spring, soft season, lifts her blooming head?
Such baffled searches mock man's prying pride,
The GOD of NATURE is your secret guide!

GILBERT WHITE, *The Naturalist's Summer-Evening Walk*

Portsmouth

The Morning come, we to the Wharfs repair,
Survey the mighty Magazines of War:
Tremendous Rows of Cannon meet our Eyes;
And Iron Deaths, in massy Mountains rise:
Store-houe of Mars! where, rang'd in Order, lay
Ten thousand Thunders for some fatal Day.
  Departing hence, the Dock we travel round,
Where lab'ring Shipwrights rattling Axes sound:
Some bend the stubborn Planks, while others rear
The lofty Mast, or crooked Timber square;
Some ply their Engines, some direct the Toil,
And carefully inspect the mighty Pile;
See ev'ry Chink securely stopt, before
The winged Castle ventures from the Shore.

STEPHEN DUCK, *A Description of a Journey to Marlborough, Bath, Portsmouth, etc.*

Stoke's Bay
(1739)

How am I pleas'd the steep ascent to gain
Where *Stoke's* tall land-mark over-looks the main,

While innocent of heat the morning beams
Play on the flood with ever-varying gleams,
And scarce the gentle zephyr's easy breeze
Russles the silver surface of the seas?
The level strand slowly the wave rolls o'er,
And faintly murmurs on the shelly shore.

*   *   *

Again my eye the lovely scene surveys,
Leaves what distracts, and chuses what may please;
The various windings of the wide-stretch'd coast,
How distant hills in doubtful skies are lost;
How *Portsmouth's* ramparts guard the sea-beat shore,
Her docks, her harbour, and her town secure:
How the fair isle,[1] at beauteous distance plac'd,
Laughs with the wealth of lavish nature grac'd,
Her woods, her fields, her meads, of chearful green,
Chequer with sweet variety the scene.
Here the tall grove surrounds the rural seat,
There russet downs the distant view compleat:
Delicious spot! scarce *Italy* can boast
A nobler soil, or more indulgent coast.

ROBERT GASELEE, *Stoke's Bay*

Southampton

The ocean liners' tow'ring funnels,
Looming over the gaunt, bent, cranes,
Merge with the town like painted turrets
Springing from the dock-side lanes.

Galleon tram-cars gong and rattle
Round the Bargate to the Quay
And the unexpected glimpses
Of a grey, unsea-like sea.

On the wharves each blear-eyed warehouse
Blunts the tang of sailors' tales;
Strictly business: care with cargoes;
Scour the cabins: stow the mails.

[1] The Isle of Wight.

Come cruising from 'The Ocean's Gateway';
Will you go 'White Star' or 'Red'?
Dancing, cocktails, 'Tourist Class',
Put to sea on a feather bed.

There are elms along The Avenue
Where General Gordon rode
And milk-bottles daily broken
On Honeysuckle Road.

JOHN ARLOTT

Cadland,[1] Southampton River

If ever sea maid, from her coral cave,
Beneath the hum of the great surge, has loved
To pass delighted from her green abode,
And, seated on a summer bank, to sing
No earthly music; in a spot like this,
The bard might feign he heard her, as she dried
Her golden hair, yet dripping from the main,
In the slant sunbeam.
                So the pensive bard
Might image, warmed by this enchanting scene,
The ideal form; but though such things are not,
He who has ever felt a thought refined;
He who has wandered on the sea of life,
Forming delightful visions of a home
Of beauty and repose; he who has loved
With filial warmth his country will not pass
Without a look of more than tenderness
On all the scene; from where the pensile birch
Bends on the bank, amid the clustered group
Of the dark hollies; to the woody shore
That steals diminished, to the distant spires
Of Hampton, crowning the long lucid wave.
White in the sun, beneath the forest-shade,
Full shines the frequent sail, like Vanity,
As she goes onward in her glittering trim,
Amid the glances of life's transient morn,
Calling on all to view her!

[1] A beautiful seat of Henry Drummond, Esq.

Vectis[1] there,
That slopes its greensward to the lambent wave,
And shows through softest haze its woods and domes,
With gray St Catherine's[2] creeping to the sky,
Seems like a modest maid, who charms the more
Concealing half her beauties.
                To the East,
Proud, yet complacent, on its subject realm,
With masts innumerable thronged and hulls
Seen indistinct, but formidable, mark
Albion's vast fleet, that like the impatient storm,
Waits but the word to thunder and flash death
On him who dares approach to violate
The shores and living scenes that smile secure
Beneath its dragon-watch!
                Long may they smile!
And long, majestic Albion (while the sound
From East to West, from Albis[3] to the Po,
Of dark contention hurtles), may'st thou rest,
As calm and beautiful this sylvan scene
Looks on the refluent wave that steals below.

W. L. BOWLES

Rhinefield

Rhinefield! as through thy solitude I rove,
Now lost amid the deep wood's gloomy night,
Doubtful I trace a ray of glimmering light;
Now where some antique oak, itself a grove,
Spreads its soft umbrage o'er the sunny glade,
Stretched on its mossy roots at early dawn,
While o'er the furze with light bound leaps the fawn,
I count the herd that crops the dewy blade:
Frequent at eve list to the hum profound
That all around upon the chill breeze floats,
Broke by the lonely keeper's wild, strange notes;
At distance followed by the browsing deer;

[1] The Isle of Wight.
[2] The highest slowly-rising eminence in the Isle of Wight, seen from the river.
[3] The Elbe.

Or the bewildered stranger's plaintive sound
That dies in lessening murmurs on the ear.

WILLIAM SOTHEBY, *A Lodge in the New Forest*

Beaulieu River

Largest of Forest snakes, by heath and scrog
    It stretches in its blue sky-borrowed coat,
For while its tail trails in a cotton bog
    It grips with foaming mouth the Solent's throat.

ANDREW YOUNG

At Boscombe

So, Florence, you have shown to me
All your wild region by the sea;
The pines, mysterious to us both,
Distorted with a sidelong growth
Of boughs irregularly spread,
And rough trunks ivy-garlanded;
The pathways indistinct and brief
Littered with droppings of the leaf;
The bents' precarious and scant
Life on the mounds extravagant
Of sand towards the abysmal sea
Crumbling for ever silently;
The rain-worn gully; the embrowned
Curve, sweeping half the horizon round,
Of low beach smooth to the content
Of the caressing element;
The glad waves' unconstrained advance,
And simultaneous resonance,
And silvery flash, the roving skiff,
And Bournemouth's pier, and Swanage cliff,
Dulling its line of keenest white
In the warm prevalence of light;
And now we sit, you smile, I sigh;
What think we, Florence, you and I?

RICHARD GARNETT, *Lines at Boscombe*

ISLE OF WIGHT

Alum Bay, Isle of Wight

From the gate
Of this home-featured Inn, which nestling cleaves
To its own shelf among the downs, begirt
With trees which lift no branches to defy
The fury of the storm, but crouch in love
Round the low snow-white walls whence they receive
More shelter than they lend,—the heart-soothed guest
Views a furze-dotted common, on each side
Wreathed into waving eminences, clothed
Above the furze with scanty green, in front
Indented sharply to admit the sea,
Spread thence in softest blue,—to which a gorge
Sinking within the valley's deepening green
Invites by grassy path; the Eastern down
Swelling with pride into the waters, shows
Its sward-tipped precipice of radiant white,
And claims the dazzling peak beneath its brow
Part of its ancient bulk, which hints the strength
Of those famed Pinnacles that still withstand
The conquering waves.

*   *   *

The giant cliffs
Scarce veiling more their lines of flint that run
Like veins of moveless blue through their bleak sides,
In moonlight than in day, shall tower as now
(Save when some moss's slender stain shall break
Into the samphire's yellow in mid-air,
To tempt some trembling life), until the eyes
Which gaze in childhood on them shall be dim.
    Yet deem not that these sober forms are all
That Nature here provides, although she frames
These in one lasting picture for the heart.
Within the foldings of the coast she breathes
Hues of fantastic beauty. Thread the gorge,
And, turning on the beach, while the low sea,
Spread out in mirrored gentleness, allows
A path along the curving edge, behold
Such dazzling glory of prismatic tints

Flung o'er the lofty crescent, as assures
The orient gardens where Aladdin plucked
Jewels for fruit no fable,—as if earth,
Provoked to emulate the rainbow's gauds
In lasting mould, had snatched its floating hues
And fixed them here; for never o'er the bay
Flew a celestial arch of brighter grace
Than the gay coast exhibits; here the cliff
Flaunts in a brighter yellow than the stream
Of Tiber wafted; then with softer shades
Declines to pearly white, which blushes soon
With pink as delicate as Autumn's rose
Wears on its scattering leaves; anon the shore
Recedes into a fane-like dell, where stained
With black, as if with sable tapestry hung,
Light pinnacles rise taper; further yet
Swells out in solemn mass a dusky veil
Of purple crimson,—while bright streaks of red
Start out in gleam-like tint, to tell of veins
Which the slow-winning sea, in distant time,
Shall bare to unborn gazers.

SIR THOMAS NOON TALFOURD, *Lines Written at the Needles Hotel, Alum Bay*

Isle of Wight

When the trippers found this island,
they publicised its charms,
And camped on it and tramped on it
And picnicked on its farms.

The paddle-boats brought the strangers
To the half-mile pier at Ryde,
In linen 'slacks' and aertex shirts,
Their women by their side.

The folk of the dolls-house island
Found the invaders strange,
And hid in their little houses,
Out of speaking range.

To the little fields came holiday camps,
Speed-boats to the river,
The little roads were dinned and thronged
By bus, and bike and 'flivver'.

To the garden isle came the tourist trade;
The Needles an afternoon trip,
'Five bob all round the Island'
In a snorting little ship.

But the first hard frost of winter
Sends the hiker to his den,
The islanders come, through unbolted doors,
Into their own again.

The foreigners' cars are ferried away,
The little roads are clear,
And island men in island pubs
Slowly quaff their beer.

In the quiet night they saunter home,
To sure, untroubled sleep:
They linger to talk at street corners
In voices unhurried and deep.

LESLIE THOMAS

4

THE WEST COUNTRY

Wessex Heights

There are some heights in Wessex, shaped as if by a kindly hand
For thinking, dreaming, dying on, and at crises when I stand
Say, on Ingpen Beacon eastward, or on Wylls-Neck westwardly
I seem where I was before my birth, and after death may be
In the lowlands I have no comrade, not even the lone man's
    friend—
Her who suffereth long and is kind; accepts what he is too weak
    to mend:
Down there they are dubious and askance; there nobody thinks
    as I,
But mind-chains do not clank where one's next neighbour is
    sky.
In the towns I am tracked by phantoms having weird detective
    ways—
Shadows of beings who fellowed with myself of earlier days
They hang about at places, and they say harsh heavy things
Men with a wintry sneer, and women with tart disparagings
Down there I seem to be false to myself, my simple self that
    was,
And is not now, and I see him watching, wondering what crass
    cause
Can have merged him into such a strange continuator as this
Who yet has something in common with himself, my chrysalis
I cannot go to the great grey Plain; there's a figure against the
    moon,
Nobody sees it but I, and it makes my breast beat out of tune
I cannot go to the tall-spired town, being barred by the forms
    now passed

For everybody but me, in whose long vision they stand there
    fast.
There's a ghost at Yell'ham Bottom chiding loud at the fall of
    the night,
There's a ghost in Froom-side Vale, thin-lipped and vague, in a
    shroud of white,
There is one in the railway train whenever I do not want it near,
I see its profile against the pane, saying what I would not hear.

As for one rare fair woman, I am now but a thought of hers,
I enter her mind and another thought succeeds me that she
    prefers;
Yet my love for her in its fulness she herself even did not know;
Well, time cures hearts of tenderness, and now I can let her go.

So I am found on Ingpen Beacon, or on Wylls-Neck to the west,
Or else on homely Bulbarrow, or little Pilsdon Crest,
Where men have never cared to haunt, nor women have walked
    with me,
And ghosts then keep their distance; and I know some liberty.

THOMAS HARDY

WILTSHIRE   *Wiltshire Downs*

    The cuckoo's double note
    Loosened like bubbles from a drowning throat
    Floats through the air
    In mockery of pipit, lark and stare.

    The stable boys thud by
    Their horses slinging divots at the sky
    And with bright hooves
    Printing the sodden turf with lucky grooves

    As still as a windhover
    A shepherd in his flapping coat leans over
    His tall sheep-crook
    And shearlings, tegs and yoes cons like a book.

    And one tree-crowned long barrow
    Stretched like a sow that has brought forth her farrow
    Hides a king's bones
    Lying like broken sticks among the stones.

ANDREW YOUNG

Stonehenge

Observatory, altar, temple, tomb,
Erected none knows when by none knows whom,
To serve strange gods or watch familiar stars,
We drive to see you in our motor-cars
And carry picture-postcards back to town
While still the unsleeping stars look coldly down.

SIR JOHN SQUIRE

In Avebury Circle

I see the white clouds blow
From cottages thick-thatched with snow
Clearer than I can read
This great stone monster without feet, wings, head;

A huge night-blackening shadow
Set up by kings in this holy meadow;
But of his fellows most
With those antique Cimmerians are lost

I wonder if King Sil
Will rise and ride from Silbury Hill
Where buried with his horse
He sits, a strange invulnerable corse,

And grey wethers that keep
On Clatford Down their lichened sleep
Drive to this ancient fold
And bring again an age of stone and gold.

ANDREW YOUNG

Salisbury: the Cathedral Close

Once more I came to Sarum Close,
    With joy half memory, half desire,
And breathed the sunny wind that rose
    And blew the shadows o'er the Spire,

And toss'd the lilac's scented plumes,
　　And sway'd the chestnut's thousand cones,
And fill'd my nostrils with perfumes,
　　And shaped the clouds in waifs and zones,
And wafted down the serious strain
　　Of Sarum bells, when, true to time,
I reach'd the Dean's, with heart and brain
　　That trembled to the trembling chime.
'Twas half my home, six years ago.
　　The six years had not alter'd it:
Red-brick and ashlar, long and low,
　　With dormers and with oriels lit.
Geranium, lychnis, rose array'd
　　The windows, all wide open thrown;
And some one in the Study play'd
　　The Wedding-March of Mendelssohn.

COVENTRY PATMORE

The White Horse of Westbury

As from the Dorset shore I travell'd home,
I saw the charger of the Wiltshire wold;
A far-seen figure, stately to behold,
Whose groom the shepherd is, the hoe his comb;
His wizard-spell even sober daylight own'd;
That night I dream'd him into living will;
He neigh'd—and, straight, the chalk pour'd down the hill;
He shook himself, and all beneath was stoned;
Hengist and Horsa shouted o'er my sleep,
Like fierce Achilles; while that storm-blanch'd horse
Sprang to the van of all the Saxon force,
And push'd the Britons to the Western deep;
Then, dream-wise, as it were a thing of course,
He floated upwards, and regain'd the steep.

CHARLES TENNYSON TURNER

DORSETSHIRE *Overlooking the River Stour*

The swallows flew in the curves of an eight
     Above the river-gleam
     In the wet June's last beam:
Like little cross-bows animate
The swallows flew in the curves of an eight
     Above the river-gleam.

Planing up shavings of crystal spray
     A moor-hen darted out
     From the bank thereabout,
And through the stream-shine ripped his way;
Planing up shavings of crystal spray
     A moor-hen darted out.

Closed were the kingcups; and the mead
     Dripped in monotonous green,
     Though the day's morning sheen
Had shown it golden and honeybee'd;
Closed were the kingcups; and the mead
     Dripped in monotonous green.

And never I turned my head, alack,
     While these things met my gaze
     Through the pane's drop-drenched glaze,
To see the more behind my back. . . .
O never I turned, but let, alack,
     These less things hold my gaze!

THOMAS HARDY

Corfe Castle

Framed in a jagged window of grey stones
These wooded pastures have a dream-like air.
You thrill with disbelief
To see the cattle move in a green field.

Grey Purbeck houses by the sun deceived
Sleep with the easy conscience of the old;
The swathes are sweet on slopes new harvested;

Householders prune their gardens, count the slugs;
The beanrows flicker flowers red as flames.

Those to whom life is a picture card
Get their cheap thrill where here the centuries stand
A thrusting mass transfigured by the sun
Reeling above the streets and crowing farms.
The rooks and skylarks are O.K. for sound,
The toppling bastions innocent with stock.

Love grows impulsive here: the best forget;
The failures of the earth will try again.
She would go back to him if he but asked.

The tawny thrush is silent; when he sings
His silence is fulfilled. Who wants to talk
As trippers do? Yet, love,
Before we go be simple as this grass.
Lie rustling for this last time in my arms.
Quicken the dying island with your breath.

ALUN LEWIS

Fifehead

'Twer' where my fondest thoughts do light,
At Fifehead, while we spent the night;
The millwheel's restèn rim wer' dry,
An' houn's held up their evenèn cry;
An' lofty, droo the midnight sky,
Above the vo'k, wi' heavy heads,
Asleep upon their darksome beds,
The stars were all awake, John.

Noo birds o' dae wer' out to spread
Their wings above the gully's bed,
An' darkness roun' the elem-tree
'D a-still'd the charmy childern's glee.
All he'ths wer' cwold but oone, where we
Wer' gaÿ, 'tis true, but gaÿ an' wise,
An' laëf'd in light o' maïden's eyes,
That glissen'd wide awake, John.

An' when we all, lik' loosen'd hounds,
Broke out o' doors, wi' merry sounds,
Our friends among the playsome team,
All brought us gwäin so vur's the stream,
But Jeäne, that there below a gleam
O' light watch'd oone o's out o' zight;
Vor willènly, vor his 'Good night',
She'd longer bide awake, John.

An' while up *Leighs* we stepp'd along
Our grassy paeth, wi' joke an' zong,
There *Plumber*, wi' its woody ground,
O' slopèn knaps a-screen'd around,
Rose dim 'ithout a breath o' sound,
The wold abode o' squiers a-gone,
Though while they lay a-sleepén on,
Their stars wer' still awake, John.

WILLIAM BARNES

Blackmoor

The primrwose in the sheäde do blow,
The cowslip in the zun,
The thyme upon the down do grow,
The clote[1] where streams do run;
An' where do pretty maïdens grow
An' blow, but where the tow'r
Do rise among the bricken tuns,
In Blackmwore by the Stour.

WILLIAM BARNES, *Blackmwore Maidens*

Oone Rule

An' while I zot, wi' thoughtvul mind,
Up where the Iwonesome Coombs do wind,
An' watch'd the little gully slide
So crookèd to the river-zide;
I thought how wrong the Stour did seem
To roll along his ramblèn stream,

---

[1] Clote, 'water-lily'.

A-runnèn wide the left o' south,
To vind his mouth, the right-hand zide.

But though his stream do teäke, at mill,
An eastward bend by Newton Hill,
An' goo to lae his welcome boon
O' daely water round Hammoon,
An' then wind off ageän, to run
By Blanvord, to the noondae zun
'Tis only bound to oone rule all,
An' that's to vall down steepest ground.

An' zoo, I thought, as we do bend
Our waÿ droo life, to reach our end,
Our God ha' gi'ed us, vrom our youth,
Oone rule to be our guide—His truth.
And zoo wi' that, though we mid teäke
Wide rambles vor our callèns' seäke,
What is, is best, we needen fear,
An' we shall steer to happy rest.

WILLIAM BARNES

View from Lewesdon Hill

From this proud eminence on all sides round
Th' unbroken prospect opens to my view,
On all sides large; save only where the head
Of Pillesdon rises, Pillesdon's lofty Pen:
So call (still rendering to his ancient name
Observance due) that rival Height south-west,
Which like a rampire bounds the vale beneath.
There woods, there blooming orchards, there are seen
Herds ranging, or at rest beneath the shade
Of some wide-branching oak; there goodly fields
Of corn, and verdant pasture, whence the kine
Returning with their milky treasure home
Store the rich dairy: such fair plenty fills
The pleasant vale of Marshwood, pleasant now,
Since that the Spring has deck'd anew the meads
With flowery vesture, and the warmer sun
Their foggy moistness drain'd; in wintry days

Cold, vapourish, miry, wet, and to the flocks
Unfriendly, when autumnal rains begin
To drench the spungy turf: but ere that time
The careful shepherd moves to healthier soil,
In the dank pasturage. Yet not the fields
Of *Evesham*, nor that ample valley named
Of the *White Horse*, its antique monument
Carved in the chalky bourne, for beauty and wealth
Might equal, though surpassing in extent,
This fertile vale, in length from LEWESDON's base
Extended to the sea, and water'd well
By many a rill; but chief with thy clear stream,
Thou nameless Rivulet, who, from the side
Of LEWESDON softly welling forth, dost trip
Adown the valley, wandering sportively.

WILLIAM CROWE, *Lewesdon Hill*

Pentridge by the River

Pentridge!—oh! my heart's a-zwellèn
Vull o' jaÿ wi' vo'k a-tellèn
   Any news o' thik wold pleäce,
An' the boughy hedges round it,
An' the river that do bound it
   Wi' his dark but glis'nèn feäce.
Vor there's noo land, on either hand
To me lik' Pentridge by the river.

Be there any leaves to quiver
On the aspen by the river?
   Doo he sheäde the water still,
Where the rushes be a-growèn,
Where the sullen Stour's a-flowèn
   Drough the meads vrom mill to mill?
Vor if a tree wer dear to me,
Oh! 'twer thik aspen by the river.

There, in eegrass[1] new a-shootèn,
I did run on even vootèn,
   Happy, over new mow'd land;

[1] Eegrass, 'the aftermath'.

Or did zing wi' zingèn drushes
While I plaïted, out o' rushes,
    Little baskets vor my hand;
Bezide the clote[1] that there did float,
Wi' yollow blossoms, on the river.

When the western zun's a-vallén,
What sh'ill vaïce is now a-callèn
    Hwome the deäiry[2] to the païls;
Who do dreve em on, a-flingèn
Wide-bow'd horns, or slowly zwingèn
    Right an' left their tufy taïls?
As they do goo a-huddled drough
The geäte a-leädèn up vrom river.

Bleaded grass is now a-shootèn
Where the vloor wer woonce our vootèn,
    While the hall wer still in pleäce.
Stwones be looser in the wallèn;
Hollow trees be nearer vallèn;
    Ev'ry thing ha' chang'd its feäce.
But still the neäme do bide the seâme—
'Tis Pentridge—Pentridge by the river.

WILLIAM BARNES

Be'mi'ster

(Beaminster)

Sweet Be'mi'ster, that bist a-bound[3]
By green an' woody hills all round,
Wi' hedges, reachèn up between
A thousan' vields o' zummer green,
Where elems' lofty heads do drow
Their sheädes vor haÿ-meakers below,
An' wild hedge-flow'rs do charm the souls
O' maïdens in their evenèn strolls.

When I o' Zunday nights wi' Jeäne
Do saunter drough a vield or leäne,

---

[1] Clote, 'water-lily'.   [3] A-bound, 'bounded'.
[2] The deäiry, 'the dairy-cows'.

Where elder-blossoms be a-spread
Above the eltrot's[1] milk-white head,
An' flow'rs o' blackberries do blow
Upon the brembles, white as snow,
To be outdone avore my zight
By Jeän's gaÿ frock o' dazzlèn white;
Oh! then there's nothèn that's 'ithout[2]
Thy hills that I do ho about,[3]—
Noo bigger pleäce, noo gaÿer town,
Beyond thy sweet bells' dyèn soun',
As they do ring, or strike the hour,
At evenèn vrom they wold red tow'r.
No: shelter still my head, an' keep
My bwones when I do vall asleep!

WILLIAM BARNES

Domicilium

(his birthplace at Higher Bockhampton, Dorset)

It faces west, and round the back and sides
High beeches, bending, hang a veil of boughs,
And sweep against the roof. Wild honeysucks
Climb on the walls, and seem to sprout a wish
(If we may fancy wish of trees and plants)
To overtop the apple-trees hard by.

Red roses, lilacs, variegated box
Are there in plenty, and such hardy flowers
As flourish best untrained. Adjoining these
Are herbs and esculents; and farther still
A field; then cottages with trees, and last
The distant hills and sky.

Behind, the scene is wilder. Heath and furze
Are everything that seems to grow and thrive
Upon the uneven ground. A stunted thorn
Stands here and there, indeed; and from a pit
An oak uprises, springing from a seed
Dropped by some bird a hundred years ago.

[1] Eltrot's, 'wild-parsnip's'. [3] I do ho about, 'I long for'.
[2] 'ithout, 'outside'.

In days bygone—
Long gone—my father's mother, who is now
Blest with the blest, would take me out to walk.
At such a time I once inquired of her
How looked the spot when first she settled here.
The answer I remember. 'Fifty years
Have passed since then, my child, and change has marked
The face of all things. Yonder garden-plots
And orchards were uncultivated slopes
O'ergrown with bramble bushes, furze and thorn:
That road a narrow path shut in by ferns,
Which, almost trees, obscured the passer-by.
Our house stood quite alone, and those tall firs
And beeches were not planted. Snakes and efts
Swarmed in the summer days, and nightly bats
Would fly about our bedrooms. Heathcroppers
Lived on the hills, and were our only friends;
So wild it was when first we settled here.'

THOMAS HARDY

At Lyme Regis

Calm, azure, marble sea,
As a fair palace pavement largely spread,
Where the grey bastions of the eternal hills
Lean over languidly,
Bosomed with leafy trees and garlanded!

Peace is on all I view;
Sunshine and peace; earth clear as heaven one hour;
Save where the sailing cloud its dusky line
Ruffles along the blue,
Brushed by the soft wing of the silent shower.

In no profounder calm
Did the great Spirit over ocean brood,
Ere the first hill his yet unclouded crest
Rear'd, or the first fair palm
Doubled her maiden beauty in the flood.

FRANCIS TURNER PALGRAVE, *At Lyme Regis*

SOMERSETSHIRE *A Song of the Baths*
(Bath)

What Angel stirrs this happy Well,
  Some Muse from thence come shew't me,
One of those naked Graces tell
  That Angels are for beauty:
The Lame themselves that enter here
  Come Angels out againe,
And Bodies turne to Soules all cleere,
  All made for joy, noe payne.

Heate never was so sweetely mett
  With moist as in this shower:
Old men are borne anew by swett
  Of its restoring pow'r:
When crippl'd joints we suppl'd see,
  And second lives new come,
Who can deny this Font to be
  The Bodies Christendome?

One Bath so fiery is you'l thinke
  The Water is all Spirit,
Whose quick'ning streames are like the drink
  Whereby we Life inheritt:
The second Poole of middle straine
  Can wive Virginity,
Tempting the blood to such a vayne
  One sexe is He and She.

The third where horses plunge may bring
  A Pegasus to reare us,
And call for pens from Bladud's wing
  For legging those that beare us.
Why should Phisitians thither fly
  Where waters med'cines be,
Physitians come to cure thereby,
  And are more cured than we.

WILLIAM STRODE

97

Letters from Bath
(1766)

FROM LETTER VII

Of all the gay Places the World can afford,
By Gentle and Simple for Pastime ador'd,
Fine Balls, and fine Concerts, fine Buildings, and Springs,
Fine Walks, and fine Views, and a Thousand fine Things,
Not to mention the sweet Situation and Air,
What Place, my dear Mother, with *Bath* can compare?
Let *Bristol* for Commerce and Dirt be renown'd,
At *Sal'sbury* Pen-Knives and Scissars be ground;
The Towns of *Devizes*, of *Bradford*, and *Frome*,
May boast that they better can manage the Loom;
I believe that they may;—but the world to refine,
In Manners, in Dress, in Politeness to shine,
O *Bath*!—let the Art, let the Glory be thine.

       *   *   *   *   *   *

Our Neighbour *Sir* Easterlyn Widgeon has swore
He ne'er will return to his Bogs any more;
The *Thickskulls* are settled; we've had Invitations
With a great many more on the Score of Relations;
The *Loungers* are come too.—Old STUCCO has just sent
His Plan for a House to be built in the *Crescent*;
'Twill soon be complete, and they say all their Work
Is as strong as *St Paul's*, or the Minster at *York*.
Don't you think 'twould be better to lease our Estate,
And buy a good House here before 'tis too late?
You never can go, my dear Mother, where you
So much have to see and so little to do.

FROM LETTER IX

But come CALLIOPE and say
How pleasure wastes the various Day:
    Whether thou art wont to rove
    By Parade, or Orange Grove,
Or to breathe a purer Air
In the Circus or the Square;
Wheresoever be thy Path,
Tell, O tell the Joys of *Bath*

     *   *   *   *

O the charming Parties made!
Some to walk the South Parade,
Some to LINCOMB's shady Groves,
Or to SIMPSON's proud Alcoves;
Some for Chapel trip away,
Then take Places for the Play:
Or we walk about in Pattins,
Buying Gauzes, cheap'ning Sattins.

CHRISTOPHER ANSTEY, *The New Bath Guide*

Bath

Chalybeate springs; chalybeate face, voice, walk;
Luke-warm chalybeate City, full of small talk;
Where even the sun, dutifully returning,
Enters our hollow crescents in half-mourning,
And winter fog stands like a hearse in waiting,
High-plumed with vapour from a Roman grating.

Chalybeate houses (ring but do not knock);
Chalybeate minds, to whom all change is shock;
With thought in colonnades and avenues
Down which we go no further than we choose,
And season tickets as our guarantees
That Death will call no sooner than we please.

Chalybeate lives, where we reserve our seat
Indefinitely, not to admit defeat;
And fashion puts new locks upon the doors
Of bankrupt bodies, evading creditors;
And hope is hired with rooms and furniture.
Cured? No. But every year we take the cure.

EISDELL TUCKER

Bath

City lulled asleep by the charm of passing years,
Sweeter smiles thy rest than the radiance round thy peers;
    Only love and lovely remembrance here have place.
Time on thee lies lighter than music on men's ears;
    Dawn and noon and sunset are one before thy face.

A. C. SWINBURNE, *A Ballad of Bath*

Hallam's Church, Clevedon

A grassy field, the lambs, the nibbling sheep,
A blackbird and a thorn, the April smile
Of brooding peace, the gentle airs that wile
The Channel of its moodiness, a steep
That brinks the flood, a little gate to keep
The sacred ground—and then that old gray pile,
A simple church wherein there is no guile
Of ornament; and here the Hallams sleep.
Blest mourner, in whose soul the grief grew song,
Not now, methinks, awakes the slumbering pain,
While Joy, with busy fingers, weaves the woof
Of Spring. But when the Winter nights are long,
Thy spirit comes with sobbing of the rain,
And spreads itself, and moans upon the roof.

T. E. BROWN

Mendip Hills Over Wells

How grand beneath the feet that company
Of steep grey roofs and clustering pinnacles
Of the massy fane, brooding in majesty
Above the town that spreads among the dells!
Hark! the deep clock unrolls its voice of power;
And sweetly-mellowed sound of chiming bells
Calling to prayer from out the central tower
Over the thickly-timbered hollow dwells.
Meet worship-place for such a glorious stretch
Of sunny prospect—for these mighty hills,
And that dark solemn Tor,[1] and all that reach
Of bright green meadows, laced with silver rills,
Bounded by ranges of pale blue, that rise
To where white strips of sea are traced upon the skies.

HENRY ALFORD

[1] Glastonbury Tor.

Nether Stowey
(1798)

But now the gentle dew-fall sends abroad
The fruit-like perfume of the golden furze:
The light has left the summit of the hill,
Though still a sunny gleam lies beautiful,
Aslant the ivied beacon. Now farewell,
Farewell, awhile, O soft and silent spot!
On the green sheep-track, up the heathy hill,
Homeward I wind my way; and lo! recalled
From bodings that have well-nigh wearied me,
I find myself upon the brow, and pause
Startled! And after lonely sojourning
In such a quiet and surrounded nook,
This burst of prospect, here the shadowy main,
Dim-tinted, there the mighty majesty
Of that huge amphitheatre of rich
And elmy fields, seems like society—
Conversing with the mind, and giving it
A livelier impulse and a dance of thought!
And now, belovéd Stowey! I behold
Thy church-tower, and, methinks, the four huge elms
Clustering, which mark the mansion of my friend;
And close behind them, hidden from my view,
Is my own lowly cottage, where my babe
And my babe's mother dwell in peace! With light
And quickened footsteps thitherward I tend,
Remembering thee, O green and silent dell!
And grateful, that by nature's quietness
And solitary musings, all my heart
Is softened, and made worthy to indulge
Love, and the thoughts that yearn for human kind.

S. T. COLERIDGE, *Fears in Solitude* (*written during the alarm of an Invasion*)

Brockley Coomb

Lines
composed while climbing the left ascent of
Brockley Coomb, May 1795

With many a pause and oft reverted eye
I climb the Coomb's ascent: sweet songsters near
Warble in shade their wild-wood melody:
Far off the unvarying Cuckoo soothes my ear.
Up scour the startling stragglers of the flock
That on green plots o'er precipices browze:
From the deep fissures of the naked rock
The Yew-tree bursts! Beneath its dark green boughs
('Mid which the May-thorn blends its blossoms white)
Where broad smooth stones jut out in mossy seats,
I rest:—and now have gained the topmost site.
Ah! what a luxury of landscape meets
My gaze! Proud towers, and Cots more dear to me,
Elm-shadow'd Fields, and prospect-bounding Sea.
Deep sighs my lonely heart: I drop the tear:
Enchanting spot! O were my Sara here.

S. T. COLERIDGE

Porlock

Porlock! thy verdant vale so fair to sight,
Thy lofty hills which fern and furze imbrown,
The waters that roll musically down
Thy woody glens, the traveller with delight
Recalls to memory, and the channel gray
Circling its surges in thy level bay.
Porlock! I shall forget thee not,
Here by the unwelcome summer rain confined;
But often shall hereafter call to mind
How here, a patient prisoner, 't was my lot
To wear the lonely, lingering close of day,
Making my sonnet by the ale-house fire,
Whilst Idleness and Solitude inspire
Dull rhymes to pass the duller hours away.

ROBERT SOUTHEY

DEVONSHIRE   *To Devon*

Haile, thou my native soile! thou blessed plot
Whose equall all the world affordeth not!
Show me who can so many crystall Rils,
Such sweet-cloath'd Vallies or aspiring Hils:
Such Wood-ground, Pastures, Quarries, welthy Mines:
Such Rocks in whom the Diamond fairely shines:
And if the earth can show the like agen,
Yet will she faile in her Sea-ruling men.

WILLIAM BROWNE, *Britannia's Pastorals*

Discontents in Devon

More discontents I never had
    Since I was born, then here;
Where I have been, and still am sad,
    In this dull Devon-shire:
Yet justly too I must confesse;
    I ne'r invented such
Ennobled numbers for the Presse,
    Then where I loath'd so much.

ROBERT HERRICK

The Tavy

As *Tavy* creepes upon
The Westerne vales of fertile *Albion*,
Here dashes roughly on an aged Rocke,
That his extended passage doth up locke;
There intricately 'mongst the Woods doth wander,
Losing himselfe in many a wry Meander:
Here amorously bent, clips some faire Mead;
And then disperst in Rils, doth measures tread
Upon her bosome 'mongst her flowery ranks:
There in another place beares downe the banks
Of some day-labouring wretch: here meets a rill,
And with their forces ioyn'd cuts out a Mill

Into an Iland, then in iocund guise
Survayes his conquest, lauds his enterprise:
Here digs a Cave at some high Mountaines foot:
There undermines an Oake, teares up his root:
Thence rushing to some Country-farme at hand,
Breaks o'er the Yeomans mounds, sweepes from his land
His Harvest hope of Wheat, of Rye, or Pease:
And makes that channell which was Shepherds lease.

WILLIAM BROWNE, *Britannia's Pastorals*

Lynton to Porlock
(Exmoor)

From Lynton when you drive to Porlock,
Just take old Tempus by the forelock—
In any case, don't hurry; time and tide—
Of course—I know. But, where the roads divide,
Upon the moor,
Be sure
To shun the *via dextra*,
And choose the marvellous ride
(One half-hour extra)
That zigzags to a gate
Nigh Porlock town—O, it is great,
That strip of Channel sea,
Backed with the prime of English Arcady!
It is not that the heather rushes
In mad tumultuous flushes
(*Trickling*'s the word I'd use);
But O, the greens and blues
And browns whereon the crimson dwells;
The buds, the bells;
That drop from arch to arch
Of pine and larch;
The scented glooms where soft-fainting culvers
Elude the eye,
And fox-gloves, like innumerous-celled revolvers
Shoot honey-tongued quintessence of July!

T. E. BROWN, *Lynton Verses*

Heddon's Mouth

Happy all, who timely know
the bright gorge, that lies below
Trentishoe and Martinhoe.
Down the vale swift Parracombe
Brawls beneath soft alder gloom,
Toward a sea of sunlit sails,
Flashing far away to Wales.

LIONEL JOHNSON, *Heddon's Mouth*

Clovelly

'Tis eve! 'tis glimmering eve! how fair the scene,
   Touched by the soft hues of the dreamy west!
Dim hills afar, and happy vales between,
   With the tall corn's deep furrow calmly blest;
Beneath, the sea, by eve's fond gale carest,
   'Mid groves of living green that fringe its side;
Dark sails that gleam on Ocean's heaving breast
   From the glad fisher-barks that homeward glide,
   To make Clovelly's shores at pleasant evening-tide.

Hearken! the mingling sounds of earth and sea,
   The pastoral music of the bleating flock,
Blent with the sea-bird's uncouth melody,
   The waves' deep murmur to the unheeding rock,
And ever and anon the impatient shock
   Of some strong billow on the sounding shore:
And hark! the rowers' deep and well-known stroke.
   Glad hearts are there, and joyful hands once more
   Furrow the whitening wave with their returning oar.

But turn where Art with votive hand hath twined
   A living wreath for Nature's grateful brow,
Where the lone wanderer's raptur'd footsteps wind
   'Mid rock, and glancing stream, and shadowy bough
Where scarce the valley's leafy depths allow
   The intruding sunbeam in their shade to dwell,
There doth the seamaid breathe her human vow—
   So village maidens in their envy tell—
   Won from her dark blue home by that alluring dell.

A softer beauty floats along the sky,
  The moonbeam dwells upon the voiceless wave;
Far off, the night-winds steal away and die,
  Or sleep in music in their ocean cave:
Tall oaks, whose strength the giant storm might brave,
  Bend in rude fondness o'er the silvery sea;
Nor can you mountain raun[1] forbear to lave
  Her blushing clusters where the waters be,
  Murmuring around her home such touching melody.

Thou quaint Clovelly! in thy shades of rest,
  When timid Spring her pleasant task hath sped,
Or summer pours from her redundant breast
  All fruits and flowers along thy valley's bed:
Yes! and when Autumn's golden glories spread,
  Till we forget near Winter's withering rage,
What fairer path shall woo the wanderer's tread,
  Sooth wearied hope and worn regret assuage?
  Lo! for firm youth a bower—a home for lapsing age.

R. S. HAWKER

The Golden Land
(Axminster)

O sweet September, in the valley
  Carved through the green hills, sheer and straight,
Where the tall trees crowd round and sally
  Down the slope sides with stately gait
And sylvan dance; and in the hollow
  Silver voices ripple and cry,
        Follow, O follow!

Follow, O follow!—and we follow
  Where the white cottages star the slope,
And the white smoke winds o'er the hollow,
  And the blithe air is quick with hope;
Till the Sun whispers, O remember!
  You have but thirty days to run,
        O sweet September!

[1] Raun, the rowan tree or mountain ash.

O sweet September, where the valley
  Leans out wider and sunny and full,
And the red cliffs dip their feet and dally
  With the green billows, green and cool;
And the green billows, archly smiling,
  Kiss and cling to them, kiss and leave them,
        Bright and beguiling,—

Bright and beguiling as She who glances
  Along the shore and the meadows along,
And sings for heart's delight, and dances
  Crowned with apples, and ruddy, and strong;—
Can we see thee, and not remember
  Thy sun-brown cheek and hair sun-golden,
        O sweet September?

F. T. PALGRAVE

On Ide Hill
(Overlooking Exeter)

O fairest native city, thou art crowned
With an enthralling beauty. Ay! a queen
Enthroned conspicuous o'er the glorious scene,
Tak'st homage from the gazing hills around.
A thousand years protecting watch and ward
These guardians have held, and loving wiles
Oft used to pleasure thee, now wreathed in smiles,
And in grey glooms anon. Their influence reared
Thy tall cathedral's majesty: it stands
In eloquent calm grandeur, and its tale
Speaks to the stars,—how works by human hands
And through man's brain the Universal Soul!
Fringes thee round with leafy dusk the vale,
And 'neath the blue a pomp of cloud doth roll!

WALTER REW

'A view of old Exeter'

Pyne, a small honest painter, well content
To limn our English landscapes, worked and went,
From 1800 onward, seventy years,
Then left the world to louden in men's ears.
Here's his 'Old Exeter'; much eyed by me
Since (how time flits!) full fifteen years ago
I bought it cheap and carried it home to be
A window on my wall making me know
Old Exeter, affectionately recorded
In the now slow-paced 'fifties.
                                    Glancing down
From some neglected meadow near the town,
He hummed and sketched that I might be afforded
This purview of the past's provincial peace.
For J. B. Pyne Old Exeter was good;
Cows in his foreground grazed and strolled and stood:
For J. B. Pyne Victorian clumps of trees
Were golden in a bland October breeze:
Large clouds, like safe investments, loitered by;
And distant Dartmoor loomed in sombre blue.
Perpetuator of that shifting sky,
It never crossed his mind that he might do
From death such things as make me stare and sigh,—
Sigh for that afternoon he thus depicted,—
That simpler world from which we've been evicted.

Here his prim figures cruise and sit and drive
In crinolines as when they were alive.
Out of the town that man and wife are going
In smart new gig, complacently unknowing
Of their great-grandchild's air-raid-worried mind:
Into the town those gentlewomen are walking
Attuned to life, of the new Bishop talking—
Pleased that the eighteenth century's left behind,
And civically unconscious, I conjecture,
Of what it gave them in good architecture.
That group beside the cypresses adds calm

And absent-minded momentary charm
To the industrious artist's composition. . . .
   When J. B. Pyne's, this was a Devon Day.
   For me it shines far far—too far—away;
   For time has changed this 'View' into a Vision.

SIEGFRIED SASSOON

Sunset on Dartmoor

      But now the sun
Is veil'd a moment, and the expansive waste
At once is wrapp'd in shade. The song has ceased
Of the rejoicing earth and sky;—the breeze
Sighs pensively along; the moorland streams
Appear less lovely, and on Fancy's ear
Complaining flow. Again the shadows fly
Before the glancing beam;—again the sun—
The conquering sun resumes his state; and he
That with Elysian forms and hues bedecks
So gloriously the skies, cheers thee,—e'en thee,—
Thou solitary one;—the very heart
Of the wild Moor is glad! The eye discerns
The mountain ridges sweep away in vast
And regular succession;—wave on wave
Rolling and glittering in the sun,—until
They reach the utmost West. The lark is up
Exulting in the bright blue heav'n;—the streams
Leap wantonly adown the laughing slopes;
And on the ear the poetry of bells,
Far borne by Auster's welcome gale, is heard;
All else is mute,—silently happy,—Earth
Reposes in the sunset.

N. T. CARRINGTON, *Dartmoor*

Wistman's Wood,[1] Dartmoor

Thy guardian oaks,
My country, are thy boast—a giant race
And undegenerate still; but of this grove—
This pigmy grove, not one has climb'd the air,
So emulously that its loftiest branch
My brush the traveller's brow. The twisted roots
Have clasp'd, in search of nourishment, the rocks,
And straggled wide, and pierced the stony soil:—
In vain; denied maternal succour, here
A dwarfish race has risen. Round the boughs
Hoary and feeble, and around the trunks,
With grasp destructive, feeding on the life
That lingers yet, the ivy winds, and moss
Of growth enormous. E'en the dull vile weed
Has fix'd itself upon the very crown
Of many an ancient oak; and thus, refused
By nature kindly aid—dishonour'd—old—
Dreary in aspect—silently decays
The lonely *Wood of Wistman*.

N. T. CARRINGTON, *Dartmoor*

Teignmouth
(Seen from the Ness)

He looked across the river stream;
    A little town was there,
O'er which the morning's earliest beam
    Was wandering fresh and fair;
No architect of classic school
Had pondered there with line and rule;
And, stranger still, no modern master
Had wasted there his lath and plaster;
The buildings in strange order lay,
As if the streets had lost their way,
Fantastic, puzzling, narrow, muddy,

---

[1] This solitary relic of Dartmoor forest—a mile or more above Two Bridges—consisting of scrubbed decrepit trees, chiefly oak, which by various causes, have been reduced to uncouth mis-shapen dwarfs.

Excess of toil from lack of study,
Where Fashion's very newest fangles
Had no conception of right angles.
But still about that humble place
There was a look of rustic grace;
'Twas sweet to see the sports and labours
And morning greetings of good neighbours,
The seamen mending sails and oars,
The matrons knitting at the doors,
The invalids enjoying dips,
The children launching tiny ships,
The beldames clothed in rags and wrinkles
Investigating periwinkles.

WINTHROP MACKWORTH PRAED, *Fragments of a Descriptive Poem*

Woodbury

On ancient Woodbury leaps dancing May
Bedecked with bluebells and the gorse's light
Of massy gold, while every birchen height
Sparkles with new-born green; the beeches ray
In emerald stain, and the hawthorn white
Drifts on the bough. Again the swallows play,
The migrant cuckoo chimes; and far away
Exe to her mother sea winds silver bright.
    On knap and knoll the solemn pines embrace,
    Darkling against the azure; where they rest,
    Moss-hidden earthwork leaves a shadow trace
    That Roman legions camped upon the west;
    But Spring from Woodbury's old patient face
    Wipes every wound and loves her withered breast.

EDEN PHILLPOTTS

Branscombe

Silver and ruddy to their forest crown
The ocean-facing cliffs and crags arise
And sea-gulls fashion secret nurseries

Within the stormy wrinkles of their frown.
A million buttercups with yellow eyes
Flood the green water-meads; a rillet brown
Under the hawthorn tumbles, twinkling down
Till in the shingle grey she faints and dies.
　　Like beads uneven strung along the street,
　　Shine cots, with sunny faces cream and white,
　　Behind their wayside gardens, very neat,
　　With rosemary scented and with roses bright;
　　And at the heart of all that radiant light
　　An old church shades her sleepers at her feet.

EDEN PHILLPOTTS

CORNWALL　　*Falmouth Haven*

　　Heere *Vale* a livelie flood, her nobler name that gives
To Falmouth; and by whom, it famous ever lives,
Whose entrance is from sea so intricatelie wound,
Her haven angled so about her barbarous sound,
That in her quiet Bay a hundred ships may ride,
Yet not the tallest mast, be of the tall'st descri'd.

MICHAEL DRAYTON, *Polyolbion*

In Falmouth Harbour

The large, calm harbour lies below
Long, terraced lines of circling light:
Without, the deep sea currents flow:
　　And here are stars, and night.

No sight, no sound, no living stir,
But such as perfect the still bay:
So hushed it is, the voyager
　　Shrinks at the thought of day.

We glide by many a lanterned mast;
Our mournful horns blow wild to warn
Yon looming pier: the sailors cast
　　Their ropes, and watch for morn.

Strange murmurs from the sleeping town,
And sudden creak of lonely oars
Crossing the water, travel down
  The roadstead, the dim shores.

A charm is on the silent bay;
Charms of the sea, charms of the land.
Memories of open wind convey
  Peace to this harbour strand.

Far off, Saint David's crags descend
On seas of desolate storm: and far
From this pure rest, the Land's drear End,
  And ruining waters are.

LIONEL JOHNSON, *In Falmouth Harbour*

Helford River

Helford River, Helford River,
  Blessed may ye be!
We sailed up Helford River
  By Durgan from the sea.

O to hear the hawser chain
  Rattle by the ferry there!
Dear, and shall we come again
    By Bosahan,
By wood and water fair?

All the wood to ransack,
  All the wave explore—
Moon on Calamansack,
  Ripple on the shore.

—Laid asleep and dreaming
  On our cabin beds;
Helford River streaming
  By two happy heads;

—Helford river, streaming
  By Durgan to the sea,
Much have we been dreaming
  Since we dreamed by thee.

Dear, and shall we dream again
   The one dream there?
All may go if that remain
   By Bosahan,
And the old face wear!

SIR A. T. QUILLER-COUCH

St Michael's Mount

St Michael's Mount, the tidal isle,
   In May with daffodils and lilies
Is kirtled gorgeously a while
   As ne'er another English hill is:
   About the precipices cling
   The rich renascence robes of Spring.

Her gold and silver, nature's gifts,
   The prodigal with both hands showers:
O not in patches, not in drifts
   But round and round, a mount of flowers—
   Of lilies and daffodils,
   The envy of all other hills.

And on the lofty summit looms
   The castle: none could build or plan it.
The foursquare foliage springs and blooms,
   The piled elaborate flower of granite,
   That not the sun can wither; no,
   Nor any tempest overthrow.

JOHN DAVIDSON

April Landscape

The cracked bell rings to Lenten service over
The April fields, lifting the mists that hover

Across the dun distances from wood to wood.
Each quiet stroke renews the familiar mood

Of a dream that has been dreamed, and again I hear
The interior, murmuring complaint of prayer.

Now the dark woods of Duporth are pierced with late
Innumerable sweet voices, separate

And clear above the burden of the sea.
The long sea-swell rolls in its symmetry

Of surf, breaking the springwhite flowers of foam
Upon the iron rocks amid the fume

And thunder of spring upon the heaving sea.
The sheltered slope is strewn with sticks that the

April winds have sown: the trees are yet bare.
A night-moth voyages on the uncertain air,

Seeking the dizzy region of the cliffs.
Somewhere in the domed sky a gull laughs

Above the turning world, and with shrill mirth
That the sea should mumble the corners of the earth.

A. L. ROWSE

Boscastle

At Castle Boterel

As I drive to the junction of lane and highway,
    And the drizzle bedrenches the waggonette,
I look behind at the fading byway,
    And see on its slope, now glistening wet,
        Distinctly yet

Myself and a girlish form benighted
    In dry March weather. We climb the road
Beside a chaise. We had just alighted
    To ease the sturdy pony's load
        When he sighed and slowed.

What we did as we climbed, and what we talked of
    Matters not much, nor to what it led,—
Something that life will not be balked of
    Without rude reason till hope is dead,
        And feeling fled.

It filled but a minute. But was there ever
  A time of such quality, since or before,
In that hill's story? To one mind never,
    Though it has been climbed, foot-swift, foot-sore,
      By thousands more.

Primaeval rocks form the road's steep border,
  And much have they faced there, first and last,
Of the transitory in Earth's long order;
    But what they record in colour and cast
      Is—that we two passed.

And to me, though time's unflinching rigour,
  In mindless rote, has ruled from sight
The substance now, one phantom figure
    Remains on the slope, as when that night
      Saw us alight.

I look and see it there, shrinking, shrinking,
  I look back at it amid the rain
For the very last time; for my sand is sinking,
    And I shall traverse old love's domain
      Never again.

THOMAS HARDY

Bodmin Moor
Plash Mill, Under the Moor

The wind leapt, mad-wolf, over the rim of the moor
At a single bound, and with furious uproar
Fell on the tree-ringed house by the deep-cut stream—
Quiet little house standing alone,
Blind, old, pale as the moon,
And sunk in some ancient grassy dream.

Through all the roaring maniac din
Outside, the shadowless stillness there within
Held. No face, all the frantic day,
Pressed the glass, watching the green apple hailstorm,
No child's heart gladdened at thought of where acorns lay,
And beechnuts, treasure for harvesting safe from harm.

Now, firewood in the ragged grass will waste, sodden
Under the winter trees; and the darkening apples lie hidden;
Or, death-brittle, float on the floor under the broken pane.
But when, next March perhaps, sunlight the colour of frost
Wavers through branches to honeycomb some flaking wall
Changeless since autumn, that will be the utmost
Hope realised: light's delicate miracle
Of grace
Still wrought on the forsaken place.

FRANCES BELLERBY

Carn Brea

How the great mountain like a rocky king
Stands silent in the tempest! Not a gust
With water laden, rushing with fierce front
Against his wrinkles, but he shakes it off,
Like filmy atoms from an insect's wing.
The thunder growls upon his splinter'd head,
Yelling from cave to cave, and every crag,
Carved by the Druid in the olden time,
When men were wont to worship on his crest,
Seems like a fiery pillar, as the flames
Leap from the clouds, and lick their knotty sides.
He, awful in his calmness, shakes his locks,
And gazes up into the solemn sky,
As if a strain of music shook the air.
O wondrous mountain, 'neath thy ribs of rock
Lie beds of precious mineral, which, when Time
With tardy feet hath crept through other years,
Shall cheer the seeker with their shining store.
Rude ridge of boulders, carn of polish'd crag!
Eternal utterer of the Deity,
I muse within thy shadow, and look up,
As on the face of the Invisible,
And sounds rush from thee in the tempest's clang,
And rattle round the portals of my soul,
Like oracles from the eternal hills;
And I have thought in childhood, when my feet
First press'd the mosses that hang down thy sides,

And bore me wondering 'mid thine isles of rock,
That on a night of tempest, wild and weird,
The Man i' the Moon had tumbled boulders down,
Which, rolling rudely, raised thee, root and rib.
I need no other monitor to show
The impress of Jehovah. Thou art full
Of the Eternal, and His voice is heard
Among the Druid temples of Carn Brea.

JOHN HARRIS

Tregardock

A mist that from the moor arose
   In sea-fog wraps Port Isaac bay,
The moan of warning from Trevose
   Makes grimmer this October day.

Only the shore and cliffs are clear.
   Gigantic slithering shelves of slate
In waiting awfulness appear
   Like journalism full of hate.

On the steep path a bramble leaf
   Stands motionless and wet with dew,
The grass bends down, the bracken's brown,
   The grey-green gorse alone is new.

Cautious my sliding footsteps go
   To quarried rock and dripping cave;
The ocean, leaden-still below,
   Hardly has strength to lift a wave.

I watch it crisp into its height
   And flap exhausted on the beach,
The long surf menacing and white
   Hissing as far as it can reach.

The dunlin do not move, each bird
   Is stationary on the sand
As if a spirit in it heard
   The final end of sea and land.

And I on my volcano edge
Exposed to ridicule and hate
Still do not dare to leap the ledge
And smash to pieces on the slate.

JOHN BETJEMAN

Trebetherick

We used to picnic where the thrift
Grew deep and tufted to the edge;
We saw the yellow foam flakes drift
In trembling sponges on the ledge
Below us, till the wind would lift
Them up the cliff and o'er the hedge.
Sand in the sandwiches, wasps in the tea,
Sun on our bathing dresses heavy with the wet,
Squelch of the bladder wrack waiting for the sea,
Fleas round the tamarisk, an early cigarette.

From where the coastguard houses stood
One used to see, below the hill,
The lichened branches of a wood
In summer silver-cool and still;
And there the Shade of Evil could
Stretch out at us from Shilla Mill.
Thick with sloe and blackberry, uneven in the light
Lonely ran the hedge, the heavy meadow was remote,
The oldest part of Cornwall was the wood as black as night
And the pheasant and the rabbit lay torn open at the throat.

But when a storm was at its height,
And feathery slate was black in rain,
And tamarisks were hung with light
And golden sand was brown again,
Spring tide and blizzard would unite
And sea came flooding up the lane.
Waves full of treasure then were roaring up the beach,
Ropes round our mackintoshes, waders warm and dry,
We waited for the wreckage to come swirling into reach,
Ralph, Vasey, Alastair, Biddy, John and I.

Then roller into roller curled
  And thundered down the rocky bay,
And we were in a water world
  Of rain and blizzard, sea and spray,
And one against the other hurled
  We struggled round to Greenaway.
    Blesséd be St Enodoc, blesséd be the wave,
    Blesséd be the springy turf, we pray, pray to thee,
    Give to our children all the happy days you gave
    To Ralph, Vasey, Alastair, Biddy, John and me.

JOHN BETJEMAN

Cornwall sea

        The utmost crag
    Of Cornwall, and the storm-encompassed isles
    Where to the sky the rude sea rarely smiles
    Unless in treacherous wrath.

P. B. SHELLEY, *Letter to Maria Gisborne*

Chough

Desolate that cry as though world were unworthy.
See now, rounding the headland, a forlorn hopeless bird,
trembling black wings fingering the blowy air,
dainty and ghostly, careless of the scattering salt.

This is the cave-dweller that flies like a butterfly,
buffeted by daws, almost extinct, who has chosen,
so gentle a bird, to live on furious coasts.

Here where sea whistles in funnels, and slaps the back
of burly granite slabs, and hisses over holes,
in bellowing hollows that shelter the female seal
the Cornish chough wavers over the waves.

By lion rocks, rocks like the heads of queens,
sailing with ragged plumes upturned, into the wind
goes delicate indifferent the doomed bird.

REX WARNER

Rough seas

From Padstow Point to Lundy Light
Is a watery grave by day and night.

ANON. (Old local saying)

Autumn in Cornwall

The year lies fallen and faded
On cliffs by clouds invaded,
With tongues of storms upbraided,
    With wrath of waves bedinned;
And inland, wild with warning,
As in deaf ears or scorning,
The clarion even and morning
    Rings of the south-west wind.

The wild bents wane and wither
In blasts whose breath bows hither
Their grey-grown heads and thither,
    Unblest of rain or sun;
The pale fierce heavens are crowded
With shapes like dreams beclouded,
As though the old year enshrouded
    Lay, long ere life were done.

Full charged with oldworld wonders,
From dusk Tintagel thunders
A note that smites and sunders
    The hard frore fields of air;
A trumpet stormier-sounded
Than once from lists rebounded
When strong men sense-confounded
    Fell thick in tourney there.

A. C. SWINBURNE, *Autumn in Cornwall*

GLOUCESTERSHIRE *Bristol*

How proud,
Opposed to Walton's silent towers, how proud,
With all her spires and fanes and volumed smoke,
Trailing in columns to the midday sun,
Black, or pale blue, above the cloudy haze,
And the great stir of commerce, and the noise
Of passing and repassing wains, and cars,
And sledges grating in their underpath,
And trade's deep murmur, and a street of masts
And pennants from all nations of the earth,
Streaming below the houses, piled aloft,
Hill above hill; and every road below
Gloomy with troops of coal-nymphs, seated high
On their rough pads, in dingy dust serene;—
How proudly amid sights and sounds like these,
Bristol, through all whose smoke, dark and aloof,
Stands Redcliff's solemn fane,—how proudly girt
With villages, and Clifton's airy rocks,
Bristol, the mistress of the Severn sea,—
Bristol, amid her merchant palaces
That ancient city, sits!

W. L. BOWLES, *Banwell Hill*

Clifton

Clifton, in vain thy varied scenes invite—
The mossy bank, dim glade, and dizzy height;
The sheep that starting from the tufted thyme,
Untune the distant churches' mellow chime.

W. S. LANDOR, *An English Scene*

In the Dim City
(BRISTOL)

City of clanging bells
And narrow, dingy streets,
Where the continuous din of traffic swells,

The throb of commerce beats.
At times, when sundown over smoky piles
Stretches a healing hand,
There comes a touch of love that reconciles,
A glory that the soul can understand.
Round dusky roofs and spires
Eddy the driven clouds of sunset fires;
With marvellous mutation
Flames the swift mystery of transfiguration.
One moment—and we deem
Thou art the magic city of a dream:
One moment—and the gloom
Hath foiled the gleam:
City of toil, and want, and mortal doom.

Close to thine ancient walls
Come subtle whisperings of the Severn Sea.
I stand upon thy quay
Amid the noisy calls,
The dissonant cries,
The clash and hurry of thy merchandise;
And with the tide that creeps
In stained impurity,
There comes a legend of far ocean deeps,
Of cave and crag and seaward mystery.
I hear the wave that leaps
In scattered foam: the sea-birds noisily
Rifle the footprints of the ebbing tide.
One moment—and the dream hath died.
Sullied and black, the water sleeps
Forgetful of the sea-fowl's wing;
City of sordid stain, and wealth, and hungering.

ARTHUR L. SALMON

Wilds in Gloucestershire

Belleve me noble Lord,
I am a stranger heere in Gloustershire,
These high wilde hilles, and rough uneeven waies
Drawes out our miles, and makes them wearisome.

WILLIAM SHAKESPEARE, *Richard II*

The fire kindled

God, that I might see
   Framilode once again!
Redmarley, all renewed,
   Clear shining after rain.

And Cranham, Cranham trees,
   And blaze of Autumn hues.
Portway under the moon,
   Silvered with freezing dews.

May Hill that Gloster dwellers
   'Gainst every sunset see;
And the wide Severn river
   Homing again to the sea.

The star of afterglow,
   Venus, on western hills;
Dymock in spring: O spring
   Of home! O daffodils!

And Malvern's matchless huge
   Bastions of ancient fires—
These will not let me rest,
   So hot my heart desires. . . .

Here we go sore of shoulder,
   Sore of foot, by quiet streams;
But these are not my rivers. . . .
   And these are useless dreams.

IVOR GURNEY

The Forest of Dean

'Now here you could not lose your way,
Although you lost it', seemed to say
Each path that ran to left or right
Through narrowing distance out of sight.

'Not here, not here', whistled a thrush
And 'Never, never', sighed a thorn-bush;
Primroses looked me in the face
With, 'O too lovely is this place'.

A larch-bough waved a loose green beard
And 'Never, never', still I heard;
'Wayfarer, seek no more your track,
It lies each side and front and back.'

ANDREW YOUNG

The Forest of Dean

The quiet congregation of the trees
Awoke to a rippled whisper. The light winged breeze
Brushed leaf against leaf, softly and delicately fingering
Silken beech and ragged oak leaf; and in the cool shadow
And wavering dapple of tremulous sunlight lingering
As weary of the hot gold glow of the buttercup meadow,
And renewing his strength in the cool green and still shade
Of the forest, deeper and deeper burrowing in
By pathway and trackway and green ride and arched glade
Over hyacinth and the white starred garlic and curled fern,
And dreaming in some unvisited haven to win
New life from the growing grass and rejoicing return
To sweep from hill to valley, from valley to hill.
The birds were still,
Only far off a cuckoo calling,
Drowsily and perpetually a far-off cuckoo calling.

ROBIN FLOWER

The Cotswolds

But *Cotswold*, be this spoke to th' onely praise of thee,
That thou of all the rest, the chosen soyle should'st bee,
Faire *Isis* to bring-forth (the Mother of great *Tames*)
With those delicious Brooks, by whose immortall streames
Her greatnesse is begunne: so that our Rivers King,
When he his long Descent shall from his Bel-sires bring,
Must needs (Great Pastures Prince) derive his stem by thee,
From kingly *Cotswolds* selfe, sprung of the third degree:
As th' old worlds Heroes wont, that in the times of yore,
On Neptune, Jove, and Mars, themselves so highly bore.

MICHAEL DRAYTON, *Polyolbion*

On Fayrford Windowes

I know no paynt of poetry
Can mend such coloured Imag'ry
In sullen inke: yet Fayrford, I
May relish thy fayre memory.

    Such is the Ecchoes faynter sound,
Such is the light when sunne is drownd;
So did the fancy looke upon
The worke before it was begunne:
Yet when those shewes are out of sight
My weaker colours may delight.

    Those Images so faythfully
Report true feature to the eye
As you may thinke each picture was
Some visage in a looking-glasse;
Not a glasse-window face, unlesse
Such as Cheapside hath: where a presse
Of paynted gallants looking out
Bedecke the casement round about
But these have holy physnomy
Each pane instructs the Laity
With silent eloquence: for here
Devotion leads the eye, not eare,
To note the catechising paynt,
Whose easy phrase doth so acquaint
Our sense with Gospell that the Creede
In such a hand the weake may reade:
Such types even yet of vertue bee,
And Christ, as in a glasse wee see.

    Behold two turtles in one cage,
With such a lovely equipage,
As they who knew them long may doubt
Some yong ones have bin stollen out.

    When with a fishing rodde the clarke
Saint Peters draught of fish doth marke,
Such is the scale, the eye, the finne,
Youd thinke they strive and leape within;
But if the nett which holds them breake,
Hee with his angle some would take.

    But would you walk a turne in Pauls?
Looke uppe; one little pane inroules

A fayrer temple: fling a stone
The Church is out o' the windowes thrown.
    Consider, but not aske your eyes,
And ghosts at midday seeme to rise:
The Saynts there, striving to descend,
Are past the glasse and downward bend.

WILLIAM STRODE

Adlestrop

Yes, I remember Adlestrop—
The name, because one afternoon
Of heat the express-train drew up there
Unwontedly. It was late June.

The steam hissed. Someone cleared his throat.
No one left and no one came
On the bare platform. What I saw
Was Adlestrop—only the name

And willows, willow-herb, and grass,
And meadowsweet, and haycocks dry,
No whit less still and lonely fair
Than the high cloudlets in the sky.

And for that minute a blackbird sang
Close by, and round him, mistier,
Farther and farther, all the birds
Of Oxfordshire and Gloucestershire.

EDWARD THOMAS

5

The Border Counties And Wales

MONMOUTHSHIRE   *Tintern*

> Five years have past; five summers, with the length
> Of five long winters! and again I hear
> These waters, rolling from their mountain springs
> With a soft inland murmur.—Once again
> Do I behold these steep and lofty cliffs,
> That on a wild secluded scene impress
> Thoughts of more deep seclusion; and connect
> The landscape with the quiet of the sky.
> The day is come when I again repose
> Here, under this dark sycamore, and view
> These plots of cottage-ground, these orchard-tufts,
> Which at this season, with their unripe fruits,
> Are clad in one green hue, and lose themselves
> 'Mid groves and copses. Once again I see
> These hedge-rows, hardly hedge-rows, little lines
> Of sportive wood run wild: and wreaths of smoke
> Sent up, in silence, from among the trees!
> With some uncertain notice, as might seem
> Of vagrant dwellers in the houseless woods,
> Or of some Hermit's cave, where by his fire
> The Hermit sits alone.

WILLIAM WORDSWORTH, *Tintern Abbey*

Castles

Upon the side, of wooddie hill full fayre,
This Castle[1] stands, full sore decayde and broke:
Yet builded once in fresh and wholesome ayre,
Full neere great Woods, and many a mighty Oke.

[1] Castle Stroge, almost cleane downe.

But sith it weares, and walles no wastes away,
In praise thereof I mynd not much to say:
Each thing decayd goes quickly out of minde,
A rotten house doth but fewe favours finde.

Three Castles fayre are in a goodly ground,
Grosmont is one, on Hill it builded was:
Skenfreth the next, in Valley it is found,
The Soyle about for pleasure there doth passe.
Whit Castle is the third of worthy fame,
The Countrey there doth beare *Whit Castles* name, —
A stately Seate, a loftie princely place, -
Whose beautie gives the simple Soyles some grace.

THOMAS CHURCHYARD, *The Worthines of Wales*

Llanthony

I

Llanthony! an ungenial clime,
And the broad wing of restless Time,
Have rudely swept thy massy walls
And rockt thy abbots in their palls.
I loved theee by thy streams of yore,
By distant streams I love thee more;
For never is the heart so true
As bidding what we love adieu.

II

Along Llanthony's ruin'd aisles we walk'd
And woods then pathless, over verdant hill
And ruddy mountain, and aside the stream
Of sparkling Hondy. Just at close of day
There by the comet's light we saw the fox
Rush from the alders, nor relax in speed
Until he trod the pathway of his sires
Under the hoary crag of Comioy.

W. S. LANDOR, *Fiesolan Musings*, and lines
To the Rev. Cuthbert Southey

HEREFORDHSIRE   *Monnow*

The road was weary; and beside the road,
  Beyond the meadow quivering in the sun,
The crystal *Monnow* murmured as it flowed;
  Monnow, the clearest of clear streams that run
By shingly reaches, where the cattle drink,
  Through islets dense with shadowy burdock-leaves,
By high red scarps, with alders on the brink,
  In glimmering pools;—a leaping troutlet weaves
Swift rings, that cross and circle, till the ripples sink.

It is the Spring! how swift her tripping feet
  Tread these sequestered valleys, though she dare
Not venture yet, where winds blow shrill and fleet,
  And all the down is washed with keener air;
Yet here each quickset hedge is green with gems;
  The bold moist king-cup stares upon the sun
From oozy creeks; the sweetbriar's polished stems
  Grow rough with crumpled tufts, and, one by one,
The cowslips wave a crown of clustered diadems.

Here will I lie a little, till the sun
  Slope westward, and the vale be brimmed with shade,
And hear the bubbling waters briskly run,
  Till every drowsy sound,—the clinking spade,
Lowing of cattle from the windy down,
  Crying of cocks, the slowly-creaking wain,
In deep content the peaceful thought shall drown,
  Ay, even the measured puffing of the train,
That hurries busy hearts from town to dusty town.

Stream, stream, thou hast a spirit, hast a soul,
  I doubt not—thou are real, as I to thee:
Neckan or Nymph, fond Fay or merry Trol,—
  Some conscious self, some breathing mystery!
No copse but hath its Dryad, each dark stone
  Its crouching Lemur: oh, the foolish dream!
We have driv'n far hence, for all their piteous moan,
  Our faithful sprites:—but thou, swift-leaping stream,
O presence, and O voice, by me art surely known!

I know the secret! how thy shivering rill
　　Leaps high on *Cusop* bluff, among the stones:
Till swelled by *Escley* brook, from *Vagar* hill,
　　Then, where by *Craswall* Chapel sleep the bones
Of grey-frocked friars, is heard a larger sound:—
　　'Tis *Olchon*, dimpling o'er his stony bed,
Olchon, from many a rood of moorland ground,
　　From heathery dingles, bare, unvisited,—
Him too thou dost enfold, and onward thou art bound.

　Onward, aye onward—fed by falling streams,
　　Still changing, yet eternally the same;—
And men are born beside thee, dream their dreams,
　　And leave the fading shadow of a name;
Still thou dost leap, and carve thy shelving shore,
　　And push each boulder further from its home,
Till, in the widening vale, thou hear'st the roar
　　Of wide-flung breakers, white with crested foam,
And drink'st the pungent brine along thy oozy floor.

A. C. BENSON, *Monnow*

SHROPSHIRE　　　*Ludlow*

The Towne doth stand most part upon an Hill,
Built well and fayre, with streates both large and wide:
The houses such, where straungers lodge at will.
As long as there the Councell lists abide,
Both fine and cleane the streates are all throughout,
With Condits cleere, and wholesome water springs:
And who that lists to walke the towne about,
Shall finde therein some rare and pleasant things:
But chiefly there the ayre so sweete you have,
As in no place ye can no better crave.

*　　*　　*

Two Bayliefes rules, one yeere the Towne throughout,
Twelve Aldermen they have therein likewise:
Who doth beare sway, as turne doth come about,
Who chosen are, by oth and auncient guise.
Good lawes they have, and open place to pleade,
In ample sort, for right and Justice sake:

A Preacher too, that dayly there doth reade,
A Schoolemaster, that doth good schollers make.
And for the Queere, are boyes brought up to sing,
And to serve God, and doe none other thing.

THOMAS CHURCHYARD, *The Worthines of Wales*

From A Shropshire Lad

XXXI

On Wenlock Edge the wood's in trouble;
His forest fleece the Wrekin heaves;
The gale, it plies the saplings double,
And thick on Severn snow the leaves.

'Twould blow like this through holt and hanger
When Uricon the city stood:
'Tis the old wind in the old anger,
But then it threshed another wood.

Then, 'twas before my time, the Roman
At yonder heaving hill would stare:
The blood that warms an English yeoman,
The thoughts that hurt him, they were there.

There, like the wind through woods in riot,
Through him the gale of life blew high;
The tree of man was never quiet:
Then 'twas the Roman, now 'tis I.

The gale, it plies the saplings double,
It blows so hard, 'twill soon be gone:
Today the Roman and his trouble
Are ashes under Uricon.

A. E. HOUSMAN

XXXIX

'Tis time, I think, by Wenlock town
  The golden broom should blow;
The hawthorn sprinkled up and down
  Should charge the land with snow.

Spring will not wait the loiterer's time
   Who keeps so long away;
So others wear the broom and climb
   The hedgerows heaped with may.

Oh tarnish late on Wenlock Edge,
   Gold that I never see;
Lie long, high snowdrifts in the hedge
   That will not shower on me.

A. E. HOUSMAN

The Quietest Places

Clunton and Clunbury,
   Clungunford and Clun,
Are the quietest places
   Under the sun.

ANON. (Old local saying)

Shrewsbury

The Towne three parts, stands in a valley loe,
Three gates there are, through which you needes must passe,
As to the height of Towne the people goe:
So Castle seemes, as twere a looking glasse,
To looke through all, and hold them all in awe,
Treangle wise, the gates and Towne doth drawe:
But Castle hill spyes out each streat so plaine,
As though an eye on them did still remaine.
In midst of Towne, fower Parish Churches are,
Full nere and close, together note that right:
The vewe farre of, is wondrous straunge and rare,
For they doe seeme a true love knot to sight:
They stand on hill, as Nature wrought a Seate
To place them flower, in stately beautie greate:
As men devout to buyld these works tooke care,
So in these daise these Temples famous are.

THOMAS CHURCHYARD, *The Worthines of Wales*

133

The Wrekin

There was a time I yet remember well,
When oft I've heard the weary reapers tell,
That when at eve the Wreken's top was clear,
Serene and bright the morning would appear,
But when dark clouds his summit should deform,
The day succeeding ever brought a storm:
And many an hour, by murm'ring brook or rill,
I've pensive mark'd the distant Wreken hill,
What time the ev'ning sun declin'd to rest,
And ruddy streaks have ting'd the peaceful west;
Then homeward have I bent my lonely way,
Musing, prophetic, on the coming day.

C. B. ASH, *Adbaston*

CHESHIRE   *Cheshire*

O! thou thrice happy Shire, confined so to bee
Twixt two so famous Floods, as *Mersey* is, and *Dee*.
Thy *Dee* upon the West from *Wales* doth thee divide;
Thy *Mersey* on the North, from the *Lancastrian* side,
Thy naturall sister Shire; and linkt unto thee so,
That *Lancashire* along with *Cheshire* still doth goe.
As tow'rds the *Derbian Peake*, and *Moreland* (which doe draw
More mountainous and wild) the high-crown'd *Shutlingslawe*
And *Molcop* be thy Mounds, with those proud hills whence rove
The lovely sister Brooks, the silvery *Dane* and *Dove*;
Cleere *Dove*, that makes to *Trent*; the other to the West.
But, in that famous Towne, most happy of the rest
(From which thou tak'st thy name), faire *Chester*, call'd of old
Carelegion; whilst proud *Rome* her conquests heere did hold,
Of those her legions known the faithfull station then,
So stoutly held to tack by those neere *North-wales* men;
Yet by her owne right name had rather called bee,
As her the *Britaine* tearm'd, *The Fortress upon Dee*,
Then vainly shee would seeme a Miracle to stand,
Th' imaginary worke of some huge Giants hand.

MICHAEL DRAYTON, *Polyolbion*

Chester

How charmed we pilgrims from the eager West,
   Where only life, and not its scene is old,
Beside the hearth at Chester's inn at rest,
   Her ancient story to each other told.

The holly-wreath and dial's moon-orbed face,
   The Gothic tankard crowned with beaded ale,
The faded aquatint of Chevy Chase,
   And heirloom Bible, harmonised the tale.

Then roamed we forth as in a wondrous dream,
   Whose visions truth could only half eclipse;
The turret shadows living phantoms seem,
   And mill-sluice brawl the moan of ghostly lips.

Night and her planet their enchantments wove,
   To wake the brooding spirits of the past;
A Druid's sickle glistened in the grove,
   And Harold's war-cry died upon the blast.

The floating mist that hung on Brewer's hill
   (While every heart-beat seemed a sentry's tramp),
In tented domes and bannered folds grew still,
   As rose the psalm from Cromwell's wary camp.

From ivied tower, above the meadows sere,
   We watched the fray with hunted Charles of yore,
When grappled Puritan and Cavalier,
   And sunk a traitor's throne on Rowton Moor.

We tracked the ramparts in the lunar gloom,
   Knelt by the peasants at St Mary's shrine;
With his own hermit mused at Parnell's tomb,
   And breathed the cadence of his pensive line.

Beneath a gable mouldering and low,
   The pious record we could still descry,
Which, in the pestilence of old De Foe,
   Proclaimed that here death's angel flitted by.

At morn the vendors in the minster's shade,
   With gleaming scales and plumage at their feet,
Seemed figures on the canvas of Ostade,
   Where mart and temple so benignly meet.

Of Holland whispered then by the sullen barge,
    We thought of Venice by the hushed canal,
And hailed each relic on time's voiceless marge,—
    Sepulchral lamp and clouded lachrymal.

The quaint arcades of traffic's feudal range,
    And giant fossils of a lustier crew;
The diamond casements and the moated grange,
    Tradition's lapsing fantasies renew.

The oaken effigies of buried earls,
    A window blazoned with armorial crest,
A rusted helm, and standard's broidered furls,
    Chivalric eras patiently attest.

Here William's castle frowns upon the tide;
    There holy Werburgh keeps aerial sway,
To warn the minions who complacent glide,
    And swell ambition's retinue to-day.

Once more we sought the parapet, to gaze,
    And mark the hoar-frost glint along the dales;
Or through the wind-cleft vistas of the haze,
    Welcome afar the mountain-ridge of Wales.

Ah, what a respite from the onward surge
    Of life, where all is turbulent and free,
To pause a while upon the quiet verge
    Of olden memories beside the Dee.

ANON.

Moonrise: Ashton-on-Mersey

Sultry has been the day, and the still air
    Of evening stirs no leaf upon the tree,—
    This level land is wilderness to me;
The full moon, rising with a ruddy glare
Over green pastures, deepens my despair:
    From fields low-lying far as eye can see
    My heavy heart cries through the heat to thee;
O wild hill-country that I deem so fair.

But yester-night I climbed the mountain-side;
    Beneath my feet, through the dim valley rolled,
        The mist wrapped all the pathway, scarce discerned;
From out the darkening moor the pee-wit cried,
    Across the heather came the night-breeze cold,
        And redly Mars above the cloud-bank burned.

J. G. F. NICHOLSON

WALES   *Welcome to Wales*

You drive in across this bridge they've built
or sleep through the railway tunnel
or step from a shaky plane on the coast.
The roads are quite modern, and the beer
is warm and generally flat.
The clocks keep the same time as Surbiton.
Our places of worship are more numerous
than the crumbling pubs, but their thin congregations
stay in bed. We have no
monopoly of compassion, but believe
no distance is too excessive
from a cold heart. Our schools
are full of children, and our seats of learning
turn out the usual quota of misfits.

Among the ancient customs, buttering-up tourists
is not one, so beware of the remnant of pride
hanging in corners. If you prick us,
we shall surely bleed. Here you can buy
what you purchase in Selfridges
and cut a small notch in your wallet for every snip.
There are plenty of bogus Tudor
expense-account restaurants; the hotels bulge
with rugby players, their supporters still happily dissecting
a try scored in 1912.
You will feel at home in the petrol fumes.

Our women are full and bloomy,
real women. Our girls
shuttle nicely in micro skirts.
(They are always a shock to the stranger.)

Our complaint is apathy, which would not
interest the visitor hungry for landscape.
We are not sure who we are, but the search
goes on. Experts fly in from abroad
to write big books about us,
to tell us who we are.

There's a splendid ritual in August
(swot up on the language first)
and singing high in the north
(book well in advance for your beds)
when the world comes rattling in motor cars
to our separate doorstep. You can eat
delicious flat cakes that are griddle-baked
and copy some recipes discovered in Caesar's time.
But our special flair is confusion: we have trouble
with our souls, and this could be tedious
if you bog yourself down in discourse
with local philosophers. On benches
in village squares, the very old keep chiselling memories.

But make no mistake, and mark this well:
we do not sell ourselves cheap,
or short, despite what the experts say.

JOHN TRIPP

GLAMORGANSHIRE *Return to Cardiff*

'Hometown'; well, most admit an affection for a city:
grey, tangles streets I cycled on to school, my first cigarette
in the back lane, and, fool, my first botched love affair.
First everything. Faded torments; self-indulgent pity.

The journey to Cardiff seemed less a return than a raid
on mislaid identities. Of course the whole locus smaller:
the mile-wide Taff now a stream, the castle not as in some black,
gothic dream, but a decent sprawl, a joker's toy façade.

Unfocused voices in the wind, associations, clues,
odds and ends, fringes caught, as when, after the doctor quit,
a door opened and I glimpsed the white, enormous face
of my grandfather, suddenly aghast with certain news.

Unable to define anything I can hardly speak,
and still I love the place for what I wanted it to be
as much as for what it unashamedly is
now for me, a city of strangers, alien and bleak.

Unable to communicate I'm easily betrayed,
uneasily diverted by mere sense reflections
like those anchored waterscapes that wander, alter, in the Taff,
hour by hour, as light slants down a different shade.

Illusory, too, that lost dark playground after rain,
the noise of trams, gunshots in what they once called Tiger Bay.
Only real this smell of ripe, damp earth when the sun comes out,
a mixture of pungencies, half exquisite and half plain.

No sooner I'd arrived than the other Cardiff had gone,
smoke in the memory, these but tinned resemblances,
where the boy I was not and the man I am not
met, hesitated, left double footsteps, then walked on.

DANNIE ABSE

The Prisoner's Walk

(Robert, Duke of Normandy, imprisoned in Cardiff Castle by
Henry I, tells of a walk with his keeper)

Wandring through forrest wide, at length we gaine
A steepe-cloud-kissing rocke, whose horned crowne
With proud imperiall looke beholds the maine,
Where Severn's dangerous waves run roling downe
From th' Holmes into the seas, by Cardiffe towne,
    Whose quicke devouring sands so dangerous been
    To those that wander Amphitrite's greene.

As there we stood, the countrie round we ey'd
To view the workmanship of Nature's hand,
There stood a mountaine, from whose weeping side
A brooke breakes forth into the low-lying land,
Here lies a plaine, and there a wood doth stand,
    Here pastures, meades, corne-fields, a vale do crowne,
    A castle here shootes up, and there a towne.

Here one with angle ore a silver streame
With banefull baite the nibling fish doth feed:
There in a plow'd-land with his painfull teame
To get the earth with childe of Ceres' seed:
    Heere sits a goatherd on a craggie rock,
    And there in shade a shepherd with his flock.

The sweet delight of such a rare prospect
Might yeeld content unto a carefull eye:
Yet downe the rock descending in neglect
Of such delight, the sunne now mounting high,
I sought the shade in vale, which low did lie,
    Where we reposde us on a greene wood side,
    Afront the which a silver streame did glide.

RICHARD NICCOLS, *Robert, Duke of Normandy*

The Rhondda

Hum of shaft-wheel, whirr and clamour
Of steel hammers overbeat, din down
Water-hag's slander. Greasy Rhondda
River throws about the boulders
Veils of scum to mark the ancient
Degraded union of stone and water.

Unwashed colliers by the river
Gamble for luck the pavements hide.
Kids float tins down dirty rapids.
Coal-dust rings the scruffy willows.
Circe is a drab.
She gives men what they know.
Daily to her pitch-black shaft
Her whirring wheels suck husbands out of sleep.
She for her profit takes their hands and eyes.

But the fat flabby-breasted wives
Have grown accustomed to her ways.
They scrub, make tea, peel the potatoes
Without counting the days.

ALUN LEWIS

BRECONSHIRE

A Memory of a Breconshire Valley

—'Patulis ubi vallibus errans,
Subjacet aëriis montibus Isca pater'
Ad Posteros.

I

I followed thee, wild stream of Paradise,
White Usk, forever showering the sunned bee
In the pink chestnut and the hawthorn tree;
And, all along, had magical surmise
Of mountains fluctuant in those vesper skies,
As unto mermen, caverned in mid-sea,
Far up the vast green reaches, soundlessly
The giant rollers form, and fall, and rise.
Above thy poet's dust, by yonder yew,
Ere distance perished, ere a star began,
His clear monastic measure, heard of few,
Through lonelier glens of mine own being ran;
And thou to me wert dear, because I knew
The God who made thee gracious, and the man.

II

If, by that second lover's power controlled,
In sweet symbolic rite thy breath o'erfills
Fields of no war with vagrant daffodils,
From distance unto distance trailing gold;
If dazzling sands or thickets thee enfold,
Transfigured Usk, where from their mossy sills
Gray hamlets kiss thee, and by herded hills
Diviner run thy shadows than of old;—
If intellectual these, O name thy Vaughan
Creator too: and close his memory keep,
Who from thy fountain, kind to him, hath drawn
Birth, energy, and joy; devotion deep;
A play of thought more mystic than the dawn;
And death at home; and centuried sylvan sleep.

LOUISE IMOGEN GUINEY

CARMARTHENSHIRE *Carmarthen*

Far, far away in wild Wales, by the shore of the boundless Atlantic,
Where the cloud-capt peaks of the North are dwarfed to the hills of the
    South,
And through the long vale to the sea, the full-fed, devious Towy
Turns and returns on itself, like the coils of a silvery snake,
A grey town sits up aloft on the bank of the clear, flowing river,
As it has sat since the days when the Romans was first in the land.
A town, with a high ruined castle and walls mantled over with ivy,
With church towers square and strong and narrow irregular streets,
And, frequent in street and lane, many-windowed high-shouldered
    chapels,
Whence all the still Sabbath ascend loud preaching and passionate prayer,
Such violent wrestling with sin, that the dogs on the pavement deserted
Wake with a growl from their dreams at the sound of the querulous voice,
And the gay youths, released from the counter and bound for the seaside
    or hillside,
Start as they wake on their way echoes of undevout feet,
And here and there a rude square, with statues of popular heroes,
A long quay with scarcely a ship, and a hoary bridge spanning the stream,
The stream which struggles in June by the shallows where children are
    swimming,
The furious flood which at Yule roars seaward, resistless along,
Though the white stream ribbons float by it, forlorn it seems, almost
    forsaken.
All the day long in the week the dumb streets are hushed in repose,
But on market or fair days there comes a throng of Welsh-speaking
    peasants
From many a lonely farm in the folds of the rain-beaten hills,
And the long streets are filled with the high pitched speech of the
    chaffering Cymry,
With a steeple-crowned hat, here and there, and the red cloaks which
    daunted the French,
Scarce in Keltic Brittany's self, or in homely Teutonic Silesia,
So foreign a crowd may you see as in this far corner of Wales.

SIR LEWIS MORRIS, *The Physicians of Myddfai*

Grongar Hill

Silent nymph, with curious eye!
Who, the purple evening, lie
On the mountain's lonely van,
Beyond the noise of busy man,
Painting fair the form of things,
While the yellow linet sings;
Or the tuneful nightingale
Charms the forest with her tale;
Come with all thy various hues,
Come, and aid thy sister Muse;
Now while Phoebus riding high
Gives lustre to the land and sky!
Grongar Hill invites my song,
Draw the landskip bright and strong;
Grongar, in whose mossy cells
Sweetly-musing Quiet dwells;
Grongar, in whose silent shade,
For the modest Muses made,
So oft I have, the even still,
At the fountain of a rill,
Sate upon a flow'ry bed,
With my hand beneath my head;
And strayed my eyes o'er Towy's flood,
Over mead, and over wood,
From house to house, from hill to hill,
'Till contemplation had her fill.
  About his chequered sides I wind,
And leave his brooks and meads behind,
And groves, and grottoes where I lay,
And vistoes shooting beams of day:
Wider and wider spreads the vale,
As circles on a smooth canal:
The mountains round, unhappy fate!
Sooner or later, of all height,
Withdraw their summits from the skies,
And lessen as the others rise:
Still the prospect wider spreads,
Adds a thousand woods and meads,
Still it widens, widens still,
And sinks the newly-risen hill.

Now I gain the mountain's brow,
What a landskip lies below!
No clouds, no vapours intervene,
But the gay, the open scene
Does the face of nature show,
In all the hues of heaven's bow!
And, swelling to embrace the light,
Spreads around beneath the sight.
    Old castles on the cliffs arise,
Proudly tow'ring in the skies!
Rushing from the woods, the spires
Seem from hence ascending fires!
Half his beams Apollo sheds
On the yellow mountain-heads!
Gilds the fleeces of the flocks:
And glitters on the broken rocks!
    Below me trees unnumber'd rise,
Beautiful in various dyes:
The gloomy pine, the poplar blue,
The yellow beech, the sable yew,
The slender fir that taper grows,
The sturdy oak with broad-spread boughs.
And beyond the purple grove,
Haunt of Phillis, queen of love!
Gaudy as the op'ning dawn,
Lies a long and level dawn,
On which a dark hill, steep and high,
Holds and charms the wand'ring eye!
Deep are his feet in Towy's flood,
His sides are cloath'd with waving wood,
And ancient towers crown his brow,
That cast an awful look below;
Whose ragged walls the ivy creeps,
And with her arms from falling keeps;
So both a safety from the wind
On mutual dependence find.
    'Tis now the raven's bleak abode;
'Tis now th' apartment of the toad;
And there the fox securely feeds; ⎫
And there the pois'nous adder breeds,⎬
Concealed in ruins, moss and weeds, ⎭
While, ever and anon, there falls

Huge heaps of hoary moulder'd walls.
Yet time has seen, that lifts the low,
And level lays the lofty brow,
Has seen this broken pile compleat,⎫
Big with the vanity of state;⎬
But transient is the smile of fate!⎭
A little rule, a little sway,
A sunbeam in a winter's day,
Is all the proud and mighty have
Between the cradle and the grave.
    And see the rivers how they run,
Thro' woods and meads, in shade and sun,
Sometimes swift, sometimes slow,
Wave succeeding wave, they go
A various journey to the deep,
Like human life to endless sleep!
Thus is nature's vesture wrought,
To instruct our wand'ring thought;
Thus she dresses green and gay,
To disperse our cares away.
    Ever charming, ever new,
When will the landskip tire the view!
The fountain's fall, the river's flow,
The woody vallies, warm and low;
The windy summit, wild and high,
Roughly rushing on the sky!
The pleasant seat, the ruin'd tow'r,
The naked rock, the shady bow'r;
The town and village, dome and farm,⎫
Each give each a double charm,⎬
As pearls upon an Æthiop's arm.⎭
    See on the mountain's southern side,⎫
Where the prospect opens wide,⎬
Where the evening gilds the tide;⎭
How close and small the hedges lie!
What streaks of meadows cross the eye!
A step methinks may pass the stream,
So little distant dangers seem;
So we mistake the future's face,
Ey'd through hope's deluding glass;
As yon summits soft and fair,
Clad in colours of the air,

Which to those who journey near,
Barren, brown, and rough appear;
Grass and flowers Quiet treads,
On the meads and mountain-heads.
Still we tread the same coarse way,
The present's still a cloudy day.

O may I with myself agree,
And never covet what I see:
Content me with an humble shade,
My passions tam'd, my wishes laid;
For while our wishes wildly roll,
We banish quiet from the soul:
'Tis thus the busy beat the air;
And misers gather wealth and care.

Now, even now, my joys run high,
As on the mountain-turf I lie;
While the wanton Zephyr sings,
And in the vale perfumes his wings;
While the waters murmur deep;
While the shepherd charms his sheep;
While the birds unbounded fly, ⎫
And with music fill the sky, ⎬
Now, even now, my joys run high. ⎭

Be full, ye courts, be great who will;
Search for peace with all your skill:
Open wide the lofty door,
Seek her on the marble floor,
In vain you search, she is not there;
In vain ye search the domes of care!
Grass and flowers Quiet treads,
On the meads and mountain-heads,
Along with Pleasure, close ally'd,
Ever by each other's side:
And often, by the murm'ring rill, ⎫
Hears the thrush, while all is still, ⎬
Within the groves of Grongar Hill. ⎭

JOHN DYER

Fern Hill
(Llangain)

Now as I was young and easy under the apple boughs
About the lilting house and happy as the grass was green,
    The night above the dingle starry,
        Time let me hail and climb
    Golden in the heydays of his eyes,
And honoured among wagons I was prince of the apple towns
And once below a time I lordly had the trees and leaves
        Trail with daisies and barley
    Down the rivers of the windfall light.

And as I was green and carefree, famous among the barns
About the happy yard and singing as the farm was home,
    In the sun that is young but once only,
        Time let me play and be
    Golden in the mercy of his means,
And green and golden I was huntsman and herdsman, the calves
Sang to my horn, the foxes on the hills barked clear and cold,
        And the sabbath rang slowly
    In the pebbles of the holy streams.

All the sun long it was running, it was lovely, the hay
Fields high as the house, the tunes from the chimneys, it was air
    And playing, lovely and watery
        And fire green as grass.
    And nightly under the simple stars
As I rode to sleep the owls were bearing the farm away.
All the moon long I heard, blessed among stables, the nightjars
        Flying with the ricks, and the horses
        Flashing into the dark.

And then to awake, and the farm, like a wanderer white
With the dew, come back, the cock on his shoulder: it was all
    Shining, it was Adam and maiden,
        The sky gathered again
    And the sun grew round that very day.
So it must have been after the birth of the simple light
In the first, spinning place, the spellbound horses walking warm
    Out of the whinnying green stable
        On to the fields of praise.

And honoured among foxes and pheasants by the gay house
Under the new made clouds and happy as the heart was long,
  In the sun born over and over,
    I ran my heedless ways,
  My wishes raced through the house high hay
And nothing I cared, at my sky blue trades, that time allows
In all his tuneful turning so few and such morning songs
  Before the children green and golden
    Follow him out of grace.

Nothing I cared, in the lamb white days, that time would take me
Up to the swallow thronged loft by the shadow of my hand,
  In the moon that is always rising,
    Nor that riding to sleep
  I should hear him fly with the high fields
And wake to the farm forever fled from the childless land.
Oh as I was young and easy in the mercy of his means,
  Time held me green and dying
    Though I sang in my chains like the sea.

DYLAN THOMAS

PEMBROKESHIRE St David's Head

Salt sprays deluge it, wild waves buffet it; hurricanes rave;
Summer and winter, the depths of the ocean girdle it round;
In leaden dawns, in golden noon-tides, in silvery moonlight
Never it ceases to hear the old sea's mystical sound.
    Surges vex it evermore
    By gray cave and sounding shore.

SIR LEWIS MORRIS, *St David's Head*

In Pembrokeshire
(1886)

Through crested grass I took my way
From my loved home. The sun was high;
The warm air slept the live-long day;
No shadowy doubt veiled the sky.

The swift train swept with rhythmic tune,
By endless pastures hurrying down,
White farm, lone chapel, castled town,
Then, fringed with weed, the salt lagune.

And last the land-locked haven blue,
Thin-sown with monstrous works of war,
And on the sweet salt air I knew
Faint sounds of cheering from afar

＊　＊　＊

The crowds are gone, the hillside bare,
The last good-nights at length are said,
The harbour crossed again, the fair
Large star of eve hangs overhead.

The shades of tardy evening fall;
Lights come in casements here and.there;
Through dewy meads on the cool air
The wandering landrails hoarsely call.

The silent roads loom ghostly white;
No veil of darkness hides the skies;
A sunless dawn appears to rise
Upon the stilly charmed night.

The day's hot concourse comes to seem
Far, far away; the eager crowd,
The upturned gaze, the plaudits loud,
In the cool silence like a dream.

And oh, sweet odours, which the air
Of the calm summer midnight deep
Draws from the rose which lies asleep,
And bowery honeysuckles fair.

Oh, perfumed night! Some tremulous bird
From the thick hedgerow seems to thrill.
No other sound but this is heard,
Save ringing horsehoofs, beating still.

Midnight is past; there comes a gleam,
Precursor of the scarce-set sun.
Through gray streets hushed as in a dream
We sweep, and the long day is done.

SIR LEWIS MORRIS, *In Pembrokeshire*, 1886

CARDIGANSHIRE *Ystwith and Aberystwith*[1]

Lo! thy graceful current laves
All beauteous Hafôd; and thy waves
Of many rills confer the Name
On yonder Seat of rising Fame,
That soon shall see a brighter day,
When promenades and villas gay,
More visited, admir'd and grand,
Shall dignify its hills and strand.

LUKE BOOKER, *The Springs of Plynlimmon*

Early Course of the Wye

Ere rose the bright-hair'd god of day,
Vaga was up, and on her way:
Adown the hoary hill[1] she glided,
By her own vagrant fancy guided;
And on, thro' verdant vallies flowing,
With cowslips dight, where herds were lowing,
Where copse-woods many a nook adorn,
And linnets warbled on the thorn.
By early journeying, she no need
Had for impetuous hurrying speed;
And therefore leisurely along
She stray'd the loveliest scenes among,
Thro' Radnor's wild and hilly plains,
Where unperverted Nature reigns,
And Eilon, stream as crystal clear,
Soon came to pay its tribute there,
With Ython, queen of numerous rills,
Sent willing from Salopian hills.
Thence, as she went thro' Builth's gay meads,
Soft whispering, as she kiss'd the reeds,
Which, bending duteous where they grew,
Hail'd with delight the nymph they knew.
There Crewyn, from a neighbouring shire,

[1]Plynlimmon.

Flow'd musically to admire
The stranger-River-Nymph; and then,
Stealing along a sylvan glen,
Delighted, from fair Brecon's side
Llewenney came, to swell her tide.

LUKE BOOKER, *The Springs of Plynlimmon*

MONTGOMERYSHIRE *In Montgomery*

Now thro' a tract all comfortless we stray
Where hills, dales, bogs, and streams obstruct the way,
And thorny woods, impervious to the day.
At length we rest, and see *Vernuvia's*[1] flood
Roll o'er rough rocks, where once *Mathraval* stood,
A royal city erst of *British* kings.
Behold what changes time revolving brings!
Now scarce a wreck of all its pomp remains,
The swain ploughs thoughtless o'er demolisht fanes.
What pure, what true delight, a thoughtful mind
Among these wild yet awful scenes must find!
When late in silent pomp the silver moon
High in the spangled arch unclouded shone;
When the pale light the prospect round display'd,
Alone and pensive o'er the fields I stray'd,
Which way soe'er I turn'd my wond'ring eyes,
Hills heap'd on hills in bright confusion rise,
Their crystal summits of pellucid snow,
Resplendent, seen among the stars to glow.
Disperst beneath, the vales o'ershadow'd lie,
Whence dusky vapours slowly mount the sky.
Here purling riv'lets sweetly fall, and there
Down dashing cataracts astound the ear.
The birds of night excursive hover round,
And savage houlings thro' the woods resound.
The peasant here enjoys the meanest lot;
Coarse are his meals and homely is his cot.

* * *

[1] The river Vernu (Vyrnwy).

In this cold region, this unfertile soil
The harvest scarce repays the ploughman's toil.
The blasted mountains, and the naked rocks,
But just with life sustain the climbing flocks,
Yet here old honesty, devoid of art,
And gen'rous love spring native in the heart.

WILLIAM VERNON, *A Journey into Wales*

MERIONETHSHIRE *Cader Idris at Sunset*

Last Autumn, as we sat, ere fall of night,
Over against old Cader's rugged face,
We mark'd the sunset from its secret place
Salute him with a fair and sudden light.
Flame-hued he rose, and vast, without a speck
Of life upon his flush'd and lonely side;
A double rainbow o'er him bent, to deck
What was so bright before, thrice glorified!
How oft, when pacing o'er these inland plains,
I see that rosy rock of Northern Wales
Come up before me! then its lustre wanes,
And all the frith and intermediate vales
Are darken'd, while our little group remains
Half-glad, half-tearful, as the vision pales!

CHARLES TENNYSON TURNER

Penmaen Pool
(For the Visitors' Book at the Inn)

Who long for rest, who look for pleasure
Away from counter, court, or school
O where live well your lease of leisure
But here at, here at Penmaen Pool.

You'll dare the Alp? you'll dart the skiff—
Each sport has here its tackle and tool:
Come, plant the staff by Cadair cliff;
Come, swing the sculls on Penmaen Pool.

What's yonder?—Grizzled Dyphwys dim:
The triple-hummocked Giant's stool,
Hoar messmate, hobs and nobs with him
To halve the bowl of Penmaen Pool.

And all the landscape under survey,
At tranquil turns, by nature's rule,
Rides repeated topsyturvy
In frank, in fairy Penmaen Pool.

And Charles's Wain, the wondrous seven,
And sheep-flock clouds like worlds of wool,
For all they shine so, high in heaven,
Shew brighter shaken in Penmaen Pool.

The Mawddach, how she trips! though throttled
If floodtide teeming thrills her full,
And mazy sands all water-wattled
Waylay her at ebb, past Penmaen Pool.

But what's to see in stormy weather,
When grey showers gather and gusts are cool?—
Why, raindrop-roundels looped together
That lace the face of Penmaen Pool.

Then even in weariest wintry hour
Of New Year's month or surly Yule
Furred snows, charged tuft above tuft, tower
From darksome darksome Penmaen Pool.

And ever, if bound here hardest home,
You've parlour-pastime left and (who'll
Not honour it?) ale like goldy foam
That frocks an oar in Penmaen Pool.

Then come who pine for peace or pleasure
Away from counter, court, or school,
Spend here your measure of time and treasure
And taste the treats of Penmaen Pool.

GERARD MANLEY HOPKINS

By Festiniog

By fair Festiniog, mid the Northern Hills
The vales are full of beauty, and the heights,
Thin set with mountain sheep, show statelier far
Than in the tamer South. There the stern round
Of labour rules,—a silent land, sometimes
Loud with the blast that buffets all the hills
Whereon the workers toil, in quarries hewn
Upon the terraced rocksides. Tier on tier,
Above the giddy depths, they edge and cling
Like flies to the sheer precipice as they strike
The thin cleft slate. For solace of their toil
Song comes to strengthen them, and songlike verse
In the old Cymric measures.

SIR LEWIS MORRIS, *Llyn y Morwynion*

Penn-y-pass

What was that place where chance with nightfall halted
Our casual journeying? Had it a name, a designation
On maps? a country, king, and government?
Had it so concrete, firm, a dignity?
Was it so many feet above sea-level
Heaved up on the wrinkling of a shrunken planet?
Had it a longitude, a point in space?
I have forgotten; but the wind swept cold,
I know, through the mountain pass, and sang in the wires
Stretched on ungainly poles up a rocky track;
Boulders had fallen from the mountain top,
Making a stairway, steps for a giant's stride,
Black boulders split from the mountain, top to base,
And man had come, rearing ungainly poles,
Stretching his wires, wires for his little news,
And the wind sang in the wire, making a lyre
Of man's contrivance when the stars were bright.
And the poles had a beauty, straight and unnatural,
Being designed for man and man's small use
Crossing the mountains; but the mountains took them,
The wind and the mountains took them, made them part

Of their greater concert, bent their straightness crooked,
Mechanical straightness of a man's designing,
Hostile to freakish Nature; Nature took them,
The poles, the wire, and sent her winds so singing
That the straightness curved to a tune, a whining tune,
Like the voice of the mountains and the mountain wind,
Lament of the heights; and chance would have it so
That we crossed the wires and intercepted the tune
On a given hour at dusk on a given day,
Once, and were gone by morning; but I think
That the wires still whine there when the wind's uneasy
Lament sighs through them and wakes them to a music
That man who set them in their mechanical straightness
Had not intended. What was that mountain pass
Where nightfall halted us in our casual journey?

V. SACKVILLE-WEST

CAERNARVONSHIRE *Snowdon*

In one of those excursions (may they ne'er
Fade from remembrance!) through the Northern tracts
Of Cambria ranging with a youthful friend,
I left Bethgelert's huts at couching-time,
And, westward took my way, to see the sun
Rise from the top of Snowdon. To the door
Of a rude cottage at the mountain's base
We came, and roused the shepherd who attends
The adventurous stranger's steps, a trusty guide;
Then, cheered by short refreshment, sallied forth.

It was a close, warm, breezeless summer night,
Wan, dull, and glaring, with a dripping fog
Low-hung and thick that covered all the sky;
But, undiscouraged, we began to climb
The mountain-side. The mist soon girt us round,
And, after ordinary traveller's talk
With our conductor, pensively we sank
Each into commerce with his private thoughts:
Thus did we breast the ascent, and by myself
Was nothing either seen or heard that checked
Those musings or diverted, save that once

The shepherd's lurcher, who, among the crags,
Had to his joy unearthed a hedgehog, teased
His coiled-up prey with barkings turbulent.
This small adventure, for even such it seemed
In that wild place and at the dead of night,
Being over and forgotten, on we wound
In silence as before. With forehead bent
Earthward, as if in opposition set
Against an enemy, I panted up
With eager pace, and no less eager thoughts.
Thus might we wear a midnight hour away,
Ascending at loose distance each from each,
And I, as chanced, the foremost of the band;
When at my feet the ground appeared to brighten,
And with a step or two seemed brighter still;
Nor was time given to ask or learn the cause,
For instantly a light upon the turf
Fell like a flash, and lo! as I looked up,
The Moon hung naked in a firmament
Of azure without cloud, and at my feet
Rested a silent sea of hoary mist.
A hundred hills their dusky backs upheaved
All over this still ocean: and beyond,
Far, far beyond, the solid vapours stretched,
In headlands, tongues, and promontory shapes,
Into the main Atlantic, that appeared
To dwindle, and give up his majesty,
Usurped upon far as the sight could reach.
Not so the ethereal vault; encroachment none
Was there, nor loss; only the inferior stars
Had disappeared, or shed a fainter light
In the clear presence of the full-orbed Moon,
Who, from her sovereign elevation, gazed
Upon the billowy ocean, as it lay
All meek and silent, save that through a rift—
Not distant from the shore, whereon we stood,
A fixed, abysmal, gloomy, breathing-place—
Mounted the roar of waters, torrents, streams
Innumerable, roaring with one voice!
Heard over earth and sea, and, in that hour,
For so it seemed, felt by the starry heavens.

WILLIAM WORDSWORTH, *The Prelude*

The Llyvon

Nor less the stream of LLYVON marks the scene,
Still glitt'ring various on the blue serene,
Reflects new beauties as his current flows,
And other skies in his deep bosom shows.—
When Vernal Suns their bright'ning influence shed,
When Summer's radiance o'er the heav'ns is spread,
When genial Autumn holds her milder reign,
And CERE's gifts enrich the yellow plain,
Old LLYVON bids his gently murm'ring wave
In softest lapse the verdant borders lave;
But when from high the fierce AQUARIUS pours
His wintry store of unremitting show'rs,
Then swells his torrent, whose resistless force,
Sublimely dreadful in its rapid course,
Deep through the subject valley sweeps along;
Hoarse murm'ring, breaks the rugged rocks among;
With sway impetuous scours the level plain,
And roaring, thund'ring, rushes to the main.

JOHN HUDDLESTONE WYNNE, *Evelina*

Misty Twilight: Y Foel Fras

Day flickered out among the mountains bleak,
    Impenetrable mist was over all,
    And, like a white flower on a sombre pall,
The lake shone steely-gray, a glimmering streak:
Chasing the shadowy waves from peak to peak
    The sea-breeze blew as night began to fall,—
    Rolled the cloud-curtain up the rocky wall,
And lifted off the veil from Nature's cheek.

The ridge gigantic loomed from out the haze,
    Its crest appeared, above whose towering crown
A great star glittered like a chrysoprase,—
    The coast below, with every twinkling town,
    The darkening straits beneath a sunset brown,
And, seaward far, the ruddy lighthouse-blaze.

J. G. F. NICHOLSON

At The Turn of The Tide: Llysfaen Head

Spectral and dim looms forth the curving coast
    As night draws down upon the shadowy bay;
    The tide that ebbed with the departed day
Comes surging back with all its thundering host:
Under the headland, where it darkens most,
    Smooth-crested billows crash with showers of spray,
    And, anchored on the tossing water-way,
One shimmering bark rocks like a pallid ghost.

Onward the foaming tidal torrents pour,—
    They break beneath the cliff with hollow boom,
And louder grows the changeless deep-toned roar;
    In wailing gusts from out the gathering gloom
The wet night-wind blows inwards on the shore,
    And drives the white sea-horses to their doom.

J. G. F. NICHOLSON

Penmanmawr

      The sun goes down.
Far off his light is on the naked crags
Of Penmanmawr, and Arvon's ancient hills;
And the last glory lingers yet awhile,
Crowning old Snowdon's venerable head,
That rose amid his mountains.

ROBERT SOUTHEY, *The Return to Wales*

Goats and Men

      Ev'n on the cliffy Height
Of *Penmenmaur*, and that Cloud-piercing Hill,
Plinlimmon, from afar the Traveller kens
Astonish'd, how the Goats their shrubby Brouze
Gnaw pendent; nor untrembling canst thou see,
How far from a scraggy Rock, whose Prominence
Half overshades the Ocean, hardy Men,

Fearless of rending Winds, and dashing Waves,
Cut Sampire, to excite the squeamish Gust
Of pamper'd luxury.

JOHN PHILIPS, *Cyder*

Menai Strait

(On crossing the Anglesea Strait to Bangor at Midnight)

'Twas midnight! from the Druid's gloomy cave,
    Where I had wander'd, tranc'd in thought, alone
    'Mid Cromlechs, and the Carnedd's funeral stone,
Pensive and slow, I sought the Menai's wave:
Lull'd by the scene, a soothing stillness laid
    My soul to rest. O'er Snowdon's cloudless brow
    The moon, that full-orb'd rose, with peaceful glow,
Beam'd on the rocks; with many a star array'd,
Glitter'd the broad blue sky; from shore to shore
    O'er the smooth current stream'd a silver light,
    Save where along the flood the lonely height
Of rocky Penmaenmaur deep darkness shed;
And all was silence, save the ceaseless roar
Of Conway bursting on the ocean's bed.

WILLIAM SOTHEBY

Beaumaris Bay

Hibernia's eastern sea here Cambria laves,
And pours on either shore its restless waves,
While Menai's currents with its waters play—
Now roll to meet, or, refluent, fill the Bay;
And, circling PRIESTHOLM, shew its oval steep,
Emerging boldly from the briny deep.

We hie where BARON-HILL attracts the Muse,
The sunny glades, the brow, the varying views—
Isles, towns, the rising hills, the spreading bay,
The Muse, delighted, owns the grand display;
Here Flora smiles, and flowers of every hue
Their glowing petals spread, and drink the dew.

Now, Muse, ascend the sylvan summits gay
That tower above the town—the valley—Bay—
Where now, unheeded, lies the heap of stones,
The altar's ruin, and the mouldering bones;
The soil once soften'd by Contrition's eyes,
On all that's mortal of ST MEUGAN lies.

Now southward, Muse, on spreading pinions bend,
A lesser Snowdon's[1] verdant sides ascend,
That rears abruptly from the lucid deep,
Its stony apex o'er the craggy steep.
The Landscape's various charms the Muse explores,
The Druid haunts, and Mona's hallowed shores,
High Afron soaring o'er the humbler isle,
The winding Menai—Daniel's mitred pile;
Thy towers, Caernarvon—triple summits, Llyn,
That distant close the vast and varied scene.
Below, amphibious Man, as whim prevails,
Trims up his little bark, and spreads his sails.

Now Nature soft'ning, from the Carnedd bends,
And gently to the humbler dale descends,
Alternate spreads the saline sheet or sands,
And checks the waves with Aber's lengthen'd strands;
Tremendous PENMAEN! there old Ocean braves,
And soars, insulting, o'er subjected waves.

RICHARD LLWYDD, *Beaumaris Bay*

DENBIGHSHIRE   *Chirk Castle*

So I tooke horse, and mounted up in haste,
From Monmouthshire, a long the coasts I ryde:
When frost and snowe, and wayward winters waste,
Did beate from tree both leaves and Sommers pryde.
I entred first, at *Chirke*, right ore a Brooke;
Where staying still, on Countrey well to looke,
A Castle fayre appeerde to sight of eye,
Whose walls were great, and towers both large and hye.

[1] 'Craig y parc'.

Full underneath the same doth Keeryock[1] run,
A raging Brooke, when rayne or snowe is greate:
It was some Prince that first this house begun,
It shewes farre of, to be so brave a Seate.
On side of hill, it stands most trim to vewe,
An old strong place, a Castle nothing newe,
A goodly thing, a princely Pallace yet,
If all within were thoroughly furnisht fit.

THOMAS CHURCHYARD, *The Worthines of Wales*

At A Fashionable Watering-Place
(Colwyn Bay)

As I have known thee once, I see thee still,
Though, to the outward sense, there lives no more
The quiet hamlet, nestling beneath the hill,
And downward straggling to a lonely shore.

One moment I, as others, see and hear,
Then, pier, parade, pavilion, melt away,
The hum of traffic dies, and to my ear
Comes but a drowsy whisper from the bay.

So, when some traveller, in hot desert sands,
Or tangled forest, looks upon the face
Of a dead city, musing long he stands,
And strives to call to life a vanished race.

He peoples there, as I unpeople here,
He calls a city back, I bid one go;
Each sees the present fade, the past appear,
One mourns the ebb of life, and one the flow.

THOMAS THORNELY

At Tremeirchion, near St Asaph
Pied Beauty

Glory be to God for dappled things—
    For skies of couple-colour as a brinded cow;

[1] Ceiriog.

For rose-moles all in stipple upon trout that swim;
Fresh-firecoal chestnut-falls; finches' wings;
   Landscape plotted and pierced—fold, fallow, and plough;
   And all trades, their gear and tackle and trim.
All things counter, original, spare, strange;
   Whatever is fickle, freckled (who knows how?)
   With swift, slow; sweet, sour, adazzle, dim;
He fathers-forth whose beauty is past change:
        Praise him.

GERARD MANLEY HOPKINS

Moonrise

I awoke in the Midsummer not to call night, | in the white
   and the walk of the morning:
The moon, dwindled and thinned to the fringe | of a finger-nail
   held to the candle,
Or paring of paradisaïcal fruit, | lovely in waning but lustreless,
Stepped from the stool, drew back from the barrow, | of dark
   Maenefa the mountain;

A cusp still clasped him, a fluke yet fanged him, | entangled
   him, not quit utterly.
This was the prized, the desirable sight, | unsought, presented
   so easily,
Parted me leaf and leaf, divided me, | eyelid and eyelid of
   slumber.

GERARD MANLEY HOPKINS

Moel Fammau

In purple heather is my sleep
On Moel Fammau; far below
   The springing rivulets leap,
   The firs wave to and fro.

This morn, the sun on Bala Lake
Broke out behind me: morrow morn
   Near Rhual I shall wake,
   Before the sun is born;

High burning over Clwyd Vale,
And reddening the mountain dew:
    While the moon lingers frail,
    High up in skies of blue.

Lovely and loved, O passionate land!
Dear Celtic land, unconquered still!
    Thy mountain strength prevails:
    Thy winds have all their will.

They have no care for meaner things;
They have no scorn for brooding dreams:
    A spirit in them sings,
    A light about them beams.

LIONEL JOHNSON

FLINTSHIRE   *Flint Castle*

                Noble Lord,
Goe to the rude Ribs of that ancient Castle

                * * *

Goe signifie as much, while here we march
Upon the Grassie Carpet of this Plaine:
Let's march without the noyse of threatning Drum,
That from this Castles tatter'd Battlements
Our faire Appointments may be well perus'd.

WILLIAM SHAKESPEARE, *Richard II*

6

The North Country

Liverpool

In Liverpool, the good old town, we miss
　　The grand old relics of a reverend past,—
Cathedrals, shrines that pilgrims come to kiss,—
　　　　Walls wrinkled by the blast.

* * *

We have our Castle Street, but castle none;
　　Redcross Street, but its legend who can learn;
Oldhall Street, too, we have, the old hall gone;
　　　　Tithebarn Street, but no barn.

Huge warehouses for cotton, rice, and corn,
　　Tea and tobacco, log and other woods,
Oils, tallow, hides that smell so foully foreign,
　　　　Yea, all things known as goods—

These we can show, but nothing to restore
　　The spirit of old times, save here and there
An ancient mansion with palatial door,
　　　　In some degenerate square.

Then rise the merchant princes of old days,
　　Their silken dames, their skippers from the strand,
Who brought their sea-borne riches, not always
　　　　Quite free from contraband.

And these their mansions, to base uses come,—
　　Harbours for fallen fair ones, drifting tars;
Some manufactories of blacking, some
　　　　Tobacco and cigars.

We have a church that one almost reveres,—
　　St Nicholas, nodding by the river-side,—
In old times hailed by ancient mariners
　　　　That came up with the tide.

Yet all so ridiculously new,
　　Except, perhaps, the river and the sky,
The waters and the immemorial blue
　　　　Forever sailing by.

ROBERT LEIGHTON, *Liverpool*

A Northern Factory Town
(Seen from an upper slum-window, Manchester)

　　A white cat strolling up the tiles;
　　And in the wind washed pants aflap,
　　Chemises, blinds, a nurse's cap,—
　　Pale patches mid the gray slate miles.

　　'Soap! Soap!'—A hoarding. Soap to shift
　　The clotted filth from this black sty!
　　Yon soap-bar, factories blindly lift
　　Their tall brick funnels to the sky.

　　And here, four hundred years flown by,
　　Grew the grass the villagers danced upon.
　　Morris and Maypole, where are they gone?
　　Chanson and Balladry? Whither? And Why?

HERBERT PALMER

Sand Dunes and Shoals
(Near Southport)

　　　　Ormeschurch and the Meales
Are our next jorney; we direct no weales
Of state, to hinder our delight. The guize
Of those chaffe sands, which doe in mountains rize,
On shore is pleasure to behould, which Hoes[1]

---

[1] Hows: a term for rising ground.

165

Are calld in Worold:[1] windie tempest blowes
Them up in heapes: tis past intelligence
With me how seas doe reverence
Unto the sands; but sands and beach and pebbles are
Cast up by rowling of the waves, a ware[2]
To make against their deluge, since the larke
And sheepe within feede lower then the marke
Of each high flood. Heere through the wasshie sholes
We spye an owld man wading for the soles
And flukes and rayes, which the last morning tide
Had stayd in nets, or did att anchor ride
Uppon his hooks; him we fetch up, and then
To our goodmorrowe, 'Welcomme gentlemen',
He sayd, and more, 'you gentlemen at ease
Who monye have, and goe where ere you please,
Are never quiett; wearye of the daye,
You now comme hether to drive time away:
Must time be driven? longest day with us
Shutts in to soone, as never tedious
Unto our buisnesse; making, mending nett,
Preparing hooks and baits, wherewith to gett
Cod, whiting, place, upon the sandie shelvs
Where with to feede the markett and our selvs.'
Happie ould blade, whoe in his youth had binne
Roving at sea when Essex Cales did winne,
So now he lives.

RICHARD JAMES, *Iter Lancastrense*

Three Hills

'Penigent, Pendle Hill, Ingleborough
Three such hills be not all England thorough.'
I long to climbe up Pendle; Pendle stands
Rownd cop[3], survaijing all the wilde moore lands,
And Malkins toure, a little cottage, where
Reporte makes caitive witches meete to sweare
Their homage to the divell, and contrive
The deaths of men and beasts.

*　*　*

[1] Wirral in Cheshire.　　　　[3] Cope.
[2] A weir or embankment.

Needs must strainge phansies poore ould wives possesse,
Whoe in those desert mystie moores doe live
Hungrie and colde, and scarce see priest to give
Them ghostlye counsell.

RICHARD JAMES, *Iter Lancastrense*

Furness Abbey

Here would the aged pilgrim gladly stay
To rest him in these hospitable halls;
Here where the night disconsolately falls
With song and story keep the night at bay.
Here did the shadowy brethren, white and grey,
Move to and fro within their stately walls,
And bind and loose the burdens of their thralls
Nor ever from the poor man turn away.
Alas! within the Abbot's painted room,
Rich with armorial rose and Eastern palms,
The ferns are growing and the harebells bloom,
And blackberry for all who ask an alms,
Where, through the vale of nightshade in the gloom,
The screech owl hoots his penitential psalms.

MARY COLERIDGE

In the Vale of Esthwaite

Magnificent
The morning rose, in memorable pomp,
Glorious as e'er I had beheld—in front,
The sea lay laughing at a distance; near,
The solid mountains shone, bright as the clouds,
Grain-tinctured, drenched in empyrean light;
And in the meadows and the lower grounds
Was all the sweetness of a common dawn—
Dews, vapours, and the melody of birds,
And labourers going forth to till the fields.

WILLIAM WORDSWORTH, *The Prelude*

On Esthwaite Lake

But now, like one who rows,
Proud of his skill, to reach a chosen point
With an unswerving line, I fixed my view
Upon the summit of a craggy ridge,
The horizon's utmost boundary; far above
Was nothing but the stars and the grey sky.
She was an elfin pinnace; lustily
I dipped my oars into the silent lake,
And, as I rose upon the stroke, by boat
Went heaving through the water like a swan;
When, from behind that craggy steep[1] till then
The horizon's bound, a huge peak,[2] black and huge,
As if with voluntary power instinct
Upreared its head. I struck and struck again,
And growing still in stature the grim shape
Towered up between me and the stars, and still,
For so it seemed, with purpose of its own
And measured notion like a living thing,
Strode after me. With trembling oars I turned,
And through the silent water stole my way
Back to the covert of the willow tree;
There in her mooring-place I left my bark,—
And through the meadows homeward went, in grave
And serious mood; but after I had seen
That spectacle, for many days, my brain
Worked with a dim and undetermined sense
Of unknown modes of being.

WILLIAM WORDSWORTH, *The Prelude*

The Thunderstorm

When Coniston Old Man was younger
And his deep-quarried sides were stronger,
Goats may have leapt about Goat's Water;
But why the tarn that looks like its young daughter
Though lying high under the fell
Should be called Blind Tarn, who can tell?

---

[1] The ridge between Hawkshead and Coniston Moors.   [2] Wetherlam.

For from Dow Crag, passing it by,
I saw it as a dark presageful eye;
And soon I knew that I was not mistaken
Hearing the thunder the loose echoes waken
About Scafell and Scafell Pike
And feeling the slant raindrops strike.

And when I came to Walna Pass
Hailstones hissing and hopping among the grass,
Beneath a rock I found a hole;
But with sharp crack and rumbling roll on roll
So quick the lightning came and went
The solid rock was like a lighted tent.

ANDREW YOUNG

Sonnets to the Duddon
'Sole Listener, Duddon'

Sole listener, Duddon! to the breeze that played
With thy clear voice, I caught the fitful sound
Wafted o'er sullen moss and craggy mound—
Unfruitful solitudes, that seemed to upbraid
The sun in heaven!—but now, to form a shade
For Thee, green alders have together wound
Their foliage; ashes flung their arms around;
And birch-trees risen in silver colonnade.
And thou hast also tempted here to rise,
'Mid sheltering pines, this Cottage rude and grey;
Whose ruddy children, by the mother's eyes
Carelessly watched, sport through the summer day,
Thy pleased associates:—light as endless May
On Infant bossoms lonely Nature lies.

Sheep-Washing

Sad thoughts, avaunt!—partake we their blithe cheer
Who gathered in betimes the unshorn flock
To wash the fleece, where haply bands of rock,
Checking the stream, make a pool smooth and clear
As this we look on. Distant Mountains hear,

Hear and repeat, the turmoil that unites
Clamour of boys with innocent despites
Of barking dogs, and bleatings from strange fear.
And what if Duddon's spotless flood receive
Unwelcome mixtures as the uncouth noise
Thickens, the pastoral River will forgive
Such wrong; nor need *we* blame the licensed joys,
Though false to Nature's quiet equipoise:
Frank are the sports, the stains are fugitive.

WILLIAM WORDSWORTH

Windermere and Hawkshead

Bright was the summer's noon when quickening steps
Followed each other till a dreary moor
Was crossed, a bare ridge clomb, upon whose top
Standing alone, as from a rampart's edge,
I overlooked the bed of Windermere,
Like a vast river, stretching in the sun.
With exultation, at my feet I saw
Lake, islands, promontories, gleaming bays,
A universe of Nature's fairest forms
Proudly revealed with instantaneous burst,
Magnificent, and beautiful, and gay.
I bounded down the hill shouting amain
For the old Ferryman; to the shout the rocks
Replied, and when the Charon of the flood
Had staid his oars, and touched the jutting pier,
I did not step into the well-known boat
Without a cordial greeting. Thence with speed
Up the familiar hill I took my way
Towards that sweet Valley where I had been reared;
'Twas but a short hour's walk, ere veering round
I saw the snow-white church upon her hill
Sit like a throned Lady, sending out
A gracious look all over her domain.
Yon azure smoke betrays the lurking town;
With eager footsteps I advance and reach
The cottage threshold where my journey closed.

WILLIAM WORDSWORTH, *The Prelude*

WESTMORLAND *Little Langdale*
(Seen from the top of Lingmoor)

All at once, behold!
Beneath our feet, a little lowly vale,
A lowly vale, and yet uplifted high
Among the mountains; even as if the spot
Had been from eldest time by wish of theirs
So placed, to be shut out from all the world!
Urn-like it was in shape, deep as an urn;
With rocks encompassed, save that to the south
Was one small opening, where a heath-clad ridge
Supplied a boundary less abrupt and close;
A quiet treeless nook, with two green fields,
A liquid pool[1] that glittered in the sun,
And one bare dwelling; one abode, no more!
It seemed the home of poverty and toil,
Though not of want: the little fields, made green
By husbandry of many thrifty years,
Paid cheerful tribute to the moorland house.
—There crows the cock, single in his domain:
The small birds find in spring no thicket there
To shroud them; only from the neighbouring vales
The cuckoo, straggling up to the hill tops,
Shouteth faint tidings of some gladder place.

WILLIAM WORDSWORTH, *The Excursion*

Langdale: Nightfall, January 4th

Dark are the shrouded hills, and vague, and the rain,
as the wind changes,
halts, and clouds over the fells
drift, and the Pleiades drown.

The hooded fells are uncertain, the track to the tarn
is lost, the fields are in flood,
and at six the lane is in darkness,
the beck is a ghost.

[1] Blea Tarn.

Night, and the day wasted, waiting,
watching, lethargic:
clouds and star-clusters are shapeless;
lamplight, dim starlight, floodland,

and fellscape, vaguely forgotten. And the wind
changes; the sky is alert:
crag, sheepfold and cairn
rise; and the mist is swept over the fells,

And the seven stars of Orion,
star-points driven home,
are nails in a buckler, or splinters
of light in the mind.

The touch of the track is a landmark,
stone underfoot,
the clouds and star-clusters are islands,
and water leaps down in the ghyll.

MICHAEL ROBERTS

Black Tarn

The road ends with the hills.
No track continues the fair and easy way
That leads in safety beside the valley lake,
Skirting the lake, the lake of candid waters
Sleek among rising fells. It is a valley
Veined by one road, one smooth and certain road,
Walled on the fell-side, walled against the boulders,
The rough fell-side, where few penurious sheep
Find a scrimp pasture, stray, crop, wander;
A road whence the traveller may scan the valley,
Seeing the lake, the prospect north and south,
The foot of the fells; and, lifting up his eyes,
Their heads, mist-dwelling;
He may explore the ferns, the little lichens,
The tiny life at fell's foot, peaty pools,
Learning their detail, finding out their habit;
This, and the general prospect of the valley,
Lie and proportion of the fells, sky, waters,
All from the road. But the road ends with the hills.

At the valley's head the road ends, making no curve
To return whence it came, but, bluntly barred,
Stops with the slope. The road's crisp gravel
Softens to turf, to swamps of spongy peat,
Boulders flung down in anger, brown streams poured
From inaccessible sources. Dull brute hills
Mount sullen, trackless; who would climb, must climb
Finding a way; steps tentative,
Thoughtful, and irrelated, steps of doubt,
Sometimes of exultation. Now see the lake
With its companion road, safe in the valley,
That bird's eye, easy conquest. Left below
That known, seen, travelled region. Sagging clouds
Veil the high hills, raze the peaks level,
Wimple in white the hidden tors, the final
Pricking of height towards sky; still through the mist
Each conquered patch spreads visible, unrolls
Its footing of turf or stone.
Faith knows the shrouded peaks, their composition,
Granite and shale, their sundered rock
Like an axe's cleavage, wedge of scars.
Faith knows they wait there, may be scaled.
But few climb higher than these middle reaches,
Difficult, wild enough; slopes to be won
Nor wholly relinquished, even when steps return
To the easy lowland, to the calm lake's shore,
For they abide in the mind, as a value held,
A gain achieved.
                    Most certainly I remember
A lonely tarn in the hills, a pool in a crater,
Lustrous as armour, wet rocks, and still, round pool.
Lustrous, but with a sheen not taken from heaven,
Not with a light as lit the lake below
In the open valley, frank and susceptible,
Receiving and giving back; but inward, sullen,
In the crater's cup, as drawing out
Some dark effulgence from subterranean depths,
Self-won, self-suffered. Stones I threw
Sank, forced the surface to a ripple,
But like a plummet dropped into earth's bowels
Were swallowed, and the satanic darkness closed
As though no wound had been.

> I have seen Black Tarn,
> Shivered it for an instant, been afraid.
> Looked into its waters, seen there my own image
> As an upturned mask that floated
> Just under the surface, within reach, beyond reach.
> There are tarns among hills, for all who climb the hills,
> Tarns suddenly stumbled on, sudden points of meaning
> Among the rough negative hills, reward
> Precious and fearful, leaving a discontent
> With the lake in the valley, and the road beside the lake,
> And the dwellings of men, the safety, and the ease.

V. SACKVILLE-WEST

The Lakes

Far from my dearest Friend, 'tis mine to rove
Through bare grey dell, high wood, and pastoral cove;
Where Derwent rests, and listens to the roar
That stuns the tremulous cliffs of high Lodore;
Where peace to Grasmere's lonely island leads,
To willowy hedge-rows, and to emerald meads;
Leads to her bridge, rude church and cottaged grounds,
Her rocky sheepwalks, and her woodland bounds;
Where, undisturbed by winds, Winander sleeps;
'Mid clustering isles, and holly-sprinkled steeps;
Where twilight glens endear my Esthwaite's shore,
And memory of departed pleasures, more.

WILLIAM WORDSWORTH, *An Evening Walk*

View From Helvellyn

There to the north the silver Solway shone,
And Criffel, by the hazy atmosphere
Lifted from off the earth, did then appear
A nodding island or a cloud-built throne.
And there, a spot half fancied and half seen,
Was sunny Carlisle; and by hillside green
Lay Penrith with its beacon of red stone.

Southward through pale blue steam the eye might glance
Along the Yorkshire fells, and o'er the rest,
My native hill, dear Ingleboro's crest,
Rose shapely, like a cap of maintenance.
The classic Duddon, Leven, and clear Kent
A trident of fair estuaries sent,
Which did among the mountain roots advance.

Westward, a region of tumultuous hills,
With here and there a tongue of azure lake
And ridge of fir, upon the eye did break.
But chiefest wonder are the tarns and rills
And giant coves, where great Helvellyn broods
Upon his own majestic solitudes,
Which even now the sunlight barely fills.

There Striding Edge with Swirrel meets to keep
The Red Tarn still when tempests rage above:
There Catsty-Cam doth watch o'er Keppel Cove
And the chill pool that lurks beneath the steep.
Far to the right St Sunday's quiet shade
Stoops o'er the dell, where Grisedale Tarn is laid
Beneath that solemn crag in waveless sleep.

The golden cliffs which from Parnassus lean
With uncouth rivets of the roots of trees,
And silent-waving pinewood terraces,
And burnished zones of hanging evergreen,—
Haunts of the antique muses though they are,
May not for dread solemnity compare,
Or savage wonders, with this native scene.

Awful in moonlight shades, more awful far
When the winds wake, are those majestic coves,
Or when the thunder feeds his muttering droves
Of swart clouds on the raven-haunted scar;
And in the bright tranquillity of noon
Most awful; lovely only in the boon
Of soft apparel wrought by twilight air.

Shall Brownrigg Well be left without a song,
Which near the summit, mid the wintry snows
In a clear vein of liquid crystal flows,
And through the pastoral months in gushes strong

175

Gleams in the eye of sunset, and from far
Holds up a mirror to the evening star,
While round its mouth the thirsty sheepflocks throng?

And now, with loitering step and minds unbent
Through hope fulfilled, we reached the vale once more;
And, wending slowly along Rydal shore,
Watched the dusk splendor which from Langdale went,
And on the hills dethroned the afternoon;
And home was gained ere yet the yellow moon
From over Wansfell her first greeting sent.

F. W. FABER, *The Ascent of Helvellyn*

Hayeswater

A region desolate and wild.
Black, chafing water: and afloat,
And lonely as a truant child
In a waste wood, a single boat:
No mast, no sails are set thereon;
It moves, but never moveth on:
And welters like a human thing
Amid the wild waves weltering.

Behind, a buried vale doth sleep,
Far down the torrent cleaves its way:
In front the dumb rock rises steep,
A fretted wall of blue and grey;
Of shooting cliff and crumbled stone
With many a wild weed overgrown:
All else, black water: and afloat,
One rood from shore, that single boat.

MATTHEW ARNOLD

On Windermere: Bowness Bay and Belle Isle

Upon the Eastern Shore of Windermere,
Above the crescent of a pleasant Bay,
There stood an Inn, no homely-featured Shed,

Brother of the surrounding Cottages,
But 'twas a splendid place, the door beset
With Chaises, Grooms, and Liveries, and within
Decanters, Glasses, and the blood-red Wine.
In ancient times, or ere the Hall was built
On the large Island, had this Dwelling been
More worthy of a Poet's love, a Hut,
Proud of its one bright fire, and sycamore shade.
But though the rhymes were gone which once inscribed
The threshold, and large golden characters
On the blue-frosted Signboard had usurp'd
The place of the old Lion, in contempt
And mockery of the rustic painter's hand,
Yet to this hour the spot to me is dear
With all its foolish pomp. The garden lay
Upon a slope surmounted by the plain
Of a small Bowling-green; beneath us stood
A grove; with gleams of water through the trees
And over the tree-tops; nor did we want
Refreshment, strawberries and mellow cream.
And there, through half an afternoon, we play'd
On the smooth platform, and the shouts we sent
Made all the mountains ring. But ere the fall
Of night, when in our pinnace we return'd
Over the dusky Lake, and to the beach
Of some small Island steer'd our course with one,
The Minstrel of our troop, and left him there,
And row'd off gently, while he blew his flute
Alone upon the rock; Oh! then the calm
And dead still water lay upon my mind
Even with a weight of pleasure, and the sky
Never before so beautiful, sank down
Into my heart, and held me like a dream.

WILLIAM WORDSWORTH

CUMBERLAND *The Vale of Keswick*
The Same Scene by Moonlight

Now sunk the sun, now twilight sunk, and night
Rode in her zenith; now a passing breeze
Sighed to the grove, which in the midnight air

Stood motionless, and in the peaceful floods
Inverted hung; for now the billow slept
Along the shore, nor heaved the deep, but spread
A shining mirror to the moon's pale orb,
Which, dim and waning, o'er the shadowy cliffs,
The solemn woods and spiry mountain tops,
Her glimmering faintness threw: now every eye,
Oppressed with toil, was drowned in deep repose;
Save that the unseen shepherd in his watch,
Propped on his crook, stood list'ning by the fold,
And gazed the starry vault and pendant moon;
Nor voice nor sound broke on the deep serene,
But the soft murmur of swift-gushing rills,
Forth-issuing from the mountains' distant steep,
(Unheard till now, and now scarce heard) proclaimed
All things at rest, and imaged the still voice
Of quiet whispering to the ear of night.

JOHN BROWN

A Recollection of the Stone Circle near Keswick

Scarce images of life, one here, one there,
Lay vast and edgeways; like a dismal cirque
Of Druid stones, upon a forlorn moor,
When the chill rain begins at shut of eve,
In dull November, and their chancel vault,
The Heaven itself, is blinded throughout night.
Each one kept shroud, nor to his neighbour gave
Or word, or look, or action of despair.

JOHN KEATS

Wastwater
Written on the Banks of Wastwater during a Calm

Is this the lake, the cradle of the storms,
Where silence never tames the mountain-roar,
Where poets fear their self-created forms,
Or, sunk in trance severe, their God adore?

Is this the lake for ever dark and loud,
With wave and tempest, cataract and cloud:
Wondrous, O Nature, is thy sovereign power,
That gives to horror hours of peaceful mirth;
For here might beauty build her summer bower!
Lo! where yon rainbow spans the smiling earth,
And clothed in glory, through a silent shower
The mighty Sun comes forth, a god-like birth;
While, 'neath his loving eye the gentle Lake
Lies like a sleeping child too blest to wake!

CHRISTOPHER NORTH

Cockermouth

Past castle, brewery, over a sandstone bridge,
A Midland Bank, 'Fletcher's Fearless Clothing',
And huge effigy of an assassinated politician,
You come upon a Georgian grand frontage,

Still the town's 'big house', built for a Sheriff,
Not long ago ransomed from demolition
(The site an ideal one for the new bus-station)
And looked at, now, by a small bust of Wordsworth.

Turn down its by-lane, leading to the river,
You'll see, fenced like a POW camp, reached by
An iron footbridge, the town's factory;
There ran a mill-race, where was once a meadow,

And Derwent shuffles by it, over stones.
And if you look up the valley toward Isel
With Blindcrake to the north, cloudcatcher fells,
Whose waters track past here to Workington.

Eighteenth-century, like some town of Portugal;
Doorways faced with stone, proportionate windows,
And painted black and white, or gayer colours;
A scale perfectly kept, appropriately small.

Born here or hereabouts then: John Dalton,
Propounder of atomic theory; Fletcher
Christian; and, juxtaposing that Bounty mutineer,
Wordsworth the poet, of all unlikely men.

Tombs of shipmasters on the hill overlook
Town roofs, the valley where the river slips away
Toward the dead ports and the Irish Sea,
Dowsed furnaces, closed mines of haematite

And coal, fortunes of Lowther and Curwen,
Slagheaps, the mansions of industralists
Shuttered and rotting, burned or derelict,
Where a prosperity of impoverishment

Flourished, and now stands memorial
There, and in small classic façades of this town,
To the era designated Augustan;
Brown leaves about the baroque headstones fall.

On one side foundries; and the other way
Those frugal, delectable mountains
Where the smallholder yeoman, an anachronism,
Hung on into the nineteenth century.

So set, equidistant between past and future,
What more likely than, just here and then,
Should have been born that Janus-headed man,
A conservator and innovator

As the machine began to gather power,
Menacing nature to smile, because subdued?
The walled garden of his childhood
Stands as it was, pondering the river.

DAVID WRIGHT

Millom Old Quarry

'They dug ten streets from that there hole,' he said,
'Hard on five hundred houses.' He nodded
Down the set of the quarry and spat in the water
Making a moorhen cock her head
As if a fish had leaped. 'Half the new town
'Came out of yonder—King Street, Queen Street, all
'The houses round the Green as far as the slagbank,
'And Market Street, too, from the Crown allotments
'Up to the Station Yard.'—'But Market Street's
'Brown freestone,' I said.—'Nobbut the facings;

'We called them the Khaki Houses in the Boer War,
'But they're Cumberland slate at the back.'

I thought of those streets still bearing their royal names
Like the coat-of-arms on a child's Jubilee Mug—
Nonconformist gables sanded with sun
Or branded with burning creeper; a smoke of lilac
Between the blue roofs of closet and coal-house:
So much that woman's blood gave sense and shape to
Hacked from this dynamite combe.
The rocks cracked to the pond, and hawthorns fell
In waterfalls of blossom. Shed petals
Patterned the scum like studs on the sole of a boot,
And stiff-legged sparrows skid down screes of gravel.

I saw the town's black generations
Packed in their caves of rock, as mussel or limpet
Washed by the tidal sky; then swept, shovelled
Back in the quarry again, a landslip of lintels
Blocking the gape of the tarn.
The quick turf pushed a green tarpaulin over
All that was mortal in five thousand lives.
Nor did it seem a paradox to one
Who held quarry and query, turf and town,
In the small lock of a recording brain.

NORMAN NICHOLSON

The Cataract of Lodore

'How does the Water,
Come down at Lodore?'
My little boy ask'd me
Thus, once on a time;
And moreover he task'd me
To tell him in rhyme.
Anon at the word,
There first came one daughter
And then came another,
To second and third
The request of their brother,
And to hear how the Water

Comes down at Lodore,
With its rush and its roar.
As many a time
They had seen it before.
So I told them in rhyme,
For of rhymes I had store;
And 't was in my vocation
For their recreation
That I should sing;
Because I was Laureate
To them and the King.

From its sources which well
In the Tarn on the fell;
From its fountains
In the mountains,
Its rills and its gills;
Through moss and through brake,
It runs and it creeps
For awhile, till it sleeps
In its own little Lake.
And thence at departing,
Awakening and starting,
It runs through the reeds
And away it proceeds,
Through meadow and glade,
In sun and shade,
And through the wood-shelter,
Among crags in its flurry,
Helter-skelter,
Hurry-scurry.
Here it comes sparkling,
And there it lies darkling;
Now smoking and frothing
Its tumult and wrath in,
Till in this rapid race
On which it is bent,
It reaches the place
Of its steep descent.

The Cataract strong
Then plunges along,
Striking and raging

As if a war waging
Its caverns and rocks among:
  Rising and leaping,
  Sinking and creeping,
  Swelling and sweeping,
  Showering and springing,
  Flying and flinging,
  Writhing and ringing,
  Eddying and whisking,
  Spouting and frisking,
  Turning and twisting,
    Around and around
   With endless rebound;
   Smiting and fighting
   A sight to delight in;
Confounding, astounding,
Dizzying and deafening the ear with its sound.

   Collecting, projecting,
   Receding and speeding,
   And shocking and rocking,
   And darting and parting,
   And threading and spreading,
   And whizzing and hissing,
   And dripping and skipping,
   And hitting and splitting,
   And shining and twining,
   And rattling and battling,
   And shaking and quaking,
   And pouring and roaring,
   And waving and raving,
   And tossing and crossing,
   And flowing and going,
   And running and stunning,
   And foaming and roaming,
   And dinning and spinning,
   And dropping and hopping,
   And working and jerking,
   And guggling and struggling,
   And heaving and cleaving,
   And moaning and groaning;

And glittering and frittering,
And gathering and feathering,
And whitening and brightening,
And quivering and shivering,
And hurrying and skurrying,
And thundering and floundering;
Dividing and gliding and sliding,
And falling and brawling and sprawling,
And driving and riving and striving,
And sprinkling and twinkling and wrinkling,
And sounding and bounding and rounding,
And bubbling and troubling and doubling,
And grumbling and rumbling and tumbling,
And clattering and battering and shattering;

Retreating and beating and meeting and sheeting,
Delaying and straying and playing and spraying,
Advancing and prancing and glancing and dancing,
Recoiling, turmoiling and toiling and boiling,
And gleaming and streaming and steaming and beaming,
And rushing and flushing and brushing and gushing,
And flapping and rapping and clapping and slapping.
And curling and whirling and purling and twirling,
And thumping and plumping and bumping and jumping,
And dashing and flashing and splashing and clashing;
And so never ending, but always descending,
Sounds and motions for ever and ever are blending,
All at once and all o'er, with a mighty uproar,
And this way the Water comes down at Lodore.

ROBERT SOUTHEY

Helvellyn

I climb'd the dark brow of the mighty Helvellyn,
  Lakes and mountains beneath me gleam'd misty and wide;
All was still, save by fits, when the eagle was yelling,
  And starting around me the echoes replied.
On the right, Striden-edge round the Red-tarn was bending,
And Catchedicam its left verge was defending,
One huge nameless rock in the front was ascending,
  When I mark'd the sad spot where the wanderer had died.

SIR WALTER SCOTT, *Helvellyn*

Glaramara

From the wild fells I return to my lowland home.
How narrow and tame these fields and gardens seem!
A vision haunts me of a lonely mountain height,
Made lonelier by an unseen raven's croak,
And a shaggy ewe bleating for her strayed lamb.
Over the rough grass I stride along
With bare feet, avoiding the sharp stones,
Pleased with the coolness of rillet and mossy bog.
I turn a hillock, and there close before me
A limestone cliff mirrored in a still tarn.
Its grave beauty holds me, and long I stand
Looking down on inverted rocks and drifting cloud,
And my own face lit by a magic glow.
I look round—mountains beyond mountains,
Over green flanks lifting scarred rock-faces
And bare crests: at their feet far below
Mid woods and meadows a lake winds and gleams.
If there be mountain spirits, then here surely
Is one of those haunts they most frequent and love.
With a memory and a regret I turn away
For the long descent to the valley and its roofs and roads.

R. C. TREVELYAN

Ennerdale

I thought of Ennerdale as of a thing
Upon the confines of my memory.
There was a hazy gleam as o'er a sheet
Of sunny water cast, and mountain side,
And much ploughed land, and cleanly cottages,
A bubbling brook, the emptying of the lake,
An indistinct remembrance of being pleased
That there were hedgerows there instead of walls,
That it was noon, and that I swam for long
In the warm lake, and dressed upon a rock:—
And this is all of verdant Ennerdale
Which I can now recover from my mind;
The current of bright years hath washed it out.

Yet do I find the memory of it still
A thing which I can lean upon, a spot
Of greenness and fresh water in my soul.
And I do feel the very knowledge good
That there is such a place as Ennerdale,
A valley and a lake of such a kind,
As though I did possess it all myself
With daily eye and ear, because I know
It is possessed by simple dalesmen there.

F. W. FABER, *Ennerdale*

Cleator Moor

From one shaft at Cleator Moor
They mined for coal and iron ore.
This harvest below ground could show
Black and red currants on one tree.

In furnaces they burnt the coal,
The ore they smelted into steel,
And railway lines from end to end
Corseted the bulging land.

Pylons sprouted on the fells,
Stakes were driven in like nails,
And the ploughed fields of Devonshire
Were sliced with the steel of Cleator Moor.

The land waxed fat and greedy too,
It would not share the fruits it grew,
And coal and ore, as sloe and plum,
Lay black and red for jamming time.

The pylons rusted on the fells,
The gutters leaked beside the walls,
The women searched the ebb-tide tracks
For knobs of coal and broken sticks.

But now the pits are wick with men,
Digging like dogs dig for a bone:
For food and life *we* dig the earth—
In Cleator Moor they dig for death.

Every waggon of cold coal
Is fire to drive a turbine wheel;
Every knuckle of soft ore
A bullet in a soldier's ear.

The miner at the rockface stands,
With his segged and bleeding hands
Heaps on his head the fiery coal,
And feels the iron in his soul.

NORMAN NICHOLSON

Summit of Skiddaw

At length here stand we, wrapt as in the cloud
In which light dwelt before the sun was born,
When the great fiat issued, in the morn
Of this fair world; alone and in a shroud
Of dazzling mist, while the wind, whistling loud,
Buffets thy streaming locks:—result forlorn
For us who up yon steep our way have worn,
Elate with hope and of our daring proud.
Yet though no stretch of glorious prospect range
Beneath our vision,—neither Scottish coast
Nor ocean-island, nor the future boast
Of far-off hills descried,—I would not change
For aught on earth this solitary hour
Of Nature's grandest and most sacred power.

HENRY ALFORD

Green-head Ghyll

If from the public way you turn your steps
Up the tumultuous brook of Green-head Ghyll,
You will suppose that with an upright path
Your feet must struggle; in such bold ascent
The pastoral mountains front you, face to face.
But courage! for around that boisterous Brook
The mountains have all opened out themselves,

And made a hidden valley of their own.
No habitation can be seen; but they
Who journey hither find themselves alone
With a few sheep, with rocks and stones, and kites
That overhead are sailing in the sky.
It is, in truth, an utter solitude.

WILLIAM WORDSWORTH, *Michael*

Nunnery Dell
(Near Kirkoswald)

The floods are roused, and will not soon be weary,
Down from the Pennine Alps how fiercely sweeps
Croglin, the stately Eden's tributary!
He raves, or through some moody passage creeps,
Plotting new mischief—out again he leaps
Into broad light, and sends, through regions airy,
That voice which soothed the nuns while on the steeps
They knelt in prayer, or sang to blissful Mary.
That union ceased; then, cleaving easy walks
Through crags, and smoothing paths beset with danger,
Came studious Taste; and many a pensive stranger
Dreams on the banks, and to the river talks.
What change shall happen next to Nunnery Dell?
Canal, and Viaduct, and Railway tell!

WILLIAM WORDSWORTH

NORTHUMBERLAND
Northumberland

Heatherland and bent-land—
Black land and white,
God bring me to Northumberland,
The land of my delight.

Land of singing waters,
And winds from off the sea,

God bring me to Northumberland,
The land where I would be.

Heatherland and bent-land,
And valleys rich with corn,
God bring me to Northumberland,
The land where I was born.

WILFRID WILSON GIBSON

Chillingham

O the high valley, the little low hill,
    And the cornfield over the sea,
The wind that rages and then lies still,
    And the clouds that rest and flee!

O the gray island in the rainbow haze,
    And the long thin spits of land,
The roughening pastures and the stony ways,
    And the golden flash of the sand.

O the red heather on the moss-wrought rock,
    And the fir-tree stiff and straight,
The shaggy old sheep-dog barking at the flock,
    And the rotten old five-barred gate!

O the brown bracken, the blackberry bough,
    The scent of the gorse in the air!
I shall love them ever as I love them now,
    I shall weary in Heaven to be there!

MARY COLERIDGE

The Cheviot

Hedgehope Hill stands high,
The Cheviot higher still:
The Cheviot's wreathed with snow
When green is Hedgehope Hill.

But at break of day
Or coming on of night,
Hedgehope Hill is dark
While Cheviot's wreathed with light.

WILFRID WILSON GIBSON

Newcastle Beer

When Fame brought the news of Great Britain's success
   And told at Olympus each Gallic defeat;
Glad Mars sent by Mercury orders express,
   To summon the deities all to a treat:
     Blithe Comus was plac'd
     To guide the gay feast,
And freely declar'd there was a choice of good cheer;
     Yet vow'd to his thinking,
     For exquisite drinking,
Their nectar was nothing to Newcastle beer.

The great god of war, to encourage the fun,
   And humour the taste of his whimsical guest,
Sent a message that moment to Moor's[1] for a tun
   Of stingo, the stoutest, the brightest and best:
     No gods, they all swore
     Regal'd so before,
With liquor so lively, so potent and clear:
     And each deified fellow
     Got jovially mellow,
In honour, brave boys, of our Newcastle beer.

*   *   *

Ye fanciful folk, for whom physic prescribes,
   Whom bolus and potion have harass'd to death!
Ye wretches, whom law and her ill-looking tribes
   Have hunted about 'till you're quite out of breath!
     Here's shelter and ease,
     No craving for fees,
No danger, no doctor, no bailiff is near!
     Your spirits this raises,
     It cures your diseases,
There's freedom and health in our Newcastle beer.

JOHN CUNNINGHAM, *Newcastle Beer*

[1] Moor's, at the sign of the Sun, Newcastle.

COUNTY OF DURHAM

Durham

This city is celebrated
In the whole empire of the Britons.
The road to it is steep.
It is surrounded with rocks,
And with curious plants.
The Wear flows round it,
A river of rapid waves;
And there live in it
Fishes of various kinds,
Mingling with the floods.
And there grow
Great forests;
There live in the recesses
Wild animals of many sorts;
In the deep valleys
Deer innumerable.
There is in this city
Also well known to men
The venerable St Cudberth;
And the head of the chaste King
Oswald, the lion of the Angli;
And Aidan, the Bishop:
Aedbert and Aedfrid,
The noble associates.
There is in it also
Aethelwold, the Bishop;
And the celebrated writer Bede;
And the Abbot Boisil,
By whom the chaste Cudberth
Was in his youth gratis instructed;
Who also well received the instructions.
There rest with these saints,
In the inner part of the Minster,
Relicks innumerable,
Which perform many miracles,
As the chronicles tell us,
And which await with them
The judgement of the Lord.

Translated from *De Situ Dunelmi* (*c.* 1100)

Durham
(1815)

The sacred pile in gothic grandeur rear'd—
Where DURHAM's mitred Princes palac'd live,
Where hospitality of open mien
And bounty dwell (an ancient British pair)—
Surmounts the eminence, and crowns the scene!

ANON. *Auckland Park*

Durham

Grey towers of Durham!

* * *

Well yet I love thy mix'd and massive piles,
Half church of God, half castle 'gainst the Scot;
And long to roam these venerable aisles,
With records stored of deeds long since forgot.

SIR WALTER SCOTT, *Harold the Dauntless*

Langley Dale

As I down Raby Park did pass,
I heard a fair maid weep and wail;
The chiefest of her song it was,
Farewell the streets of Langley dale!

The bonny Mavis cheers his mate,
The Thristle-cock sings in the glen,
But I may never hope to rove
Within sweet Langley dale again.

The Gowan blooms beside the brae,
The Primrose shaws its blossom pale,
But I must bid adieu for aye
To all the sweets of Langley dale.

The days of peace are past and fled,
Youth's golden hairs to silver turn,
Each bonny flow'ret droops its head
By Langley dale and mossy burn.

False Suthrons crop each lovely flower,
And strew their blossoms on the gale:
Our foes have spoil'd the sweetest bower—
Alas for bonny Langley dale!

ANON.

Cocken Woods are Bonnie

The shadows o' evenin' owre Cocken were creepin',
  An' blackbirds were warblin' their notes lane an' clear;
The ruins o' Finchale their lane watch were keepin',
  And rumlie an' low was the song o' oor Wear.
As lanely I sauntered, the fair scene enjoyin',
  A birdie frae bush tap the brackens amang,
Gae lilt true and saftenin', my heart a' decoyin',
  Enraptured I listened to its bonnie sang.

Song of the Birdie

I hae come frae a fair south'ren clime,
  Where orange groves bonnilie bloom,
I hae sang on sierras sublime,
  Where zephyrs are charged wi' perfume,
I hae warbled 'mang rich growin' vines,
  An' aft by some clear stream fand rest,
Tho' in glades o' maist flowery designs,
  I ne'er saw a nook for a nest.
      But Cocken woods are bonnie,
        An' Cocken dells are fair,
      Brighter far than ony,
        Nane wi' them compare.

I hae sought repose in sunnier lands,
  Where scenes maist enchantin's abound,
An' the blue seas roll on golden strands,
  Alas! 'twas not there to be found.

But a breeze frae the far northern skies
  Aince ruffled my longin' wee breast,
Whisprin' saftly, Come fly where I rise,
  I ken o' a nook for a nest,
      In Cocken woods sae bonnie,
       An' Cocken dells sae fair,
     Brighter far than ony,
       Nane wi' them compare.

Its liltie sae lovely the wee birdie endit,
  And flutt'rin' a weel, flew sae blithely awa;
Responsive my thochts a' in unison blendit,
  For fairer than Finchale I ken nane e'er saw.
Tho' lands may be famous wi' mountains and valleys,
  And ruins historic fu' grandly appear,
Yet Nature at Cocken has made her ain palace,
  Sae seek not for beauty, while flows on the Wear.

SIR WILLIAM ALLAN

Along the Wear

Where scenes of The feasted eye may stray
Where scenes of plenty glad the happy day:
The groves, the meads, the pastures fill'd with sheep;
Yon gilded hills, where corn, ready to reap,
Employs the hook; what groupes of men around,
In eager labour, clothe the furrow'd ground:
Where CROXDALE with its woods adorns the view
And far extends the stretching avenue,
The work of art! or further bear the eye,
Where the horizon's faintly lost in sky!
There yonder hill with MERRINGTON is crown'd,
Just rising, from the far extending ground;
Whilst all below, the grove, the hill, the mead,
With hamlets mix'd, irregularly spread,
Compose the prospect.

ANON. *Butterby*

Roker Cliffs

To Roker Cliffs let us away,
While yet the shining sun
Reflects so bright the cliffs' proud height,
On sparkling waves that run.
Along the silv'ry sand-bound beach
We'll spend the summer day,
And we will bathe in curling wave
By Roker Cliffs so grey.

By Roker Cliffs I oft have strayed
And viewed the driving storm,
The frowning rocks, the great wave mocks,
And breaks its sweeping form;
The Cliffs so grim the white sea-foam
With a heathery down bedews.
High, high in the air, 'mid tempest's glare
Sweep round the wild sea mews.

O Roker Cliffs, with awe I view
Thy pillar'd caverns grand,
And wonder oft, as I gaze aloft,
If reared by Titan's hand.
The sea may lash thee with its might
And Time thy face may tear,
But sea and Time, tho' both combine,
Thy beauties cannot wear.

SIR WILLIAM ALLAN

YORKSHIRE   *The Moorland Map*

Our maps are music and our northern titles,
  Like wind among the grass and heather, grieve.
Our maps are candid charts of desolation
  And wear the Pennine weather on their sleeve.

There's Howl Moor, Wetshaw, Winterings and Gutters,
  Mirk Fell and Dirty Pool and Hagworm Hill,
Fog Close, Cold Syke, Ravock, and Crooks Altar,
  And Loups and Wham and Whaw and Rotten Gill.

Our maps are music and they sing the miners'
  Old wrestle with the rocks for yield of lead:
There's Old Gang, Windegg, Eskeleth, and Crackpot,
  And Racca Vein, forsaken. They are dead.

Our maps are music and they sing the farmers'
  Long battle to wring fodder from fell:
There's Stony Mea and Nettlepot and Sour Nook,
  There's Pasture End and Halfpenny, and Farewell.

IVOR BROWN

The Call of the Fells

I would that I were home again
Smelling the Yorkshire loam again
  And the sweet flowers stealing sunwards in the ghylls.
Oh, to hear the wild lambs calling
And the silver streams down-falling
  Where Wharfe and Swale come rushing from the hills!

And to hear the rough moor voices
At yon inn where life rejoices,
  And to drink fower pints o' ale wi' Yorkshire Jan!
How I'd love to see old faces
And walk free in rocky places,
  And forget I am a star-struck singing-man.

And to flick a line, and angle
Where the milk-white pebbles spangle
  The borders of the little fleeting streams!
Pack my fishing rod and basket.
No, but no! I may not ask it.
  I must feast my heart on shadows—Dreams!—Dreams!

HERBERT PALMER

NORTH RIDING

From the Watch-Tower

Far in the chambers of the west,
The gale had sigh'd itself to rest;
The moon was cloudless now and clear,
But pale, and soon to disappear.
The thin grey clouds wax dimly light
On Brusleton and Houghton height;
And the rich dale, that eastward lay,
Waited the wakening touch of day,
To give its woods and cultured plain,
The towers and spires, to light again.
But, westward, Stanmore's shapeless swell,
And Lunesdale wild, amd Kelton-fell,
And rock-begirdled Gilmanscar,
And Arkingarth, lay dark afar;
While, as a livelier twilight falls,
Emerge proud Barnard's bannered walls.
High crown'd he sits, in dawning pale,
The sovereign of the lovely vale.
What prospects, from his watch-tower high,
Gleam gradual on the warder's eye!—
Far sweeping to the east, he sees
Down his deep woods the course of Tees,
And tracks his wanderings by the steam
Of summer vapours from the stream;
And ere he pace his destined hour
By Brackenbury's dungeon-tower,
These silver mists shall melt away,
And dew the woods with glittering spray.
Then in broad lustre shall be shown
That mighty trench of living stone,
And each huge trunk that, from the side,
Reclines him o'er the darksome tide,
Where Tees, full many a fathom low,
Wears with his rage no common foe;
For pebbly-bank, nor sand-bed here,
Nor clay-mound, checks his fierce career,
Condemn'd to mine a channell'd way,
O'er solid sheets of marble grey.

Nor Tees alone, in dawning bright,
Shall rush upon the ravish'd sight;
But many a tributary stream
Each from its own dark dell shall gleam:
Staindrop, who, from her sylvan bowers,
Salutes proud Raby's battled towers;
The rural brook of Egliston,
And Balder, named from Odin's son;
And Greta, to whose banks ere long
We lead the lovers of the song;
And silver Lune, from Stanmore wild,
And fairy Thorsgill's murmuring child,
And last and least, but loveliest still,
Romantic Deepdale's slender rill.
Who in that dim-wood glen hath stray'd,
Yet longed for Roslin's magic glade?
Who, wandering there, hath sought to change
Even for that vale so stern and strange,
Where Cartland's crags, fantastic rent,
Through her green copse like spires are sent?
Yet, Albin, yet the praise be thine,
Thy scenes and story to combine!
Thou bid'st him, who by Roslin strays,
List to the deeds of other days;
'Mid Cartland crags thou show'st the cave,
The refuge of thy champion brave;
Giving each rock its storied tale,
Pouring a lay for every dale,
Knitting, as with a moral band,
Thy native legends with thy land,
To lend each scene the interest high
Which genius beams from Beauty's eye.

SIR WALTER SCOTT, *Rokeby*

The Woods: Appleton House

When first the Eye this Forrest sees
It seems indeed as *Wood* not *Trees*:
As if their Neighbourhood so old
To one great Trunk them all did mold.

There the huge Bulk takes place, as ment
To thrust up a *Fifth Element*;
And stretches still so closely wedg'd
As if the Night within were hedg'd.

Dark all without it knits; within
It opens passable and thin;
And in as loose an order grows,
As the *Corinthean Porticoes*.
The arching Boughs unite between
The Columnes of the Temple green;
And underneath the winged Quires
Echo about their tuned Fires.

The *Nightingale* doth here make choice
To sing the Tryals of her Voice,
Low Shrubs she sits in, and adorns
With Musick high the squatted Thorns.
But highest Oakes stoop down to hear,
And listning Elders prick the Ear.
The Thorn, lest it should hurt her, draws
Within the Skin its shrunken claws.

But I have for my Musick found
A Sadder, yet more pleasing Sound:
The *Stock-doves*, whose fair necks are grac'd
With Nuptial Rings their Ensigns chast;
Yet always, for some Cause unknown,
Sad pair unto the Elms they moan.
O why should such a Couple mourn,
That in so equal Flames do burn!

Then as I careless on the Bed
Of gelid *Straw-berryes* do tread,
And through the Hazles thick espy
The hatching *Throstles* shining Eye;
The *Heron* from the Ashes top,
The eldest of its young lets drop,
As if it Stork-like did pretend
That *Tribute* to *its Lord* to send.

But most the *Hewel's*[1] wonders are
Who here has the *Holt-felsters*[2] care.

[1] Woodpecker.   [2] Wood-cutter.

He walks still upright from the root,
Meas'ring the Timber with his Foot;
And all the way, to keep it clean,
Doth from the Bark the Wood-moths glean.
He, with his Beak, examines well
Which fit to stand and which to fell.

The good he numbers up, and hacks;
As if he mark'd them with the Ax.
And where he, tinkling with his Beak,
Does find the hollow Oak to speak,
That for his building he designs,
And through the tainted Side he mines.
Who could have thought the *tallest Oak*
should fall by such a *feeble Strok'*

* * *

And see how chance's better Wit
Could with a Mask my studies hit!
The Oak-leaves me embroyder all,
Between which Caterpillars crawl:
And Ivy, with familiar trails,
Me licks, and clasps, and curles, and hales.
Under this *antick Cope* I move
Like some great *Prelate of the Grove,*

Then, languishing with ease, I toss
On Pallets swoln of Velvet Moss;
While the Wind, cooling through the Boughs,
Flatters with Air my panting Brows.
Thanks for my Rest ye *Mossy Banks,*
And unto you *cool Zephyrs* Thanks,
Who, as my Hair, my Thoughts too shed,
And winnow from the Chaff my Head.

How safe, methinks, and strong, behind
These Trees have I incamp'd my Mind;
Where Beauty, aiming at the Heart,
Bends in some Tree its useless Dart;
And where the World no certain Shot
Can make, or me it toucheth not.
But I on it securely play,

And gaul its Horsemen all the Day.
Bind me ye *Woodbines* in your 'twines,
Curle me about ye gadding *vines*,
And Oh so close your Circles lace,
That I may never leave this Place:
But, lest your Fetters prove too weak,
Ere I your Silken Bondage break,
Do you, O *Brambles*, chain me too,
And courteous *Briars* nail me through.

ANDREW MARVELL: *Upon Appleton House*

Scarborough
(1813)

In June, when May-flowers and May-flies
Paronomastically rise,
Ere yet the dog-star shoots his fire,
Prayers on all sides assail the 'Squire
From craving wife and coaxing daughters;
'Your hunting o'er, your hounds in quarters,
And ere the moors demand your gun,
Full two months' interval to run—
Oh! as you promised, Scarbro' show us,
In the old coach you well can stow us:
Yourself included, we're but seven,
Betty, as eighth, keeps both sides even.
Do, pray Sir, without *and* or *if*,
Take a month's lodging on the Cliff.'

* * *

O Scarbro'! queen of sea-side joys,
Which no domestic care alloys,
Far from the petty jangling war
Of housemaid, and of housekeeper!
Throned on thy cliffs, how proudly thou
Survey'st the varied scene below:
In curve exact thy mansions bending,
And to the watery marge descending:

201

Upon that marge, in modest state,
Hygeia throwing wide her gate[1]
(A better Cytherea she,
Risen newly from the ambient sea)
To indigent infirmity:
The temple, castle, double mole,
Port, spa, and circling round the whole,
Of beauty and of strength the zone,
The ocean's azure girdle thrown!
Thy pleasures ever charm the young,
The morning stroll—stroll all day long:
Joy, triumph, health at once they give,
To see, to conquer, and to live;
And *vidi, vici, vixi*, plain
Records the bright and brief campaign.

   Nor hither 'Squires alone resort
With water to dilute their port,
Walk off the aches which riding gave,
And tip the go-by to the grave—
That only *port* they still would pass,
As Time's their only hated *glass*:—
For Scarbro' parsons quit their church,
For Scarbro' schoolmasters their birch;
And York and Lancaster agree
To sip their amicable tea.

FRANCIS WRANGHAM, *The Cornelian Party*

WEST RIDING   *Fountains Abbey*

Abbey! for ever smiling pensively,
  How like a thing of nature dost thou rise,
  Amid her loveliest works! as if the skies,
Clouded with grief, were arched thy roof to be,
And the tall trees were copied all from thee!
  Mourning thy fortunes,—while the waters dim
  Flow like the memory of thy evening hymn;
Beautiful in their sorrowing sympathy,
As if they with a weeping sister wept,

[1] The Warm Sea Bathing Infirmary.

Winds name thy name! But thou, though sad, art calm,
And Time with thee his plighted troth hath kept;
   For harebells deck thy brow, and at thy feet,
   Where sleep the proud, the bee and redbreast meet,
Mixing thy sighs with nature's lonely Psalm.

EBENEZER ELLIOTT

Haworth in May

The crowded graveyard, the tall solemn trees,
The dark tower and the narrow climbing street,
At every turn the grim blue distances,
The gray roofs and the hill-winds blowing sweet—

Here at the world's end in this house of stone
Gazing upon the tombs and the far hills,
Lived Genius, daughter of the Air and Fire,
The lovely victim of the harsh world's ills.

Then afterward we found a long green dale
Walled up the heaven, with all its scattered farms,
And lean fields parcelled out with dun stone walls
And ragged clouds piled on the moor's faint arms.

In the gray ash-tree sang the blackbirds of May,
And a remote ancestral beauty blessed
The granges and the groves, the water troughs
Flooded with upland crystal, and caressed

The hillsides with a magic wing, and I
Was near to tears whene'er I thought of thee,
Most glorious of that cabined falcon-brood,
Virgin and poet, huntress, Emily. . . .

WILFRED ROWLAND CHILDE

Leeds

                Wide around
Hillock and valley, farm and village, smile;
And ruddy roofs, and chimney-tops appear,

Of busy Leeds, up-wafting to the clouds
The incense of thanksgiving: all is joy;
And trade and business guide the living scene,
Roll the full cars, adown the winding Aire
Load the slow-sailing barges, pile the pack
On the long tinkling train of slow-pac'd steeds.
As when a sunny day invites abroad
The sedulous ants, they issue from their cells
In bands unnumber'd, eager for their work;
O'er high, o'er low, they lift, they draw, they haste
With warm affection to each other's aid;
Repeat their virtuous efforts, and succeed.
Thus all is here in motion, all is life:
The creaking wain brings copious store of corn;
The grazier's sleekly kine obstruct the roads;
The neat-dress'd housewives, for the festal board
Crown'd with full baskets, in the field-way paths
Come tripping on; th' echoing hills repeat
The stroke of axe and hammer; scaffolds rise,
And growing edifices; heaps of stone,
Beneath the chisel, beauteous shapes assume
Of frieze and column. Some, with even line,
New streets are marking in the neighb'ring fields,
And sacred domes of worship. Industry,
Which dignifies the artist, lifts the swain,
And the straw cottage to a palace turns,
Over the work presides. Such was the scene
Of hurrying Carthage, when the Trojan chief
First view'd her growing turrets. So appear
Th' increasing walls of busy Manchester,
Sheffield, and Birmingham, whose redd'ning fields
Rise and enlarge their suburbs.

JOHN DYER, *The Fleece*

Bramham Park

If thro' the glades I turn my raptur'd eyes,
What various views, what lovely landskips rise?
Here a once-hospitable mansion stands
'Midst fruitful plains, and cultivated lands;

There russet heaths, with fields of corn between,
And peaceful cotts, and hamlets intervene:
These far-stretch'd views direct me to admire
A tower dismantled, or a lofty spire,
Or farm imbosom'd in some aged wood,
Or lowing herds that crop the flowery food;
Thro' these, irriguous vales, and lawns appear,
And fleecy flocks, and nimble-footed deer:
Sun-glittering villas, and bright streams are seen,
Gay meads, rough rocks, hoar hills, and forests green.

* * *

O! what descriptive eloquence can tell
The woods, and winding walks of Boscobell?
The various vistas, and the grassy glades,
The bowery coverts in sequester'd shades?
Or where the wandering eye with pleasure sees
A spacious amphitheatre of trees?
Or where the differing avenues unite,
Conducting to more pompous scenes the sight?
Lo! what high mounds immense divide the moor,
Stretch'd from the southern to the northern shore!
These are but relicks of the Roman way,
Where the firm legions march'd in dread array,
Where rode the hero in his iron car,
And big with vengeance roll'd the mighty war.

FRANCIS FAWKES, *Bramham Park*

Barnsley and District

Judy Sugden! Judy, I made you caper
With rage when I said that the British Fascist
Sheet your father sold was a jolly good paper

And you had agreed and I said, Yes, it holds
Vinegar, and everyone laughed and imagined
The feel of fish and chips warm in its folds.

That was at Hood Green. Under our feet there shone
The modest view, its slagheaps amethyst
In distance and white walls the sunlight flashed on.

If your father's friends had succeeded, or if I
Had canvassed harder for the Peace Pledge Union,
A world of difference might have leapt to the eye

In a scene like this which shows in fact no change.
That must have been the summer of '39.
I go back sometimes, and find nothing strange—

Short-circuiting of politics engages
The Grammar School masters still. Their bright sixth-formers sport
Nuclear Disarmament badges.

And though at Stainborough no bird's-nesting boy
Nor trespasser from the town in a Sunday suit
Nor father twirling a stick can now enjoy

Meeting old Captain Wentworth, who in grey
And ancient tweeds, gun under arm, keen-eyed
And unemployable, would give a gruff Good-day,

His rhododendrons and his laurel hedge
And tussocked acres are no more unkempt
Now that the Hall is a Teachers' Training College.

The parish primary school where a mistress once
Had every little Dissenter stand on the bench
With hands on head, to make him out a dunce;

Black backs of flour-mills, wafer-rusted railings
Where I ran and ran from colliers' boys in jerseys,
Wearing a blouse to show my finer feelings—

These still stand. And Bethel and Zion Baptist,
Sootblack on pavements foul with miners' spittle
And late-night spew and violence, persist.

George Arliss was on at the Star, and Janet Gaynor
Billed at the Alhambra, but the warmth
Was no more real then, nor the manners plainer.

And politics has no landscape. The Silesian
Seam crops out in prospects felt as deeply
As any of these, with as much or as little reason.

DONALD DAVIE

EAST RIDING   *April in Holderness*
A Village

Remote from all
the voices of the world, remote
from cities and the cries,
bewildered, of their sad humanities,
—red roofs grouped round a grey church tower,
a blur of grey stone wall—
remote
the village stands,
at peace upon its native lands
under its native skies.

The lights of early April fall
soft on its suburb of pale yellow ricks;
the century-mellowed bricks
of its old houses, like a faded flower,
glow dimly in the feeble sun; the brown
branches of naked trees, like drifts
of smoke from smouldering leaves,
—brown drifts that float
on windless days low down—
draw round it in a silent crowd;
and from their midst the church tower lifts
its weary strength on high,
its patient strength against a sky
of sudden blue and sudden cloud.
Starlings about the slanted eaves
chatter of spring, while, far aloft
and almost out of sight,
the larks on their spasmodic flight
let fall
note after note,
clear and delirious and soft,
the song that holds with outstretched hands
heaven and earth together.

So, in this early April weather,
—red roof and grey church tower,
pale brick and blur of wall—
remote from all
the voices of the world, remote
the village stands.
J. REDWOOD ANDERSON

Humberside
Turn of Tide

The wide
sweep of the Humber; the first hint
of coming night;
along the riverside,
pale, here and there, a yellow light;
and in the fluid amber of the west,
the sun's last copper glint.

Dumb are the freighter's loud appeals;
the cranes
stand mute; from the long warehouse-walls
no echoes wake: on idle wheels,
on idle pulleys, idle chains,
a growing silence falls.

Like travellers who rest,
the great ships lie—
ships that have sailed the seas of all the world
and known the winds of every sky;
like travellers who dream—
the steamer with no pennant of thin steam,
the three-mast schooner with all canvas furled.

Shoreward, out of the wet,
shoreward, since noon,
shoreward, upon the footsteps of the moon,
shoreward, in wide
long swell and wave on wave asweep,
shoreward, as if to force
the river backward to its source,
shoreward, out of the deep
the tide has set.

To the dry seaweed where it hung
grey
to the dry ridge all day,
to the dry limpets where they clung
to pier and jetty, pile and rock,
and all the barnacles among
the old stones of the tumbled mole,
the tide

—ripple and surge and foam,
laughter and swish and shock—
the tide has come,
to give them back a living soul
and set them in their ancient home.

And to the fishing-boats that lay
idle all day,
idle upon the sloping beach,
the tide
has come with its soft speech
of blue horizons out of reach;
the tide
has set each lazy rowing-boat
once more afloat.

The tide has kissed the battlement
of cliffs along the coast of Kent;
and hid the Norfolk wilderness
of salt sea-marshes with its cold caress;
while, on the shores of Holderness,
the wall
of the black earth, repeatedly,
has broken—with a sob, repeatedly,
the fragments of the dry land fall
and crumble in the sea.

And up the wide
reach of the rivers flows the tide.

Up past the Pool of London, where
the lighters at their moorings ride,
past bridge on bridge, and tower on tower,
to Westminster:
past all the lights that make the Thames
a road of royal diadems.

And, far inland, the fields that sleep
between the Orwell and the Stour
laugh as they hear their rivers rise,
and from the eyes
of shallow creek and reedy pool,
now with clear water full,
look up in beauty to the skies.

Until past Spurn the currents sweep,
and the great Humber opens wide
his mouth to drain the cup,
wave after wave, of splendour and pride
the sea has lifted up.

Shoreward, out of the wet,
shoreward, upon the footsteps of the moon,
shoreward, since noon,
the tide has set.

Then,
suddenly and silently,
—the sun has sunk, the wind is dead,
only a stray cloud overhead
drifts dully red against the sky,
only one white star burns—
suddenly and silently,
the tide
turns.

Suddenly and silently:
and, all along the Humberside,
the ships,
as if they felt athwart their sleep
the summons of the changing deep,
stir gently and, without a sound,
swing round.

One after one, in slow eclipse,
red lights go out;
masts draw together till they rise
not three, but one, against the skies,
as each ship goes about;
then,
masts that were one are three again,
and, one by one, the clear
green lights appear.

Seaward, into the vast
world of the ocean and the night,
seaward, as if in flight
before the river's downward might,
seaward, with roar and swift

laugh of the after-drift,
seaward, with wide
long swell and wave on wave asweep,
seaward, into the deep,
the tide falls fast.

J. REDWOOD ANDERSON

The River Humber

No wonder
The river Humber
Lies in a silken slumber.

For it is dawn
And over the newly warm
Earth the mists turn,

Wrapping their gentle fringes
Upon the river where it hinges
Upon the perfect sleep of perfected images.

Quiet in the thoughts of its felicity,
A graven monument of sufficiency
Beautiful in every line the river sleeps complacently.

And hardly the dawn distinguishes
Where a miasma languishes
Upon the waters' farther reaches.

Lapped in the sleeping consciousness
Of its waves' happiness
Upon the mudbanks of its approaches,

The river Humber
Turns again to deeper slumber,
Deeper than deeps in joys without number.

STEVIE SMITH

THE EAST COUNTRY

The Fens

Wandering by the river's edge,
I love to rustle through the sedge
And through the woods of reed to tear
Almost as high as bushes are.
Yet, turning quick with shudder chill,
As danger ever does from ill,
Fear's moment ague quakes the blood,
While plop the snake coils in the flood
And, hissing with a forked tongue,
Across the river winds along.
In coat of orange, green, and blue
Now on a willow branch I view,
Grey waving to the sunny gleam,
Kingfishers watch the ripple stream
For little fish that nimble bye
And in the gravel shallows lie.

Eddies run before the boats,
Gurgling where the fisher floats,
Who takes advantage of the gale
And hoists his handkerchief for sail
On osier twigs that form a mast—
While idly lies, nor wanted more,
The spirit that pushed him on before.

There's not a hill in all the view,
Save that a forked cloud or two
Upon the verge of distance lies
And into mountains cheats the eyes.
And as to trees the willows wear
Lopped heads as high as bushes are;

Some taller things the distance shrouds
That may be trees or stacks or clouds
Or may be nothing; still they wear
A semblance where there's nought to spare.

Among the tawny tasselled reed
The ducks and ducklings float and feed.
With head oft dabbing in the flood
They fish all day the weedy mud,
And tumbler-like are bobbing there,
Heels topsy turvy in the air.
The geese in troops come droving up,
Nibble the weeds, and take a sup;
And, closely puzzled to agree,
Chatter like gossips over tea.
The gander with his scarlet nose
When strife's at height will interpose;
And, stretching neck to that and this,
With now a mutter, now a hiss,
A nibble at the feathers too,
A sort of 'pray be quiet do',
And turning as the matter mends
He stills thems into mutual friends;
Then in a sort of triumph sings
And throws the water oer his wings.

Ah, could I see a spinney nigh,
A puddock riding in the sky
Above the oaks with easy sail
On stilly wings and forked tail,
Or meet a heath of furze in flower,
I might enjoy a quiet hour,
Sit down at rest, and walk at ease,
And find a many things to please.
But here my fancy's moods admire
The naked levels till they tire,
Nor een a molehill cushion meet
To rest on when I want a seat.

Here's little save the river scene
And grounds of oats in rustling green
And crowded growth of wheat and beans,
That with the hope of plenty leans
And cheers the farmer's gazing brow,

Who lives and triumphs in the plough—
One sometimes meets a pleasant sward
Of swarthy grass; and quickly marred
The plough soon turns it into brown,
And, when again one rambles down
The path, small hillocks burning lie
And smoke beneath a burning sky.
Green paddocks have but little charms
With gain the merchandise of farms;

And, muse and marvel where we may,
Gain mars the landscape every day—
The meadow grass turned up and copt,
The trees to stumpy dotterels lopt,
The hearth with fuel to supply
For rest to smoke and chatter bye;
Giving the joy of home delights,
The warmest mirth on coldest nights.
And so for gain, that joy's repay,
Change cheats the landscape every day,
Nor trees nor bush about it grows
That from the hatchet can repose,
And the horizon stooping smiles
Oer treeless fens of many miles.
Spring comes and goes and comes again.
And all is nakedness and fen.

JOHN CLARE

The Great Level of the Fenns[1]

Here thrives the lusty Hemp, of Strength untam'd,
Whereof vast Sails and mighty Cables fram'd
Serve for our Royal Fleets, Flax soft and fine
To the East Countrey's envy; could we joyn
To *England's* Blessings *Holland's* industry,
We all the world in wealth should far outvie.

Here grows proud Rape, whose price and plenty foyls
The *Greenland* Trade, and checks the *Spanish* Oyls,

[1] 300,000 Acres of Fenny Ground, lying within the Counties of *Norfolk, Suffolk, Cambridge* and the Isle of *Ely, Huntingdon, Northampton* and *Lincolne.*

Whose branch thick, large, and tall, the Earth so shrowds,
As heaps of Snow the *Alps*, or pregnant Clouds
The azure Sky, or like that Heavenly Bread
Which in the Wilderness God's bounty shed.

After long Tillage, it doth then abound
With Grass so plentiful, so sweet, so sound,
Scarce any tract but this can Pastures shew
So large, so rich. And, if you wisely Sow,
The fine *Dutch* clover with such Beauty spreads
As if it meant t'affront our English Meads.

The Gentle Ozier, plac't in goodly ranks,
At small Expence, upon the comely Banks,
Shoots forth to admiration here, and yields,
Revenues certain as the Rents of Fields,
And for a Crown unto this blest Plantation,
Almost in every Ditch, there's Navigation.

To scan all its Perfections would desire
A Volume, and as great a Skill require
As that which Drayn'd the Countrey; in one word,
It yields whate're our Climate will afford;
And did the Sun with kinder beams reflect,
You might Wine, Sugar, Silk and Spice expect.

ANON (c. 1680), *The Great Level of the Fenns*

Bedford Level
(Cambridgeshire)

Was wont with hairy fleeces to deform;
And, smiling with her lure of summer flow'rs,
The heavy ox, vain-struggling, to ingulph;
Till one, of that high-honoured patriot name,
RUSSELL, arose, who drained the rushy fen,
Confined the waves, bid groves and gardens bloom,
And through his new creation led the Ouze,
And gentle Camus, silver-winding streams:
Godlike beneficence; from chaos drear
To raise the garden and the shady grove.

Yet much may be performed, to check the force
Of nature's rigour: the high heath, by trees
Warm-sheltered, may despise the rage of storms:
Moors, bogs, and weeping fens, may learn to smile,
And leave in dykes their soon-forgotten tears.
Labour and art will ev'ry aim achieve
Of noble bosoms. Bedford Level, erst
A dreary pathless waste, the coughing flock.

JOHN DYER

The Ouse

Next these the plenteous Ouse came far from land,
    By many a city, and by many a towne,
    And many rivers taking under hand
    Into his waters, as he passeth downe,
    The Cle, the Were, the Grant, the Sture, the Rowne.
    Thence doth by Huntingdon and Cambridge Flit,
    My mother Cambridge, whom as with a Crowne
    He doth adorne, and is adorn'd of it
With many a gentle Muse, and many a learned wit.

EDMUND SPENSER, *The Fairie Queene*

'The Old West River'[1]

Larks are singing round the Old West River,
Coot are calling from the reeds below,
Golden shafts of morning break and shiver,
Where the swallows, dipping, darting, come and go.

Scarce the name of what thou wast is left thee—
Ouse is borne in shackles to the sea;
They that of thy store and strength bereft thee
Spared thee nothing but thy liberty.

Trickling runlets weep thy degradation,
And in tears their tiny tribute pay,
Healing drops that kept thee from stagnation,
When thy native springs were borne away.

[1] The old bed of the Ouse.

Emblem art thou of a form forsaken
By its quickening soul, a creed outworn;
Husk thou art, from which the seed is shaken;
Truth, from all its living context torn.

All that made thee great has gone for ever;
None shall lead thine exiled waters home;
Yet some there are that love the Old West River,
And share its peace, when by its banks they roam.

THOMAS THORNELY

LINCOLNSHIRE   *Lincoln*

I lik'd the motion, and made haste away
To *Lincolne*, which was 50 mile, that Day:
Which City in the 3 King *Edwards* Raigne,
Was th' onely staple, for this Kingdome's gaine
For Leather, Lead and Wooll, and then was seene
Five times ten Churches there, but now Fifteene.
A brave Cathedral Church there now doth stand,
That scarcely hath a fellow in this Land:
'Tis for a Godly use, a goodly Frame,
And beares that blessed Virgin *Maries* name.

JOHN TAYLOR,
A very Merrie Wherrie-Ferry Voyage

The Fens near Lincoln

From thence we past a Ditch of Weeds and Mud,
Which they doe (falsly) there call *Forcedike*[1] Flood:
For I'l be sworne, no flood I could finde there,
But dirt and filth, which scarce my Boat would beare,
'Tis 8 miles long, and there our paines was such
As all our travell did not seeme so much,
My men did wade and draw the Boate like Horses,

[1] It is a passage cut thorow the Land eight miles from *Lincolne* into *Trent*, but through either the peoples poverty or negligence, it is growne up with weedes, and mudde, so that in the Summer it is in many places almost dry.

And scarce could tugge her on with all our forces:
Moyl'd, toyl'd, myr'd, tyr'd, stil lab'ring, ever doing,
Yet were we 9 long hours that 8 miles going.
At last when as the Day was well-nigh going.
We gat from *Forcedikes* floodlesse flood to *Trent*.

JOHN TAYLOR,
A very Merrie Wherrie-Ferry Voyage

Boston

Oh, Boston, Boston, thou hast nought to boast on
But a grand sluice and a high steeple
And a coast as souls are lost on.

ANON.

Stamford to Grantham

From *Stamford* as along my tract tow'rd *Lincolne* straines,
What Shire is there can shew more valuable Vaines
Of soyle then is in mee? or where can there be found,
So faire and fertile fields, or Sheep-walks nere so sound?
Where doth the pleasant ayre resent a sweeter breath?
What Countrey can produce a delicater Heath,
Then that which her faire Name from *Ancaster* doth hold?
Through all the neighboring Shires, whose praise shall still be told,
Which *Flora* in the Spring doth with such wealth adorne,
That *Bever* needs not much her company to scorne,
Though shee a Vale lye low, and this a Heath sit hye,
Yet doth she not alone, allure the wondring eye
With prospect from each part, but that her pleasant ground
Gives all that may content, the well-breath'd Horse and Hound:
And from the *Britans* yet, to shew what then I was,
One of the *Roman* Wayes neere through my midst did passe:
Besides to my much praise, there hath been in my mould
Their painted Pavements found, and Armes of perfect gold.
They neere the *Saxons* raigne, that in this tract did dwell,
All other of this Isle, for that they would excell

For Churches every where, so rich and goodly rear'd
In every little Dorpe, that after-times have fear'd
T'attempt so mighty workes; yet one above the rest,
In which is may be thought, they strove to doe their best,
Of pleasant *Grantham* is, that Pyramis so hye,
Rear'd (as it might be thought) to overtop the skie,
The Traveller that strikes into a wondrous maze,
As on his Horse he sits, on that proud height to gaze.

MICHAEL DRAYTON, *Polyolbion*

NORFOLK   *Ruins of Walsingham*

Bitter, bitter, oh! to behould
    the grasse to growe
Where the walles of Walsingam
    so statly did shewe.
Such were the workes of Walsingam
    while shee did stand!
Such are the wrackes as now do shewe
    of that holy-land!
Levell, levell, with the ground
    the towres doe lie,

Which with their golden glitteringe tops
    pearsed once to the skye!
Wher weare gates, no gates ar now;
    the waies unknowen,
Wher the presse of peares did passe,
    while her fame far was blowen,
Oules do scrike wher the sweetest himnes
    lately weer songe;
Toades and serpentes hold their dennes
    wher the Palmers did thronge.

ANON. *A Lament for Walsingham*

Thetford

The poets, one and all, were wont to choose
Some fabled, fav'rite Goddess, as their muse.
But gratitude alone my mind inspires,

No other Muse my simple pen requires.
When erst in youth's gay prime and uncontrolled
O Thetford! round thy flow'ry fields I've strolled,
From Tutt-Hill's eminence and Croxton's height,
Have view'd thine ancient ruins with delight,
Thy sloping hills and wooded vallies gay,
Whose silv'ry Ouse meand'ring winds his way.
Though then, each lofty mound, each ruin'd tower
Told but of war, and time's destructive power;
And thou, they pristine grandeur long had'st lost,
Nor more of Kings, or mighty chiefs could boast;
Yet heartfelt joys beneath they roots I found,
And peace, with all the social blessings crown'd.
To tune his reed, and sing they healing streams,
Then enter'd not the Bard's enraptur'd dreams,
But now the Muse exultingly may sing,
The well attested virtues of they Spring;
Since eruditation and clear truth unite
To chase all fear, and set the judgment right.

GEORGE BLOOMFIELD

Holkham Hall

Where Holkham rears in graceful pride
   Her marble halls and created towers,
And stretches o'er the champaign wide
   Her lengthened suite of social bowers;

Where, led by Leicester's forming hand,
   To Nature Art her succour gives,
Touches the desert with her wand,
   And sculpture breathes and painting lives;

Sheltered beneath this friendly dome,
   Far from the world's tumultuous rage,
I ope the venerated tome,
   And read, and glow along the page.

*   *   *

But happier far the moments fly
   When, resting from my lengthened toil,
I meet with Cole's benignant eye,
   And share his kind approving smile;

Friend of his country and mankind,
  To more than titled honours born;
Who looks with independent mind
  On all the venal tribes with scorn.

His the firm soul to freedom true,
  The open heart, the liberal hand
That from the rock the waters drew,
  And bade the bounteous stream expand,

To clothe the plain with brighter green,
  The soil with richer harvests bless,
And pour on all the cultured scene
  The glow of life and happiness:

Not with scant hand the pittance small
  To starving industry to give;
But grant their general rights to all,
  And as he lives, let others live.

And sees, with all a parent's pride,
  His healthful village train display'd,
To heal the woundsin nature's side,
  By tyrants and by heroes made.

WILLIAM ROSCOE

The Coast: Norfolk

As on the highway's quiet edge
He mows the grass beside the hedge,
The old man has for company
The distant, grey, salt-smelling sea,
A poppied field, a cow and calf,
The finches on the telegraph.

Across his faded back a hone,
He slowly, slowly scythes alone
In silence of the wind-soft air, .
With ladies' bedstraw everywhere,
With whitened corn, and tarry poles,
And far-off gulls like risen souls.

FRANCES CORNFORD

Blakeney

As in her days of power and state,
The great church stands, uplifting high
Her lantern—long the guiding eye
Of commerce—Surely they were great.

Who so could build, and, day by day,
From sheltered homes could valiantly
Go forth to meet so wild a sea
As that which booms beyond the bay.

Those days are gone. There sound no more
The capstan song, the welcoming hails,
As some stout trader, fraught with bales
From eastland marts, draws near the shore.

For not to Anglian ports today
Turns England with her swollen needs.
They perished, but they sowed the seeds
Of empire ere they passed away.

Not all has gone; to marsh and lea
Still the migrating myriads flock,
To preen their plumes, and ease the shock
Of their long battling o'er the sea.

Not all is lost, for Beauty flies
From hearts that keep no place for her,
And with the wild sea-lavender
Builds here a home for outraged eyes,

That late have looked where, seamed and scarred,
Lies what men reverenced once. May all
Who hear the bells of Blakeney call,
Against a like despoiling guard.

THOMAS THORNELY

Cromer

It is an Ancient Market Towne that stands
Upon a lofty Cliffe of mouldring Sands:
The Sea against the Cliffes doth daily beate,

And every tyde into the Lande doth eate,
The Towne is poore, unable by Expence,
Against the raging Sea to make defence:
And everyday it eateth further in,
Still wasting, washing downe the sand doth win,
That if some course be not tane speedily,
The Town's in danger in the Sea to lye.
A goodly Church stands on these brittle grounds,
Not many fairer in Great *Britaines* bounds:
And if the Sea shall swallow't, as some feare,
Tis not ten thousand pounds the like could rare.

JOHN TAYLOR,
A very Merrie Wherrie-Ferry Voyage

SUFFOLK   *Spring at Euston*

Fled now the sullen murmurs of the North,
The splendid raiment of the SPRING peeps forth;
Her universal green and the clear sky
Delight still more and more the gazing eye.
Wide o'er the fields, in rising moisture strong,
Shoots up the simple flower, or creeps along
The mellow'd soil; imbibing fairer hues,
Or sweets from frequent showers and evening dews;
That summon from their sheds the slumb'ring plows,
While health impregnates every breeze that blows.
No wheels support the diving, pointed, share;
No groaning ox is doom'd to labour there;
No helpmates teach the docile steed his road;
(Alike unknown the ploughboy and his goad;)
But, unassisted through each toilsome day,
With smiling brow the ploughman cleaves his way,
Draws his fresh parallels, and, wid'ning still,
Treads slow the heavy dale, or climbs the hill:
Strong on the wing his busy followers play,
Where writhing earth-worms meet th' unwelcome day;
Till all is chang'd, and hill and level down
Assume a livery of sober brown:
Again disturb'd, when *Giles* with wearying strides
From ridge to ridge the ponderous harrow guides;

223

His heels deep sinking every step he goes,
Till dirt adhesive loads his clouted shoes.
Welcome green headland! firm beneath his feet;
Welcome the friendly bank's refreshing seat;
There, warm with toil, his panting horses browse
Their shelt'ring canopy of pendent boughs;
Till rest, delicious, chase each transient pain,
And new-born vigour swell in every vein.
Hour after hour, and day to day succeeds;
Till every clod and deep-drawn furrow spreads
To crumbling mould; a level surface clear,
And strew'd with corn to crown the rising year;
And o'er the whole *Giles* once transverse again,
In earth's moist bosom buries up the grain.

ROBERT BLOOMFIELD, *The Farmer's Boy*

Newmarket

From BALSHAM hill hark to the drum
That beats around, 'come let them come'.
And yet it is no point of war,
As when fierce DAVILA was there,
Who fram'd the ditch: whilst high was seen
His Raven hov'ring o'er the green.
How my heart beats with eager speed!
What joy in man! how neighs the steed!
Unstabled hunters scour the plain.
Young Piper there would stretch the rein.
Lay by the law, resign the gown,
For rural sports exchange the town.
The spring serene does friends invite,
To mix with thousands in delight.
She that in the chariot rides,
He who the fretful horse bestrides:
The heir, that on the turf rebounds,
Which to the hoof or wheel resounds;
Crowds that from NEWMARKET spread,
And o'er the heath confus'dly tread.
Why all these sporters in your eye
List to the word impetuously

'They're off, they're off', now here now gone,
And quick the vig'rous race is run.
Scarce breath allow'd, or time to lay
Who loses or who wins the day.

KENRICK PRESCOT, *To the Counsellor*

Walsham-le-Willows

Peace past understanding shall tarry in Walsham-le-Willows,
No village had ever a name with so lovely a burden,
And there under blue and white clouds, pastured deep in warm summer
     May the worn heart find healing.

Thus I thought: and the ways were made sweeter with lime-trees in
  blossom,
Pale flowers a-swing to bees drifting with honey-drunk murmur;
And bent willows stood rooted in meads whose yellow-turned haycocks
     The white pullets plundered.

The cool stream flowed on half asleep and quiescent in beauty,
Old cottages pondered benignly their musk and blown roses,
The elms launched their great shadow ships floating deep green and silver
     Over meadows sun-golden.

And peace fluttered down like a sleep upon Walsham-le-Willows,
Like a dove that returns from the pool in the valley at sunset,
Dewy-feathered flies back to her mate and the nest on the hedge-top,
     Stilled a worn heart with healing.

CLAUDE COLLEER ABBOTT

Playford

Upon a hill-side green and fair
  The happy traveller sees
White cottages peep here and there
  Between the tufts of trees;
With a white farm-house on the brow,
And an old grey Hall below
  With moat and garden round;

And on a Sabbath wandering near
Through all the quiet place you hear
  A Sabbath-breathing sound
Of the church-bell slowly swinging
  In an old grey tower above
The wooded hill, where birds are singing
  In the deep quiet of the grove;—
And when the bell shall cease to ring,
And the birds no longer sing,
And the grasshopper is heard no more,
  A sound of praise, of prayer,
  Rises along the air,
Like the sea murmur from a distant shore.

BERNARD BARTON

Dunwich

The last church-tower of Dunwich was destroyed by the sea
in November 1919

Last of a score of towers,
To fling defiant music o'er the sea,
That lion-like roared round and now devours,
Thy vigil ends, Dunwich has ceased to be!

E'en while she crowned her state
With mitred pomp in her meridian day,
The foe had rolled his thunders to her gate
And hurled afar the challenge of his spray.

And now we mourn the fall
From lone sea-bluff of her last lingering shrine;
It fell, as on Byzantium's ruined wall
Fell, midst the Paynim, Rome's last Constantine.

Beyond that ruthless main,
Still, swollen or shrunk, her old-time rivals stand,
But they that Dunwich seek shall seek in vain,
They find but moaning sea and shifting sand.

THOMAS THORNELY

A frowning coast: Country near Aldeburgh

I grant indeed that fields and flocks have charms
For him that grazes or for him that farms;
But when amid such pleasing scenes I trace
The poor laborious Natives of the place,
And see the mid-day sun, with fervid ray,
On their bare heads and dewy temples play;
While some, with feebler heads and fainter hearts,
Deplore their fortune, yet sustain their parts:
Then shall I dare these real ills to hide
In tinsel trappings of poetic pride?

No; cast by Fortune on a frowning coast,
Which neither groves nor happy valleys boast;
Where other cares than those the Muse relates,
And other Shepherds dwell with other Mates;
By such examples taught, I paint the Cot,
As Truth will paint it, and as Bards will not:
Nor you, ye Poor, of letter'd scorn complain,
To you the smoothest song is smooth in vain;
O'ercome by labour, and bow'd down by time,
Feel you the barren flattery of a rhyme?
Can Poets soothe you, when you pine for bread,
By winding myrtles round your ruin'd shed?
Can their light tales your weighty griefs o'erpower,
Or glad with airy mirth the toilsome hour?

Lo! where the heath, with withering brake grown o'er,
Lends the light turf that warms the neighbouring poor;
From thence a length of burning sand appears,
Where the thin harvest waves its wither'd ears;
Rank weeds, that every art and care defy,
Reign o'er the land, and rob the blighted rye:
There thistles stretch their prickly arms afar,
And to the ragged infant threaten war;
There poppies nodding, mock the hope of toil;
There the blue bugloss paints the sterile soil;
Hardy and high, above the slender sheaf,
The slimy mallow waves her silky leaf;
O'er the young shoot the charlock throws a shade,
And clasping tares cling round the sickly blade;
With mingled tints the rocky coasts abound,
And a sad splendour vainly shines around.

GEORGE CRABBE, *The Village*

Dwellings of the poor: Aldeburgh

Farewell to these; but all our Poor to know,
Let's seek the winding Lane, the narrow Row,
Suburbian Prospects, where the Traveller stops
To see the sloping Tenement on props,
With building Yards inmix'd, and humble Sheds and Shops;
Where the *Cross-Keys* and *Plumber's-Arms* invite
Laborious Men to taste their coarse Delight;
Where the low Porches, stretching from the Door,
Gave some Distinction in the Days of Yore,
Yet now neglected, more offend the eye,
By Gloom and Ruin, than the Cottage by:
Places like these the noblest Town endures,
The gayest Palace has its Sinks and Sewers.

Here is no Pavement, no inviting Shop,
To give us shelter when compell'd to stop;
But plashy Puddles stand along the Way,
Fill'd by the Rain of one tempestuous Day;
And these so closely to the Buildings run,
That you must ford them, for you cannot shun;
Though here and there convenient Bricks are laid,
And door-side Heaps afford their dubious aid.

Lo! yonder Shed; observe its Garden-Ground,
With the low, Paling, form'd of Wreck, around:
There dwells a Fisher; if you view his Boat,
With Bed and Barrel—'tis his House afloat;
Look at his House, where Ropes, Nets, Blocks abound,
Tar, Pitch and Oakum—'tis his Boat aground:
That Space enclos'd, but little he regards,
Spread o'er with relicks of Masts, Sails and Yards:
Fish by the Wall, on Spit of Elder, rest,
Of all his Food, the cheapest and the best,
By his own Labour caught, for his own Hunger dress'd.

Here our Reformers come not; none object
To Paths polluted, or upbraid Neglect;
None care that ashy Heaps at doors are cast,
That Coal-dust flies along the blinding Blast:
None heed the stagnant Pools on either side,
Where new-launch'd Ships of infant Sailors ride:
Rodneys in rags here British Valour boast,

And lisping *Nelsons* fright the Gallic Coast.
They fix the Rudder, set the swelling Sail,
They point the Bowsprit, and they blow the Gale:
True to her Port, the Frigate scuds away,
And o'er that frowning Ocean finds her Bay:
Her Owner rigg'd her, and he knows her worth,
And sees her, fearless, Gunwale-deep go forth;
Dreadless he views his Sea, by Breezes curl'd,
When inch-high Billows vex the watery World.
   There, fed by Food they love, to rankest size,
Around the dwellings *Docks* and *Wormwood* rise;
Here the strong *Mallow* strikes her slimy Root,
Here the dull *Nightshade* hangs her deadly Fruit;
On hills of Dust the *Henbane's* faded green,
And pencill'd Flower of sickly scent is seen:
At the Wall's base the fiery Nettle springs,
With Fruit globose and fierce with poison'd Stings;
Above (the Growth of many a Year) is spread
The yellow Level of the *Stone-crop's* Bed;
In every Chink delights the *Fern* to grow,
With glossy Leaf and tawny Bloom below:
These, with our *Sea-weeds*, rolling up and down,
Form the contracted Flora of the Town.
   Say, wilt thou more of Scenes so sordid know?
Then will I lead thee down the dusty Row;
By the warm Alley and the long close Lane,—
There mark the fractured Door and paper'd Pane,
Where flags the noon-tide Air, and, as we pass,
We fear to breathe the putrefying Mass:
But fearless yonder Matron; she disdains
To sigh for Zephyrs from ambrosial Plains;
But mends her Meshes torn, and pours her Lay
All in the stifling Fervour of the Day.
   Her naked Children round the Alley run,
And roll'd in Dust, are bronz'd beneath the Sun;
Or gambol round the Dame, sho, loosely dress'd,
Woos the coy Breeze to fan the open Breast:
She, once a Handmaid, strove by decent art
To charm her Sailor's Eye and touch his Heart;
Her Bosom then was veil'd in Kerchief clean,
And Fancy left to form the Charms unseen.

But when a Wife, she lost her former Care,
Nor thought on Charms, nor time for Dress could spare;
Careless she found her Friends who dwelt beside,
No rival Beauty kept alive her Pride:
Still in her bosom Virtue keeps her place,
But Decency is gone, the Virtues' Guard and Grace.
   See that long boarded Building!—By these Stairs
Each humble Tenant to that Home repairs—
By one large Window lighted—it was made
For some bold Project, some design in Trade:
This fail'd,—and one, a Humorist in his way,
(Ill was the humour), bought it in decay;
Nor will he sell, repair, or take it down;
'Tis his,—what cares he for the talk of Town?
'No! he will let it to the Poor;—a Home
Where he delights to see the Creatures come:'
'They may be Thieves;'—'Well, so are richer Men;'
'Or Idlers, Cheats, or Prostitutes:'—'What then?'
'Outcasts pursued by Justice, vile and base;'—
'They need the more his Pity and the Place:'
Convert to System his vain Mind has built,
He gives Asylum to Deceit and Guilt.
   In this vast Room, each Place by habit fix'd,
All Sexes, Families, and Ages mix'd,—
To union forced by Crime, by Fear, by Need,
And all in Morals and in Modes agreed;
Some ruin'd Men, who from Mankind remove;
Some ruin'd Females, who yet talk of Love;
And some grown old in Idleness—the prey
To vicious Spleen, still railing through the Day;
And Need and Misery, Vice and Danger bind
In sad Alliance each degraded Mind.
   That Window view!—oil'd Paper and old Glass
Stain the strong Rays, which, though impeded, pass,
And give a dusty Warmth to that huge Room,
The conquer'd Sunshine's melancholy gloom;
When all those Western Rays, without so bright,
Within become a ghastly glimmering Light,
As pale and faint upon the Floor they fall,
Or feebly gleam on the opposing Wall:
That Floor, once Oak, now piec'd with Fir unplan'd,
Or, where not piec'd, in places bor'd and stain'd;

That wall once whiten'd, now an odious sight,
Stain'd with all Hues, except its antient White;
The only Door is fasten'd by a Pin,
Or stubborn Bar, that none may hurry in:
For this poor Room, like Rooms of greater pride,
At times contains what prudent Men would hide.
　　Where'er the Floor allows an even space,
Chalking and Marks of various Games have place;
Boys without foresight, pleas'd in Halters swing;
On a fix'd Hook Men cast a flying Ring;
While Gin and Snuff their female Neighbours share,
And the black Beverage in the fractured Ware.
　　On swinging Shelf are things incongruous stor'd,—
Scraps of their Food,—the cards and Cribbage-board,—
With Pipes and Pouches; while on Peg below,
Hang a lost Member's Fiddle and its Bow:
That still reminds them how he'd dance and play,
Ere sent untimely to the Convicts' Bay.
　　Here by a Curtain, by a Blanket there,
Are various Beds conceal'd, but none with care;
Where some by Day and some by Night, as best
Suit their Employments, seek uncertain Rest;
The drowsy Children at their pleasure creep
To the known Crib, and there securely sleep.
　　Each end contains a Grate, and these beside
Are hung Utensils for their boil'd and fry'd—
All used at any hour, by Night, by Day,
As suit the Purse, the Person, or the Prey.
　　Above the Fire, the Mantel-Shelf contains
Of China-Ware some poor unmatch'd remains;
There many a Tea-cup's gaudy fragment stands,
All placed by Vanity's unwearied hands;
For here she lives, e'en here she looks about,
To find some small consoling Objects out:
Nor heed these Spartan Dames their House, nor sit
'Mid Cares domestic,—they nor sew nor knit;
But of their Fate discourse, their Ways, their Wars,
With arm'd Authorities, their 'Scapes and Scars:
These lead to present Evils, and a Cup,
If Fortune grant it, winds Description up.
High hung at either end, and next the Wall,
Two ancient Mirrors show the forms of all,

In all their force;—these aid them in their Dress,
But with the good, the Evils too express,
Doubling each look of Care, each token of Distress.

GEORGE CRABBE, *The Borough*

Aldborough, from the terrace

Thy old Moot-Hall is but a relique hoar!
   Thy time-worn Church stands lonely on the hill!
   And he who sojourns here when winds are shrill
In winter—peradventure might deplore
The poor old Borough,—Borough now no more!
   Yet, on a summer day, 'tis pleasant still
   From this fair eminence to gaze at will
Over the town below, and winding shore.

BERNARD BARTON

The Alde

How near I walked to Love,
How long, I cannot tell.
I was like the Alde that flows
Quietly through green level lands,
So quietly, it knows
Their shape, their greenness and their shadows well;
And then undreamingly for miles it goes
And silently, beside the sea.

Seamews circle over,
The winter wildfowl wings,
Long and green the grasses wave
Between the river and the sea.
The sea's cry, wild or grave,
From bank to low bank of the river rings;
But the uncertain river though it crave
The sea, knows not the sea.

Was that indeed salt wind?
Came that noise from falling
Wild waters on a stony shore?
Oh, what is this new troubling tide
Of eager waves that pour
Around and over, leaping, parting, recalling? . . .
How near I moved (as day to same day wore)
And silently, beside the sea!

JOHN FREEMAN

ESSEX   *Colchester*

The broad High street of good old Colchester
May match with any street in any town,
Ending in old East Hill—where once I dwelt,
And which I have climbed some twenty thousand times—
Where I brewed beer of excellent quality,
Which I could confidently recommend
As genuine, wholesome, and invigorating,
And thereby earned a comfortable living.
I hope my poetry may prove as good.

           *   *   *

Our grand old Castle overtops the town
With walls that promise to stand firm till doomsday.
Who shall reveal its undiscovered records?
. . . Beneath the Castle on the northern side,
Beyond the Roman ruinous town-wall,
Where the small river winds along the meadows,
An old lop-sided humble flour-mill stands;
Behind it is a clump of ancient willows,
So large and venerable that any artist
Would notice and enjoy their fine effect;
Beyond them is a small but cheerful meadow,
Brilliant and gay with buttercups and daisies
When the warm breath of Summer comes each year;
The playing place for countless generations
Of the small population of the town—
Delighted childhood kicking up its heels.
. . . There in the mill-dam boys and grown up men,
Gifted with large development of hope,

And blessed as well with admirable patience,
Angle for fish that never will be caught.

           *   *   *

The town looks very nobly from the north
When the descending sun gleams richly on it.
There proudly stands the ancient Roman castle,
Half hidden by a grove of stately trees;
There is St James's ivy-covered tower,
And there St Peter's lifts his lofty brow;
While old St Mary's rears her battered form,
Telling to all her story of the siege,
Her fine stone tower being topped by vulgar bricks,
From whence the one-eyed gunner smote the foe,
Until himself in turn was smitten down.

JAMES HURNARD, *The Setting Sun*

Kelvedon

How pleasant are the meads of Kelvedon,
Where in my youthful days I played at will,
And which I now revisit in my age,
How sweetly winds its little humble river—
Known by its sounding name, the Blackwater—
Through the green level meadows it refreshes,
Where lowing heifers indolently graze,
And sheep repose or idly chew the cud.
The river, when I was the miller's son,
To me was a perpetual dear delight;
But not for any beauty it possessed
That my philosophy was conscious of.
How eagerly I used to bathe in it
When sultry summer days made the earth pant;
But that which most of all delighted me
Were the small fish that glanced within its waters.
How many pleasant hours have I expended
Angling for gudgeons in the pebbly stream,
Myself a happy gudgeon all the while,
The patient votary of distant hope.

JAMES HURNARD, *The Setting Sun*

Romford Market

With human bellow, bovine glare,
Glittering trumpery, gaudy ware,
The life of Romford market-square
      Set all our pulses pounding;
The gypsy drover with his stick,
The huckster with his hoary trick,
The pork with fat a good foot thick,
      And sausages abounding:

Stalls of apples, piles of cake,
Stacks of kippers, haddock, hake,
Great slabs of toffee that they make,
      Which urchins eye and pray for;
Divine abundance! glorious day!
We stayed as long as we could stay,
Then upped our loads and went our way
      With all that we could pay for.

Then homeward bound by Clockhouse Lane
We jabbered of our golden gain,
And not in our too usual strain
      Of rancorous dissension;
Here is the little onion-hoe
We bought that day, so long ago;
Worn down—but so are one or two
      More things that I could mention.

Threading the silent, mist-bedewed
And darkening thicks of Hainault wood,
We reached that cottage, low and rude,
      Which was so loved a dwelling;
By the black yew, solemn and still,
Under the brow of Crabtree Hill—
Ah, dear it was, and ever will
      Be dear beyond all telling.

Dry hornbeam twigs roared up in flame,
The kettle quivered to the same:
When home the weary Parents came
      The sausages were frying;
The tea was brewed, the toast was brown;
We chattered of our day in town—

Outside, the leaves went whispering down
    And autumn owls were crying.

Our market-day was done. But we
Enshrine it still in memory,
For it was passed in perfect glee,
    By youth and health begotten;
My Romford on the Essex plain!
My upland woods! while you remain,
One humble jewel we retain,
    One day is unforgotten.

RUTH PITTER

Archaeology
(Wimbish)

They say a church once stood in this Anglian field.
But there's no village here it could have served.
The district is a plateau, wide and wild,
Where winds meet, and scrub-bush only has thrived
For centuries, except on one lonely farm.

Here in its acres set grim and taciturn,
An outpost of humanity, it holds
Authority of a field or two; no more.
The wind is master here, and grudgingly yields
A yearly crop of corn, too thin for flour.

But in the early summer, when the tyrant
Relents for a month, and growing lenient
Breaks into bramble-flowers, and eglantine,
And all the little outlaws man dismisses
From garden beds and honestly hoed fields,
Then the dim murmurs of old homes, and guesses
About a church once sanctifying these wilds,
Are proved in barley. Where it rises green
A deeper hue of tall blades, cruciform,
Reveals the old foundations. No need to search
By gossip or legend. There stands the living church.

RICHARD CHURCH

Tilbury
(1588)

In Essex faire, that fertill soile,
  upon the hill of Tilsburie:
To give our Spanish foes the foile,
  in gallant campe they now do lie.

THOMAS DELONEY, *The Queenes visiting of the Campe at Tilsburie*

Tilbury Docks[1]
(1940)

Factory chimneys loosen their slow hair,
Paying out clouds that shrink without a shower,
While terra-cotta copings, privets, railings
—Each prong the same sham Graeco-Roman spear—
Darken with dry unrunning rain. I'm looking
Southward across the river to a town;
Shops going broke behind their flashy windows,
And churches dingily devout, where the Word
Exhorts one scattered somnolent pew—or so
The fanciful eye might read a blur of walls
Impersonally windowed, wedged beneath
A pile of cloud, now dense and traversed by
A sea-gull like some friendly plane, now hung
In dripping shreds, one vast defeated flag.
But here, close to the stream, where we have pitched
Our flapping home, dry-docks and wharfs compose
An uneventful siding of the Sea,
A tidal pond. Here, on each high tide visit,
He bulges under stationary keels,
Creeps up the pier, and noses into corners
Like the caretaker of a rambling grange
Doing the daily round; and cranes in couples
Lean their inquisitive necks over the horizon,
Wanting the last of the sun. We found ourselves
In Nature's no-man's-land; for when they had made
River and Sea shake hands through floating doors,

[1] Originally entitled 'Ground Defence'.

Submerged, and opening both ways into water,
This patch remained, the lock being cut, dead ground,
A dump. Cow-parsley opens at the air
Her crowded parasols of snow, neck-high
Coarsely profuse, and smelling of stale bread;
Thistles, outnumbered, stab their claim between,
Tufted with shaving brushes of soft seed,
Clocks of the wind, that offer nothing to
The reconnoitring bee; and where she can,
Convolvulus prepares her silent bugles
Low in the undergrowth, where night by night
Invisible nomads of the dew steal forth
To pitch their mushrooms—a competitive scrum,
Seething, prolific, and all born of rubbish,
Fly-bothered, we began our ground defences
And tore midsummer's carpet. Gradually
The smooth politeness of our hands wore off,
As memories long buried in the bone
Started from racial sleep to give our spirits
Their second wind. How often had we climbed
The sheer slope to its interesting crown,
Sat on a weal of earth that barely showed
The gale whose every broad assault retook
The wall in mockery of the Iberian ghosts
Bunched at the rampart where they fell. We sat
Close to the sun, while England, telling her treasures,
Drew off her mists, unravelled at our feet
Her patterned boundaries; orchard and holt,
The same jigsaw as when the Capuchins
Argued their hedges, sole memorial
Of the anonymous saints—unless some tithe-barn
Sport a remaindered gargoyle at the door.
We were detached, picnicking on the ridge,
Probing the rabbit-holes for flints; but now
The ancestral hill-men moved in our blood, renerved
Our arms with their barbarian pith, so far
Had we sunk back across the centuries
To shake them from their graves. We hacked through time
Doubly, for every spadeful disinterred
The 'nineties. There were leg-and-armless dolls;
Shepherd and shepherdess, an Arcadian group,
Wooing without their heads; shivers of plates

Once excellent with catering that cheerly
Contributed a respite of well-being
To one lost hunger, one forgotten day
Fifty forgotten sad lost years ago
—Mementoes of what blunders? Breakfast-time,
A hansom pausing at the door, someone
Not concentrating on her mop, a heart-jump,
Then Harriet running crimson to her room,
Hugging the guilty shards, from that hot moment
Mysteriously gone, until we found them
Wasting their stencilled cherries on a worm.
   Midnight, someone's on guard, watching the searchlights,
Finger-tips of a tense, blindfolded Island,
Fumble the stars indented like a page
Of braille. The exploring breeze halts at our tent
As on a rock, and spouts, a breaker of air;
Poles creak, canvas recoils, the hurricane lamp
Turned down into a sanctuary glimmer,
Swing on its wire and throws across the roof
A wobbling shadow-cobweb. My friends, like bundles
Dropped from a height, snooze, flat out, under greatcoats,
Buttons obediently shined; Muschamp,
Surveyor, Mellins, architect, and Crump,
The resonant actor, Bailey too, whose thumbs
Can tell at a touch the qualities of fur:
Each with a talent which is death to hide
Lodged in him useless—stript of their difference
Down to the bare humanity—dour friendship,
A common hate their only common ground.
And yet how like the inverted warmth of ice
Would be this warmth of heart, were violence
Alone our bond! No, somewhere there's a hope
Crosses our false with true, and by whose grace
We trust to be forgiven. Dawn's overdue:
The eastward barriers wear a molten look,
Cock-sparrow skims the grass. Soon we'll be up
And doing the Ancient Briton, sunk to the waist
In Yesterday, our picks discovering
Dishes and dolls, like manners and ideals,
Turning to fossils, as it were, by numbers,
—*One*. . . . Black then to the trench. We'll stuff our sandbags
Plump with the butter-fingered past, salvage

None of these dust-bin burials, that when
Our earth has been defended, we may fashion
Newness in all things, even from these ruins.
Dig fast, dig deep. To-morrow's building-time.

CHRISTOPHER HASSALL

CAMBRIDGESHIRE

Residence at Cambridge

It was a dreary morning when the wheels
Rolled over a wide plain o'erhung with clouds,
And nothing cheered our way till first we saw
The long-roofed chapel of King's College lift
Turrets and pinnacles in answering files,
Extended high above a dusky grove.

Advancing, we espied upon the road
A student clothed in gown and tasselled cap,
Striding along as if o'ertasked by Time,
Or covetous of exercise and air;
He passed—nor was I master of my eyes
Till he was left an arrow's flight behind.
As near and nearer to the spot we drew,
It seemed to suck us in with an eddy's force.
Onward we drove beneath the Castle; caught,
While crossing Magdalene Bridge, a glimpse of Cam;
And at the *Hoop* alighted, famous Inn.

My spirit was up, my thoughts were full of hope;
Some friends I had, acquaintances who there
Seemed friends, poor simple school-boys, now hung round
With honour and importance: in a world
Of welcome faces up and down I roved;
Questions, directions, warning and advice,
Flowed in upon me, from all sides; fresh day
Of pride and pleasure! to myself I seemed
A man of business and expense, and went
From shop to shop about my own affairs,
To Tutor or to Tailor, as befel,
From street to street with loose and careless mind.

I was the Dreamer, they the Dream; I roamed
Delighted through the motley spectacle;
Gowns grave, or gaudy, doctors, students, streets,
Courts, cloisters, flocks of churches, gateways, towers:
Migration strange for a stripling of the hills,
A northern villager.
                    As if the change
Had waited on some Fairy's wand, at once
Behold me rich in monies, and attired
In splendid garb, with hose of silk, and hair
Powdered like rimy trees, when frost is keen.
My lordly dressing-gown, I pass it by,
With other signs of manhood that supplied
The lack of beard.—The weeks went roundly on,
With invitations, suppers, wine and fruit,
Smooth housekeeping within, and all without
Liberal, and suiting gentleman's array.

The Evangelist St John my patron was:
Three Gothic courts are his, and in the first
Was my abiding-place, a nook obscure;
Right underneath, the College kitchens made
A humming sound, less tuneable than bees,
But hardly less industrious; with shrill notes
Of sharp command and scolding intermixed.
Near me hung Trinity's loquacious clock,
Who never let the quarters, night or day,
Slip by him unproclaimed, and told the hours
Twice over with a male and female voice.
Her pealing organ was my neighbour too;
And from my pillow, looking forth by light
Of moon or favouring stars, I could behold
The antechapel where the statue stood
Of Newton with his prism and silent face,
The marble index of a mind for ever
Voyaging through strange seas of Thought, alone.

WILLIAM WORDSWORTH, *The Prelude*

Cambridge

Thence to Cambridge, where the Muses
Haunt the Vine-bush, as their use is;
Like sparks up a Chimney warming,
Or Flyes near a Dung-hill swarming,
In a Ring they did enclose me,
Vowing they would never lose me.
  'Bout midnight for drinke I call S^r,
As I had drunk nought at all S^r
But all this did little shame me,
Tipsy went I, tipsy I came:
Grounds, greenes, groves, are wet and homely,
But the Schollers wondrous comely.

RICHARD BRAITHWAIT, *Barnabees Journall,*
       His Northerne Journey, Third Part

Cambridge

I past beside the reverend walls
  In which of old I wore the gown;
  I roved at random through the town,
And saw the tumult of the halls;

And heard once more in college fanes
  The storm their high-built organs make,
  And thunder-music, rolling, shake
The prophet blazoned on the panes;

And caught once more the distant shout
  The measured pulse of racing oars
  Among the willows; paced the shores
And many a bridge, and all about

The same gray flats again, and felt
  The same, but not the same; and last
  Up that long walk of limes I past
To see the rooms in which he dwelt.

Another name was on the door:
  I lingered; all within was noise
  Of songs, and clapping hands, and boys
That crashed the glass and beat the floor;

Where once we held debate, a band
   Of youthful friends, on mind and art,
   And labour, and the changing mart,
And all the framework of the land;

When one would aim an arrow fair,
   But send it slackly from the string;
   And one would pierce an outer ring,
And one an inner, here and there;

And last the master-bowman, he,
   Would cleave the mark. A willing ear
   We lent him. Who, but hung to hear
The rapt oration flowing free

From point to point, with power and grace
   And music in the bounds of law,
   To those conclusions when we saw
The God within him light his face,

And seem to lift the form, and glow
   In azure orbits heavenly-wise;
   And over those ethereal eyes
The bar of Michael Angelo.

LORD TENNYSON, *In Memoriam*

Cambridge

Ye brown o'er-arching groves,
That Contemplation loves,
Where willowy Campus lingers with delight!
Oft at the blush of dawn
I trod your level lawn,
Oft woo'd the gleam of Cynthia silver-bright
In cloisters dim, far from the haunts of Folly,
With Freedom by my side, and soft-ey'd Melancholy.

THOMAS GRAY, *Ode for Music*

Cambridge Revisited

Down by the bridge the lovers walk,
Above the leaves there rolls the talk
Of lighted rooms. Across the lawn
Clare's greyness prophesies the dawn.
River and grass and classic weight,
As if the Fellows meditate
Socratically, the masculine
Beauty of th' athletic line,
Squared brow or pediment, and look
For Greek ghosts out of Rupert Brooke.
Grey stone, slow river, heavy trees,
I once had my share of these;
But now, within the central wood,
I neglect the wise and good:
And London smoke, and middle age,
Open on a grimier page.

JULIAN BELL

The Backs
(1853)

Dropping down the river,
Down the glancing river,
Through the fleet of shallops,
Through the fairy fleet,
Underneath the bridges
Carved stone and oaken,
Crowned with sphere and pillar,
Linking lawn with lawn,
Sloping swards of garden,
Flowering bank to bank;
'Midst the golden noontide,
'Neath the stately trees,
Reaching out their laden
Arms to overshade us;
'Midst the summer roses,
Whilst the winds were heavy
With the blossom odours,
Whilst the birds were singing
From their sleepless nests.

Dropping down the river
Down the branchéd river,
Through the hidden outlet
Of some happy stream,
Lifting up the leafy
Curtain that o'erhung it,
Fold on fold of foliage
Not proof against the stars.

JAMES PAYN, *The Backs*

The Devourers

Cambridge town is a beleaguered city;
   For south and north, like a sea,
There beat on its gates, without haste or pity,
   The downs and the fen country.

Cambridge towers, so old, so wise,
   They were builded but yesterday,
Watched by sleepy gray secret eyes
   That smiled as at children's play.

Roads south of Cambridge run into the waste,
   Where learning and lamps are not,
And the pale downs tumble, blind, chalk-faced,
   And the brooding churches squat.

Roads north of Cambridge march through a plain
   Level like the traitor sea.
It will swallow its ships, and turn and smile again—
   The insatiable fen country.

Lest the downs and the fens should eat Cambridge up,
   And its towers be tossed and thrown,
And its rich wine drunk from its broken cup,
   And its beauty no more known—

Let us come, you and I, where the road runs blind,
   Out beyond the transient city,
That our love, mingling with earth, may find
   Her imperishable heart of pity.

ROSE MACAULAY

Balsham Bells

Sweet waft their rounds those tuneful brothers five,
Learn brothers hence with harmony to live.
At eve the swains stir up the pleasing sounds,
Themselves repast, with music fills the grounds.
These notes abroad, each other noise is still,
Dusk, and clear peals do all the region fill.
The crescent moon just sheds an instant light,
Stars, and sweet sounds spread all abroad delight.
The herds in music chew the feasts of day,
Peals strike the ear, the eyes stars bright and gay.
The village cur intoxicated lies,
He lists to music and his anger dies.

KENRICK PRESCOT, *Balsham Bells*

The Old Vicarage, Grantchester
(Café des Westens, Berlin, May 1912)

Just now the lilac is in bloom,
All before my little room;
And in my flower-beds, I think,
Smile the carnation and the pink;
And down the borders, well I know,
The poppy and the pansy blow. . . .
Oh! there the chestnuts, summer through,
Beside the river make for you
A tunnel of green gloom, and sleep
Deeply above; and green and deep
The stream mysterious glides beneath,
Green as a dream and deep as death.
—Oh damn! I know it! and I know
How the May fields all golden show,
And when the day is young and sweet,
Gild gloriously the bare feet
That run to bathe. . . .
                          Du lieber Gott!
Here am I, sweating, sick, and hot,
And there the shadowed waters fresh
Lean up to embrace the naked flesh.

Temperamentvoll German Jews
Drink beer around;—and *there* the dews
Are soft beneath a morn of gold.
Here tulips bloom as they are told;
Unkempt about those hedges blows
An English unofficial rose;
And there the unregulated sun
Slopes down to rest when day is done,
And wakes a vague unpunctual star,
A slippered Hesper; and there are
Meads towards Haslingfield and Coton
Where *das Betreten's* not *verboten*. . . .

εἴθε γενοίμην . . . would I were
In Grantchester, in Grantchester!—
Some, it may be, can get in touch
With Nature there, or Earth, or such.
And clever modern men have seen
A Faun a-peeping through the green,
And felt the Classics were not dead,
To glimpse a Naiad's reedy head,
Or hear the Goat-foot piping low; . . .
But these are things I do not know.
I only know that you may lie
Day long and watch the Cambridge sky,
And, flower-lulled in sleepy grass,
Hear the cool lapse of hours pass,
Until the centuries blend and blur
In Grantchester, in Grantchester. . . .
Still in the dawnlit waters cool
His ghostly Lordship swims his pool,
And tries the strokes, essays the tricks,
Long learnt on Hellespont, or Styx,
Dan Chaucer hears his river still
Chatter beneath a phantom mill.
Tennyson notes, with studious eye,
How Cambridge waters hurry by . . .
And in that garden, black and white,
Creep whispers through the grass all night;
And spectral dance, before the dawn,
A hundred Vicars down the lawn;
Curates, long dust, will come and go
On lissom, clerical, printless toe;

And oft between the boughs is seen
The sly shade of a Rural Dean . . .
Till, at a shiver in the skies,
Vanishing with Satanic cries,
The prim ecclesiastic rout
Leaves but a startled sleeper-out,
Grey heavens, the first bird's drowsy calls,
The falling house that never falls.

God! I will pack, and take a train,
And get me to England once again!
For England's the one land, I know,
Where men with Splendid Hearts may go;
And Cambridgeshire, of all England,
The shire for Men who Understand;
And of *that* district I prefer
The lovely hamlet Grantchester.
For Cambridge people rarely smile,
Being urban, squat, and packed with guile;
And Royston men in the far South
And black and fierce and strange of mouth;
At Over they fling oaths at one,
And worse than oaths at Trumpington,
And Ditton girls are mean and dirty,
And there's none in Harston under thirty,
And folks in Shelford and those parts
Have twisted lips and twisted hearts,
And Barton men make Cockney rhymes,
And Coton's full of nameless crimes,
And things are done you'd not believe
At Madingley, on Christmas Eve.
Strong men have run for miles and miles,
When one from Cherry Hinton smiles;
Strong men have blanched, and shot their wives,
Rather than send them to St Ives;
Strong men have cried like babes, bydam,
To hear what happened at Barbraham.
But Grantchester! ah, Grantchester!
There's peace and holy quiet there,
Great clouds along pacific skies,
And men and women with straight eyes,
Lithe children lovelier than a dream,
A bosky wood, a slumbrous stream,

And little kindly winds that creep
Round twilight corners, half asleep.
In Grantchester their skins are white;
They bathe by day, they bathe by night;
The women there do all they ought;
The men observe the Rules of Thought.
They love the Good; they worship Truth;
They laugh uproariously in youth;
(And when they get to feeling old,
They up and shoot themselves, I'm told). . . .

Ah, God! to see the branches stir
Across the moon at Grantchester!
To smell the thrilling-sweet and rotten
Unforgettable, unforgotten
River-smell, and hear the breeze
Sobbing in the little trees.
Say, do the elm-clumps greatly stand,
Still guardians of that holy land?
The chestnuts shade, in reverend dream,
The yet unacademic stream?
Is dawn a secret shy and cold
Anadyomene, silver-gold?
And sunset still a golden sea
From Haslingfield to Madingley?
And after, ere the night is born,
Do hares come out about the corn?
Oh, is the water sweet and cool,
Gentle and brown, above the pool?
And laughs the immortal river still
Under the mill, under the mill?
Say, is there Beauty yet to find?
And Certainty? and Quiet kind?
Deep meadows yet, for to forget
The lies, and truths, and pain? . . . oh! yet
Stands the Church clock at ten to three?
And is there honey still for tea?

RUPERT BROOKE

Ely

Of all the *Marshland* Iles, I *Ely* am the Queene:
For Winter each where sad, in me lookes freshe and greene.
The Horse, or other beast, o'rway'd with his owne masse,
Lies wallowing in my Fennes, hid over head in grasse:
And in the place where growes ranke Fodder for my Neat;
The Turffe which beares the Hay, is wondrous needfull Peat:
My full and batning earth, needs not the Plowmans paines;
The Rils which runne in me, are like the branched vaines
In humane Bodies seene; those Ditches cut by hand,
From the surrounding *Meres*, to winne the measured land,
To those choyce waters, I most fitly may compare,
Wherewith nice women use to blanch their Beauties rare.
Hath there a man beene borne in me, that never knew
Of *Watersey* the *Leame*, or th' other cal'd the *New*.
The *Frithdike* neer'st my midst, and of another sort,
Who ever fish'd, or fowl'd, that cannot make report
Of sundry *Meres* at hand, upon my Westerne way,
As *Ramsey mere*, and *Ug*, with the great Whittelsey:
Of the abundant store of Fish and Fowle there bred,
Which whilst of *Europes* Iles Great *Britaine* is the Head,
No *Meres* shall truely tell, in them, then at one draught,
More store of either kinds hath with the Net been caught:
Which though some pettie Iles doe challenge them to be
Their owne, yet must those Iles likewise acknowledge me
Their soveraigne. Nor yet let that Islet *Ramsey* shame,
Although to *Ramsey-Mere* shee onely gives the name;
Nor *Huntingdon*, to me thought she extend her grounds,
Twit me that I at all usurpe upon her Bounds.
Those *Meres* may well be proud, that I will take them in,
Which otherwise perhaps forgotten might have bin.
Beside my towred *Phane*, and my rich Citied seat,
With Villages and Dorpes, to make me most compleat.

MICHAEL DRAYTON, *Polyolbion*

HUNTINGDONSHIRE
Kimbolton Park

—Nor less imperious that extended shade
By reverend oaks, the growth of ages, made;
Save where wide avenues that shade divide,
And shew the woodland in its utmost pride.
Here let the huntsman wind the echoing horn,
Cheer his swift steed, and wake the rosy morn;
Let dogs and men in noisy concert join,
And sportsmen call the harmony divine:
The Muse delights not, fond of pensive ease,
In disssipation, or pursuits like these.

    *   *   *

To Peace then sacred be the shady grove!
Be there no murmurs heard—but those of love:
Love, fled from noise and cities, haunts the glade,
The falling fountains, and the silent shade,
Inspires each warbling songster in the bower,
Breathes in each gale, and blossoms in each flower.
When every object thus their charms combine,
What bosom can resist the power divine?

    *   *   *

But lo! my Muse! the humid drops descend,
And parting shepherds to the hamlet tend,
O! quit the task those beauties to display,
That fairer spring with each returning day!
So Reynolds thus, presuming on his art
To trace those charms, my Lord![1] that win your heart,
Sees softer smiles when'er he lifts his eye,
That bid him throw his baffled pencil by.

BENJAMIN HUTCHINSON, *Kimbolton Park*

---

[1] The Duke of Manchester.

Stilton

Thence to Stilton, slowly paced,
With no bloome nor blossome graced,
With no plums nor apples stored,
But bald, like an old mans forehead;
Yet with Innes so well provided,
Guests are pleas'd when they have tride it.

RICHARD BRAITHWAIT, *Barnabees Journall, His Northerne Journey, Third Part*

THE MIDLANDS

In Praise of Peterborough

Golden fruit and blossoms red,
And a home at Medehamsted!
Towerèd Medehamsted, of all
Tronèd queen and principal,
Queen of fen and billowing lowland,
Sawtre, Yaxley, Stamford, Crowland!
Where the westered sun each eve
Miles of waving meadows' heave
Gilds, and his upturnèd glows
On the wondrous minster throws;
Gifts with transitory gold
Vanished kings, and abbots old,
That in their nichèd sconces seem
Living lamps that pray and dream.
Peter's shrine, to Hereward
Erst that gave the knightly sword,
Still to things that flit and flee
Harbour safe and hostelry!
When these eyes beheld thee last
In shimmering noons that quickly passed,
Pigeons circled, swallows flew,
Thrushes built within the yew,
Yea, the sparrow found a nest
Underneath thy sunlit crest,
Tiny lives a shelter gained
In thy borders crevice-veined,
Where snapdragon and featherfew
And golden-freckled wallflower grew!

EDWARD THOMPSON

NORTHAMPTONSHIRE
Northamptonshire Fens

The lake that held a mirror to the sun
Now curves with wrinkles in the stillest place.
The autumn wind sounds hollow as a gun,
And water stands in every swampy place.
Yet in these fens peace, harmony, and grace,
The attributes of nature, are allied.
the barge with naked mast, in sheltered place
Beside the brig, close to the bank is tied,
While small waves plash by its bulky side.

JOHN CLARE

Dyke Side
(Helpston)

The frog croaks loud, and maidens dare not pass
But fear the noisome toad and shun the grass;
And on the sunny banks they dare not go
Where hissing snakes run to the flood below.
The nuthatch noises loud in wood and wild,
Like women turning skreeking to a child.
The schoolboy hears and brushes through the trees
And runs about till drabbled to the knees.
The old hawk winnows round the old crow's nest;
The schoolboy hears and wonder fills his breast.
He throws his basket down to climb the tree
And wonders what the red blotched eggs can be:
The green woodpecker bounces from the view
And hollos as he buzzes bye 'kew kew'.

JOHN CLARE

Remembrances

Summer's pleasures they are gone like to visions every one,
And the cloudy days of autumn and of winter cometh on.
I tried to call them back, but unbidden they are gone

Far away from heart and eye and forever far away.
Dear heart, and can it be that such raptures meet decay?
I thought them all eternal when by Langley Bush I lay,
I thought them joys eternal when I used to shout and play
On its bank at 'clink and bandy', 'chock' and 'taw' and 'ducking stone',
Where silence sitteth now on the wild heath as her own
Like a ruin of the past all alone.

When I used to lie and sing by old Eastwell's boiling spring,
When I used to tie the willow boughs together for a swing,
And fish with crooked pins and thread and never catch a thing,
With heart just like a feather, now as heavy as a stone;
When beneath old Lea Close oak I the bottom branches broke
To make our harvest cart like so many working folk,
And then to cut a straw at the brook to have a soak.
O I never dreamed of parting or that trouble had a sting,
Or that pleasures like a flock of birds would ever take to wing,
Leaving nothing but a little naked spring.

When jumping time away on old Crossberry Way,
And eating awes like sugarplums ere they had lost the may,
And skipping like a leveret before the peep of day
On the roly poly up and downs of pleasant Swordy Well,
When in Round Oak's narrow lane as the south got black again
We sought the hollow ash that was shelter from the rain,
With our pockets full of peas we had stolen from the grain;
How delicious was the dinner time on such a showery day!
O words are poor receipts for what time hath stole away,
The ancient pulpit trees and the play.

When for school oer Little Field with its brook and wooden brig,
Where I swaggered like a man though I was not half so big,
While I held my little plough though twas but a willow twig,
And drove my team along made of nothing but a name,
'Gee hep' and 'hoit' and 'woi'—O I never call to mind
These pleasant names of places but I leave a sigh behind,
On the only aged willow that in all the field remains,
And nature hides her face while they're sweeing in their chains
And in a silent murmuring complains.

Here was commons for their hills, where they seek for freedom still,
Though every common's gone and though traps are set to kill
The little homeless miners—O it turns my bosom chill
When I think of old Sneap Green, Puddock's Nook and Hilly Snow,
Where bramble bushes grew and the daisy gemmed in dew

And the hills of silken grass like to cushions to the view,
Where we threw the pismire crumbs when we'd nothing else to do,
All levelled like a desert by the never weary plough,
All banished like the sun where that cloud is passing now
And settled here for ever on its brow.

O I never thought that joys would run away from boys,
Or that boys would change their minds and forsake such summer joys;
But alack I never dreamed that the world had other toys
To petrify first feelings like the fable into stone,
Till I found the pleasure past and a winter come at last,
Then the fields were sudden bare and the sky got overcast
And boyhood's pleasing haunt like a blossom in the blast
Was shrivelled to a withered weed and trampled down and done,
Till vanished was the morning spring and set the summer sun
And winter fought her battle strife and won.

By Langley Bush I roam, but the bush hath left its hill,
On Cowper Green I stray, tis a desert strange and chill,
And the spreading Lea Close oak, ere decay had penned its will,
To the axe of the spoiler and self-interest fell a prey,
And Crossberry Way and old Round Oak's narrow lane
With its hollow trees like pulpits I shall never see again,
Enclosure like a Buonaparte let not a thing remain,
It levelled every bush and tree and levelled every hill
And hung the moles for traitors—though the brook is running still
It runs a sicker brook, cold and chill.

O had I known as then joy had left the paths of men,
I had watched her day and night, be sure, and never slept agen,
And when she turned to go, O I'd caught her mantle then,
And wooed her like a lover by my lonely side to stay;
Ay, knelt and worshipped on, as love in beauty's bower,
And clung upon her smiles as a bee upon a flower,
And gave her heart my posies, all cropt in a sunny hour,
As keepsakes and pledges all to never fade away;
But love never heeded to treasure up the may,
So it went the common road to decay.

JOHN CLARE

Wansford

Thence to Wansforth-brigs, a river
And a wife will live for ever;
River broad, an old wife jolly,
Comely, seemely, free from folly:
Gates and gardens neatly gracious,
Ports, and Parks and pastures spatious.

RICHARD BRAITHWAIT, *Barnabees Journall,
His Northerne Journey, Third Part*

Emmonsail's Heath in Winter

I love to see the old heath's withered brake
Mingle its crimpled leaves with furze and ling,
While the old heron from the lonely lake
Starts slow and flaps his melancholy wing,
And oddling crow in idle motions swing
On the half rotten ashtree's topmost twig,
Beside whose trunk the gipsy makes his bed.
Up flies the bouncing woodcock from the brig
Where a black quagmire quakes beneath the tread,
The fieldfares chatter in the whistling thorn
And for the awe round fields and clover rove,
And coy bumbarrels twenty in a drove
Flit down the hedgerows in the frozen plain
And hang on little twigs and start again.

JOHN CLARE

The Cherwell

O silent Cherwell! once wert thou
A minstrel river; thou didst flow
Gently as now, but all along
Was heard that sweet itinerant song,
Which thou hadst learnt in coming down
From the rich slope of Helidon,
The green-capped hill that overlooks

257

Fair Warwick's deep and shady brooks,
And blithe Northampton's meadow nooks,
Tamest of Counties! with a dower
Of humblest beauty rich, a power
Only by quiet minds obeyed,
And by the restless spurned,—scant shade,
And ruddy fallow, and mid these
Rare meadows, foliage-framed, which please
The leisure-loving heart, and line
Where the slow-footed rivers shine,
Upon whose reedy waters swim
The roving sea-birds, on the brim
Of flooded Nenna, in a fleet
With a golden lustre lit,
What time the short Autumnal day
Sets o'er the tower of Fotheringay.

F. W. FABER, *The Cherwell*

BEDFORDSHIRE

The Lament of Woburn

Hail! sepulchre of mighty dead
Congenial to the Poet's tread;
Thine is the glen I love to pace,
Thine is the tale I love to trace;
Dear are the walls, thy thronged town,
Remembrance of thine old renown,
And though thy names have pass'd away,
They leave behind a beamy ray.

Yes, *Woburn*, tho' thy cloister'd pile,
Thy groined roof, thy fretted aile,
With holy Abbots, great and just,
Are mingled in one common dust!
Yet hast thou glories—thou canst claim
The memory of unsullied fame.

*   *   *   *

Peace gilds that roof, yet once that wall
Hath known the stern oppressor's thrall;
The moon that set on *Tingrith's* bower
Saw *Woburn* sadden'd in that hour;
The sun that rose on *Kymble's* hill
Beheld her children weeping still.
'Woe' might each native voice exclaim,
For *Woburn* was a ruin'd name.

J. T. M., *The Lament of Woburn*
(Gentleman's Magazine, 1821)

Ampthill and Houghton

How gracefully the green and swelling mound
    Stoops to the valley!—Not unblest who roves
Or lingers on its brink, while smiles, around
    Far stretched, this lovely scene, these plains and groves.

Soon HOUGHTON's chequered hills appear (a name
    Allied to AMPTHILL) crowned with many a tree
In shape and hue not differing, nor the same,
    Such should the kindred forms of sisters be![1]

The terraced walk, the turf that gently swells,
    Adorn them both;—before th' enchanted eye
The spreading oaks along their shady dells
    And their rough knolls, in rival beauty, lie.

And, in this moment, as yon golden globe
    Full in the horizon flaming, braves the west,
Both share th' impartial splendor, in a robe
    From the same loom,—of heaven's own colours, drest.

It clothes this woodland promontory now,
    Which from the rising vapours, as they sail
Along the meadow, rears its lofty brow,
    And with a leafy rampart bounds the vale.

Here will I pause.—How quick the sunny breaks
    O'er thy grey tower, romantic MILBROOK, pass!
What hues beneath the slanting beam it takes,

[1]   Facies non omnibus una,
Nec diversa tamen, qualem decet esse sororum.   Ovid.

Till evening blends them in one shadowy mass!
And lo! where, nearer still, in tufted trees
  Half hidd'n, and ivy-clasp'd, rude forms arise
Of antique masonry,—the shattered frieze
  Beneath them, and the broken column lies.

Stranger, these pinnacles, and roofless walls,
  And clustering chimneys, mark the spot where stood
Chambers now tenantless, and spacious halls,
  The mansion of the 'fair, and wise, and good'.

Here, in the fabric which her hands had raised,
  Dwelt 'Sydney's sister, Pembroke's mother',[1]—here
On all so bright and beautiful she gazed,
  Blessing, and blest, through many a changeful year.

HENRY LUTTRELL, *Lines written
at Ampthill Park,* 1818

The Ouse near Sharnbrook

Slow winding stream! how stilly dost thou glide,
  'Twixt level meadows of a charming green,
  Whereon pied cattle, and white sheep, are seen!
And brilliant flowers gleam out from either side,
Like sparkling jewels on a beauteous bride;
  While silvery pollards o'er thy margins lean,
  Like grey-hair'd men of venerable mein,
Holding low converse o'er thy list'ning tide,
  Beneath whose wave disport the bream and dace,
And little minstrels pipe within thy bowers;
  Where dragon-flies their prey do fiercely chase.—
On, on thou flowest, like the gliding hours,—
  Save when arous'd by floods—at equal pace
Fed by earth's ceaseless springs, and heaven's blest showers.

W. B. GRAHAM

---

[1] Houghton Park was purchased, and its building erected, by Mary, Countess of Pembroke.

Dunstable

On yonder mountain top, behold
The hallow'd work of days of old,
The ancient knolls that crown the steep,
The shrines where fallen heroes sleep.
Haply when Britons fought in vain,
And slavery clank'd her iron chain,
They heard the victors' haughty cry,
Saw freedom lay expiring by;
Disdain'd from wounds and death to fly,
And only fought to bravely die.
There oft the lonely shepherd stands,
To overlook the neighbouring lands,
Nor thinks beneath his feet are spread
The ashes of the mighty dead.
Not from old Pisgah's towering height
That shepherd view'd a fairer sight,
When far and wide he saw expand
The beauty of the promis'd land.
How ample to the wandering eyes
The variegated prospect lies;
There pleasant villages are seen,
And shady groves that intervene.
The green wood waves upon the hill,
And softly winds the silver rill,
While many a steepled dome appears
Grown reverend in the vale of years;
Embower'd in shade there seem to reign
The guardian spirits of the plain.

GEORGE DERBYSHIRE,[1] *Dunstable*

BUCKINGHAMSHIRE

My County

We do not sell our secrets like
The other shires try to do.
And those bred here alone will find
The secrets of the chosen few.

[1] Parish clerk of Dunstable

Nor Bideford, nor Parracombe,
Nor Dart, nor Devon's Plymouth Hoe;
But plain, ungarnished Luggershaw,
Marsh Gibbon, Brill and Hampden Row;
For Exe and Teign and Culm and Tawe
And cream and cider, tor and hoe
Are only common property
For anyone to see and know,
But the lips of the men of Bucks alone
By Chiltern air are purified.
The barren breasts of Ivinghoe,
And ridge and bottom are their guide.
We find it hard to worship pike,
Crag, dale, moor, moss and lonely fell;
For Great and Little, ham, ton, den,
Low, end and green have cast their spell.
No secret lies in Striding Edge,
Great Gable, Coniston Old Man,
But Boddington, Coombe Hill and Kop
Shall hoard the song our hearts began.
No Stickletarn, no Bassenthwaite,
No Cumberland or Appleby—
The Thames, the Ouse, the Chess, the Thame,
Are waters good enough for me.
Llanberis, Barmouth, Bala, coed,
Cwm, afon, moel, fach and llyn
For them. For us, the Icknield Way,
Where the plain ends and the woods begin.
The chalk in this, our native land,
Was scattered with a liberal hand.
The holly hedges, massive, tall
And changeless, stand from fall to fall;
And in our woods, the cherry trees
Blossom forth just when they please.
Along the milk-and-honey Vale
Shall the broken speech of Bucks prevail,
Rushing, like an all-cleansing stream
Our thoughts go where the bloodstones gleam.
Fresh flints will come to our poor eyes
Glittering under Chiltern skies.
Like the sure, deep throb of a distant train
Our history echoes in my brain;

So, when our woods, the vale, have gone
This shall remain, surpassed by none.

H. EVELYN HOWARD

Eton

Ye distant spires, ye antique towers,
That crown the wat'ry glade,
Where grateful Science still adores
Her HENRY's holy Shade;
And ye, that from the stately brow
Of WINDSOR's heights th' expanse below
Of grove, of lawn, of mead survey,
Whose turf, whose shade, whose flowers among
Wanders the hoary Thames along
His silver-winding way.

THOMAS GRAY,
Ode on a Distant Prospect of Eton College

Weston Park, NEAR Olney, & The Ouse

How oft upon yon eminence our pace
Has slacken'd to a pause, and we have borne
The ruffling wind, scarce conscious that it blew,
While Admiration feeding at the eye,
And still unsated, dwelt upon the scene.
Thence with what pleasure have we just discern'd
The distant plough slow moving, and beside
His lab'ring team, that swerv'd not from the track,
The sturdy swain diminish'd to a boy!
Here Ouse, slow winding through a level plain
Of spacious meads with cattle sprinkled o'er,
Conducts the eye along his sinuous course
Delighted. There, fast rooted in their bank,
Stand, never overlook'd, our fav'rite elms,
That screen the herdsman's solitary hut;
While far beyond, and overthwart the stream
That, as with molten glass, inlays the vale,

The sloping land recedes into the clouds;
Displaying on its varied side the grace
Of hedge-row beauties numberless, square tow'r,
Tall spire, from which the sound of cheerful bells
Just undulates upon the list'ning ear,
Groves, heaths, and smoking villages remote.
Scenes must be beautiful, which, daily view'd,
Please daily, and whose novelty survives
Long knowledge and the scrutiny of years.
Praise justly due to those that I describe.

* * *

Descending now (but cautious, lest too fast)
A sudden steep, upon a rustic bridge
We pass a gulph, in which the willows dip
Their pendent boughs, stooping as if to drink.
Hence, ancle deep in moss and flow'ry thyme,
We mount again, and feel at every step
Our foot half sunk in hillocks green and soft,
Rais'd by the mole, the miner of the soil.
He, not unlike the great ones of mankind,
Disfigures Earth: and, plotting in the dark,
Toils much to earn a monumental pile,
That may record the mischiefs he has done.
The summit gain'd, behold the proud alcove,
That crowns it! yet not all its pride secures
The grand retreat from injuries impress'd
By rural carvers, who with knives deface
The pannels, leaving an obscure, rude name,
In characters uncouth and spelt amiss.
So strong the zeal t' immortalize himself
Beats in the breast of man, that ev'n a few,
Few transient years, won from th' abyss abhorr'd
Of blank oblivion, seem a glorious prize,
And even to a clown. Now roves the eye;
And, posted on this speculative height,
Exults in its command. The sheepfold here
Pours out its fleecy tenants o'er the glebe.
At first, progressive as a stream, they seek
The middle field; but scatter'd by degrees,
Each to his choice, soon whiten all the land.
There, from the sunburnt hayfield, homeward creeps

The loaded wain; while, lighten'd of its charge,
The wain that meets it passes swiftly by;
The boorish driver leaning o'er his team
Vocif'rous, and impatient of delay.
Nor less attractive is the woodland scene,
Diversified with trees of ev'ry growth,
Alike, yet various. Here the gray smooth trunks
Of ash, of lime, or beech, distinctly shine,
Within the twilight of their distant shades;
There, lost behind a rising ground, the wood
Seems sunk, and shorten'd to its topmost boughs.
No tree in all the grove but has its charms,
Though each its hue peculiar; paler some,
And of a wannish gray; the willow such,
And poplar, that with silver lines his leaf,
And ash far-stretching his umbrageous arm;
Of deeper green the elm; and deeper still,
Lord of the woods, the long-surviving oak.
Some glossy leav'd, and shining in the sun,
The maple, and the beech of oily nuts
Prolific, and the lime at dewy eve
Diffusing odours; nor unnoted pass
The sycamore, capricious in attire,
Now green, now tawny, and, ere autumn yet
Have chang'd the woods, in scarlet honours bright.
O'er these, but far beyond (a spacious map
Of hill and valley interpos'd between),
the Ouse, dividing the well-water'd land,
Now glitters in the sun, and now retires,
As bashful, yet impatient to be seen.

WILLIAM COWPER, *The Task*

OXFORDSHIRE   *Thyrsis*

How changed is here each spot man makes or fills!
In the two Hinkseys nothing keeps the same;
    The village street its haunted mansion lacks,
And from the sign is gone Sibylla's name,
    And from the roofs the twisted chimney-stacks;
        Are ye too changed, ye hills?

See, 'tis no foot of unfamiliar men
　　To-night from Oxford up your pathway strays!
　　　Here came I often, often, in old days;
　　Thyrsis and I; we still had Thyrsis then.

Runs it not here, the track by Childsworth Farm,
　　Past the high wood, to where the elm-tree crowns
　　　The hill behind whose ridge the sunset flames?
　　The signal-elm, that looks on Ilsey Downs,
　　　The Vale, the three lone wears, the youthful Thames?—
　　　　This winter-eve is warm,
　　Humid the air; leafless, yet soft as spring,
　　　The tender purple spray on copse and briers;
　　　And that sweet City with her dreaming spires,
　　She needs not June for beauty's heightening,

Lovely all times she lies, lovely to-night!
　　Only, methinks, some loss of habit's power
　　　Befalls me wandering through this upland dim;
　　Once pass'd I blindfold here, at any hour,
　　　Now seldom come I, since I came with him.
　　　　That single elm-tree bright
　　Against the west—I miss it! is it gone?
　　　We prized it dearly; while it stood, we said,
　　　Our friend, the Scholar-Gipsy, was not dead;
　　While the tree lived, he in these fields lived on.

*　*　*

Well! wind-dispersed and vain the words will be,
　　Yet, Thyrsis, let me give my grief its hour
　　　In the old haunt, and find our tree-topp'd hill!
　　Who, if not I, for questing here hath power?
　　　I know the wood which hides the daffodil,
　　　　I know the Fyfield tree,
　　I know what white, what purple fritillaries
　　　The grassy harvest of the river-fields,
　　　Above by Ensham, down by Sandford, yields,
　　And what sedged brooks are Thames's tributaries;

I know these slopes; who knows them if not I?—
　　But many a dingle on the loved hill-side,
　　　With thorns once studded, old, white-blossom'd trees,
　　Where thick the cowslips grew, and, far descried,
　　　High tower'd the spikes of purple orchises,

Hath since our day put by
The coronals of that forgotten time.
    Down each green bank hath gone the ploughboy's team,
    And only in the hidden brookside gleam
Primroses, orphans of the flowery prime.

Where is the girl, who, by the boatman's door,
    Above the locks, above the boating throng,
        Unmoor'd our skiff, when, through the Wytham flats,
    Red loosestrife and blond meadow-sweet among,
        And darting swallows, and light water-gnats,
            We track'd the shy Thames shore?
Where are the mowers, who, as the tiny swell
    Of our boat passing heaved the river-grass,
        Stood with suspended scythe to see us pass?—
They all are gone, and thou art gone as well.

                        *   *   *

But hush! the upland hath a sudden loss
    Of quiet;—Look! adown the dusk hill-side,
        A troop of Oxford hunters going home,
    As in old days, jovial and talking, ride!
        From hunting with the Berkshire hounds they come.
            Quick, let me fly, and cross
Into yon further field!—'Tis done; and see,
    Back'd by the sunset, which doth glorify
    The orange and pale violet evening-sky,
        Bare on its lonely ridge, the Tree! the Tree!

MATTHEW ARNOLD, *Thyrsis*

Oxford and her Doctors

Emperour of Germany:
        Trust me Plantagenet these *Oxford* schooles
        Are richly seated neere the river side:
        The mountaines full of fat and fallow deere,
        The batling pastures laid with kine and flocks,
        The towne gorgeous with high built colledges,
        And schollers seemely in their grave attire,
        Learned in searching principles of art.
        What is thy judgement, *Jacques Vandermast*?

267

Vandermast:
>   That lordly are the buildings of the towne,
>   Spatious the romes and full of pleasant walkes;
>   But for the doctors, how that they be learned,
>   It may be meanly, for ought I can heere.

ROBERT GREENE, *The Honorable Historie
of Frier Bacon and Frier Bungay*

Oxford

Ye fretted pinnacles, ye fanes sublime,
Ye towers that wear the mossy vest of time;
Ye massy piles of old munificence,
At once the pride of learning and defence;
Ye cloisters pale, that, lengthening to the sight,
To contemplation, step by step, invite;
Ye high-arched walks, where oft the whispers clear
Of harps unseen have swept the poet's ear;
Ye temples dim, where pious duty pays
Her holy hymns of ever-echoing praise;—
Lo! your loved Isis, from the bordering vale,
With all a mother's fondness bids you hail!

THOMAS WARTON, *Oxford*

Duns Scotus's Oxford

Towery city and branchy between towers;
Cuckoo-echoing, bell-swarmèd, lark-charmèd, rook-racked, river-
    rounded;
The dapple-eared lily below thee; that country and town did
Once encounter in, here coped and poisèd powers;

Thou hast a base and brickish skirt there, sours
That neighbour-nature thy grey beauty is grounded
Best in; graceless growth, thou hast confounded
Rural rural keeping—folk, flocks and flowers.

Yet ah! this air I gather and release
He lived on; these weeds and waters, these walls are what
He haunted who of all men most sways my spirits to peace;

Of realty the rarest-veinèd unraveller; a not
Rivalled insight, be rival Italy or Greece;
Who fired France for Mary without spot.

GERARD MANLEY HOPKINS

Oxford

My music-loving Self this afternoon
(Clothed in the gilded surname of Sassoon)
Squats in the packed Sheldonian and observes
An intellectual bee-hive perched and seated
In achromatic and expectant curves
Of buzzing, sunbeam-flecked, and overheated
Accommodation. Skins perspire . . . But hark! . . .
Begins the great *B minor Mass* of Bach.

The choir sings *Gloria in excelsis Deo*
With confident and well-conducted *brio*.
Outside, a motor-bike makes impious clatter,
Impinging on our Eighteenth-Century trammels.
God's periwigged: He takes a pinch of snuff.
The music's half-rococo . . . Does it matter
While those intense musicians shout the stuff
In Catholic Latin to the cultured mammals
Who agitate the pages of their scores? . . .

Meanwhile, in Oxford sunshine out of doors,
Birds in collegiate gardens rhapsodize
Antediluvian airs of worm-thanksgiving.
To them the austere and buried Bach replies
With song that from ecclesiasmus cries
Eternal *Resurrexit* to the living.

Hosanna in excelsis chants the choir
In pious contrapuntal jubilee.
Hosanna shrill the birds in sunset fire.
And Benedictus sings my heart to Me.

SIEGFRIED SASSOON

North Oxford

Belbroughton Road is bonny, and pinkly bursts the spray
Of prunus and forsythia across the public way,
For a full spring-tide of blossom seethed and departed hence,
Leaving land-locked pools of jonquils by sunny garden fence.

And a constant sound of flushing runneth from windows where
The toothbrush too is airing in this new North Oxford air
From Summerfields to Lynam's, the thirsty tarmac dries,
And a Cherwell mist dissolveth on elm-discovering skies.

Oh! well-bound Wells and Bridges! Oh! earnest ethical search
For the wide high-table λογος of St C. S. Lewis's Church.
This diamond-eyed Spring morning my soul soars up the slope
Of a right good rough-cast buttress on the housewall of my hope.

And open-necked and freckled, where once there grazed the cows,
Emancipated children swing on old apple boughs,
And pastel-shaded book rooms bring New Ideas to birth
As the whitening hawthorn only hears the heart beat of the earth.

JOHN BETJEMAN

Oxford

Over, the four long years! And now there rings
One voive of freedom and regret: *Farewell!*
Now old remembrance sorrows, and now sings:
But song from sorrow, now, I cannot tell.

City of weathered cloister and worn court;
Gray city of strong towers and clustering spires:
Where art's fresh loveliness would first resort;
Where lingering art kindled her latest fires.

Where on all hands, wondrous with ancient grace,
Grace touched with age, rise works of goodliest men:
Next Wykeham's art obtain their splendid place
The zeal of Inigo, the strength of Wren.

Where at each coign of every antique street,
A memory hath taken root in stone:
There, Raleigh shone; there, toiled Franciscan feet;
There, Johnson flinched not, but endured, alone.

There, Shelley dreamed his white Platonic dreams;
There, classic 'Landor throve on Roman thought;
There, Addison pursued his quiet themes;
There, smiled Erasmus, and there, Colet taught.

And there, O memory more sweet than all!
Lived he, whose eyes keep yet our passing light;
Whose crystal lips Athenian speech recall;
Who wears Rome's purple with least pride, most right.

That is the Oxford, strong to charm us yet:
Eternal in her beauty and her past.
What, though her soul be vexed? She can forget
Cares of an hour: only the great things last.

Only the gracious air, only the charm,
And ancient might of true humanities:
These, nor assault of man, nor time, can harm;
Not these, nor Oxford with her memories.

Together have we walked with willing feet
Gardens of plenteous trees, bowering soft lawn:
Hill, whither Arnold wandered; and all sweet
June meadows, from the troubling world withdrawn:

Chapels of cedarn fragrance, and rich gloom
Poured from empurpled panes on either hand:
Cool pavements, carved with legends of the tomb;
Grave haunts, where we might dream, and understand.

Over, the four long years! And unknown powers
Call to us, going forth upon our way:
Ah! turn we, and look back upon the towers,
That rose above our lives, and cheered the day.

Proud and serene, against the sky, they gleam:
Proud and secure, upon the earth, they stand:
Our city hath the air of a pure dream,
And hers indeed is an Hesperian land.

Think of her so! the wonderful, the fair,
The immemorial, and the ever young:
The city, sweet with our forefathers' care;
The city, where the Muses all have sung.

Ill times may be; she hath no thought of time:
She reigns beside the waters yet in pride.

Rude voices cry: but in her ears the chime
Of full, sad bells brings back her old springtide.

Like to a queen in pride of place, she wears
The splendour of a crown in Radcliffe's dome.
Well fare she, well! As perfect beauty fares;
And these high places, that are beauty's home.

LIONEL JOHNSON

Blenheim Palace

Atria longè patent; sed nec cœnantibus usquam
Nec somno locus est: quàm bene non habitas!

MART. *Epig.*

See, sir, here's the grand approach,
This way is for his Grace's coach;
There lies the bridge, and here's the clock,
Observe the lion and the cock,
The spacious court, the colonnade,
And mark how wide the hall is made!
The chimneys are so well designed,
They never smoke in any wind.
This gallery's contrived for walking,
The windows to retire and talk in;
The council-chamber for debate,
And all the rest are rooms of state.

   'Thanks, sir,' cried I, ''tis very fine,
But where d'ye sleep, or where d'ye dine?
I find by all you have been telling,
That 'tis a house, but not a dwelling.'

ALEXANDER POPE

Village sketch
(Bampton-in-the-Bush)

Horses, their heads together under a tree;
Elm trees and oaks, mantled in glistening green;
Streams silver-brimmed, the stream-divided lea,

Wide-rising ground with barley thronged or bean:
A town-end of good houses, something grave,
Gray, square, and windowing far; cypress and yew
Topping a long gray wall; five poplars wave
Above the dark-plumed wall; against high blue
Spear-flashing white the spire, and windcock new
Aloft the spire, proud plaything of these gales
Which bring more violent wreaths of cloud and swirl
Of whistling rain; the storm's great ghost assails
The boys with bat and ball, the blue-capped girl
Who leans with her young love against the pales;
While over the level the terrier speeds and springs,
Hoping to catch the swallows in their low swift rings.

EDMUND BLUNDEN

Oxford Bells

So have I stood at eve on Isis' banks
To hear the merry Christ Church bells rejoice.
So have I sate too in thy honour'd shades,
Distinguished Magdalen, on Cherwell's brink,
To hear thy silver Wolsey tones so sweet
And so, too, have I paus'd and held my oar,
And suffer'd the slow stream to bear me home,
While Wykeham's peal along the meadow ran.

JAMES HURDIS, *The Village Curate*

Bab-Lock-Hythe

In the time of wild roses
As up Thames we travelled
Where 'mid water-weeds ravelled
The lily uncloses,

To his old shores the river
A new song was singing,
And young shoots were springing
On old roots for ever.

273

Dog-daisies were dancing,
And flags flamed in cluster,
On the dark stream a lustre
Now blurred and now glancing.

A tall reed down-weighing,
The sedge-warbler fluttered;
One sweet note he uttered,
The left it soft-swaying.

By the bank's sandy hollow
My dipt oars went beating,
And past our bows fleeting
Blue-backed shone the swallow.

High woods, heron-haunted,
Rose, changed, as we rounded
Old hills greenly mounded,
To meadows enchanted;

A dream ever moulded
Afresh for our wonder,
Still opening asunder
For the stream many-folded;

Till sunset was rimming
The West with pale flushes;
Behind the black rushes
The last light was dimming;

And the lonely stream, hiding
Shy birds, grew more lonely,
And with us was only
The noise of our gliding.

In cloud of gray weather
The evening o'erdarkened.
In the stillness we hearkened;
Our hearts sang together.

LAURENCE BINYON

On Westwell Downs

When Westwell Downes I gan to tread,
Where cleanely wynds the greene did sweepe,
Methought a landskipp there was spread,
Here a bush and there a sheepe:
    The pleated wrinkles of the face
    Of wave-swolne earth did lend such grace,
    As shadowings in Imag'ry,
    Which both deceive and please the eye.

The sheepe sometymes did tread the maze
By often wynding in and in,
And sometymes round about they trace
Which milkmayds call a Fairie ring:
    Such semicircles have they runne,
    Such lynes acrosse so trymly spunne
    The sheppeards learn whenere they please
    A new Geometry with ease.

The slender food upon the downe
Is allwayes even, allwayes bare,
Which neither spring nor winter's frowne
Can ought improve or ought impayre:
    Such is the barren Eunuches chynne,
    Which thus doth evermore begynne
    With tender downe to be orecast
    Which never comes to haire at last.

Here and there twoe hilly crests
Admiddst them hugg a pleasant greene,
And these are like twoe swelling breasts
That close a tender falle betweene.
    Here would I sleepe, or read, or pray
    From early morne to flight of day:
    But harke! a sheepe-bell calls mee upp,
    Like Oxford colledge bells, to supp.

WILLIAM STRODE

Vale
(Oxfordshire)

In Beckley from the high green woods
The eye looks down on sheeted floods,
Blue visionary solitudes,
Where many a thick-leaved hillock broods
On lonely Otmoor starkly grand,
And shining leagues of silent land,
Which the horizon's endless line
Does in an azure mist confine.

From Beckley the hid paths go down
To many a blessèd fairy town,
To many a hidden wandering way,
And the hushed flood of virgin Ray,
To Merton and to Ambrosden,
To Charlton, tower of fortunate men,
Lost in the gentian-coloured fen,
Whereof I am a citizen,
But shall not take youth there again.
(Rememberest thou, my soul, that noon
Watched by the still blue face of June,
The sacred water stealing slow,
The flowery dykes, how sweet they flow!
The starry lilies, golden and white,
The blossom of iris burning bright,
The dreaming distance infinite?)

From Beckley slowly wandering
Those roads meet many a pleasant thing,
Wood Eaton veiled in towering trees,
Noke nodding lapped in drowsy leas,
Cloaked Waterperry, nurse of peace,
And Elsfield, whence the traveller sees,
Faint, royal-crowned, majestical,
A distant vision, dear and small,
Apparent in the leafy dale,
Proud as a king's town in a tale,
The city of our blessedness,
The towers that are her gloriousness,
The spires that are her splendid joy—
So seems she to the gazing boy.

Ah, now my joy is not the same:
In Charlton under sunset-flame,
When all the dim marsh-lands aspire
Toward the orange western fire,
And in the vanèd tower the bell
Rings, and the hour is very well,
And the infinite plain is changèd all
To a vast blue blossom magical,
And a few stars shine, and the spring-dews fall:
In Beckley, when the flowers are out,
And in rich woods and cuckoos shout,
And scattered all around appear
The dancing babes of the jubilant year,
Green spurges, hyacinths, orchises,
A glory in the shade of the trees:
Ah, now I cannot laugh and sing,
And drink the sweet earth triumphing:
For now I am a man and find
The world is not made after my mind,
As it is made after the mind of a boy.
Good-bye, my lovely sister joy!

WILFRED ROWLAND CHILDE, *Vale*

WARWICKSHIRE   *Warwick*

Now WARWICK claims the promis'd Lay, supreme
In this her midland Realm! Precedence due,
And long maintain'd! For her kind Nature rais'd,
The rocky Hill, a gentle Eminence,
For Health and Pleasure form'd! where her gay Tribes
Indulge the social Walk; once gloomy Haunt
Of solitary Monks! now beauteous Seat
Of rural Elegance! around whose Skirts
Parks, Meadows, Groves, their mingled Graces join,
And AVON pours his tributary Urn.

RICHARD JAGO, *Edge-hill*

Ichington & Leamington

Where LEAME and ICHENE own a kindred Rise,
And haste their neighb'ring Currents to unite,
New Hills arise, new Pastures green, and Fields
With other Harvests crown'd; with other Charms
Villas, and Towns with other Arts adorn'd.
There ICHINGTON its downward Structures views
In ICHENE'S passing Wave which, like the Mole,
Her subterraneous Journey long pursues,
Ere to the Sun she gives her lucid Stream.
Thy Villa, LEAMINGTON! her sister Nymph
In her fair Bosom shews; while on her Banks,
As further she her liquid Course pursues,
Amidst surrounding Woods his ancient Walls
BIRB'RY conceals, and triumphs in the Shade.

RICHARD JAGO, *Edge-hill*

On Swift Joining Avon Near Rugby

Silent and modest Brook! who dippest here
Thy foot in Avon as if childish fear
Withheld thee for a moment, wend along;
        Go, follow'd by my song,
Sing in such easy numbers as they use
Who turn in fondness to the Tuscan Muse
And such as often have flow'd down on me
        From my own Fiesole.
I watch thy placid smile, nor need to say
        That Tasso wove one loose lay,
And Milton took it up to dry the tear
        Dropping on Lycidas's bier.
In youth how often at thy side I wander'd!
What golden hours, hours numberless, were squander'd
        Among thy sedges, while sometimes
        I meditated native rhymes,
And sometimes stumbled upon Latian feet;
        Then, where soft mole-built seat
        Invited me, I noted down
        What must full surely win the crown,

But first impatiently vain efforts made
On broken pencil with a broken blade.
       Anon, of lighter heart, I threw
       My hat where circling plover flew,
And once I shouted till, instead of plover,
There sprang up half a damsel, half a lover.
I would not twice be barbarous; on I went. . . .
And two heads sank amid the pillowing bent.
       Pardon me, gentle Stream, if rhyme
Holds up these records in the face of Time:
Among the falling leaves some birds yet sing,
And Autumn hath his butterflies like Spring.
Thou canst not turn thee back, thou canst not see
       Reflected what hath ceased to be:
       Haply thou little knowest why
       I check this levity, and sigh.
Thou never knewest her whose radiant morn
   Lighted my path to Love; she bore thy name,
She whom no Grace was tardy to adorn,
   Whom one low voice pleas'd more than louder fame:
She now is past my praises; from her urn
       To thine, with reverence due, I turn.
O silver-braided Swift! no victim ever
       Was sacrificed to thee,
Nor hast thou carried to that sacred River
Vases of myrrh, nor hast thou run to see
A band of Maenads toss their timbrels high
Mid *oi-evohes* to their Deity.
But holy ashes have bestrewn thy stream
       Under the mingled gleam
Of swords and torches, and the chaunt of Rome,
       When 'Wiclif's lowly tomb
       Thro' its thick briars was burst
       By frantic priests accurst;
For he had enter'd and laid bare the lies
That pave the labyrinth of their mysteries.
       We part . . . but one more look!
       Silent and modest Brook.

W. S. LANDOR

Rugby to Peterborough Line
A Song from Bradshaw

By *Rockingham* and *Harborough* the road ran fair and wide,
And who would want a better way, to tramp it or to ride?
At *Wansford*, heads were shaken then, at *Wakerley* and *Barrowden*,
When first they saw the railwaymen invade the countryside.

The turf that fringed the King's highway was broad and fresh and green,
And if the road was deep in mud the grass was always clean.
—'Twas horrid, at the railway's birth, from *Nassington* to
    Theddingworth,
To see the banks of naked earth the metals ran between!

At *Welford*, for the coaching horn, they heard the whistling steam,
The couplings clanked in *Castor*, for the clatter of the team:
And peasants walking in the dark near *Yelvertoft* and *Stanford Park*,
Would pause upon their way to mark the passing engine's gleam.

But now the grass has grown again upon the broken ground,
The whistling of the engines is an old, accustomed sound;
And down the line, from *Clifton Mill* as far as *Orton Waterville*,
Are little country stations, still, where quiet can be found.

COLIN ELLIS

The Rectory Remembered

And many places lures us in the bound,
So wide a pleasance, of the Rectory ground.
The drive, pale pebbly river, swirls between
A shaggy hayfield and the fresh-cut green,
Banded with silver, of trim lawns that ride
Down to a hidden curve. On that smooth side
Prodigious rhododendron-clumps their bold
Bonnets of crimson from dark mounds unfold,
And fir-like, small, uncandled Christmas-trees
Stiffen in glaucous sprays. How unlike these,—
Disdaining by such uniform to please,—
The busy deserts of the hayfield spread!
Here dragon-flies their thin bright needles thread
Zigzagging; here, through breathless afternoon
Flicker the Blues, and float the Whites, and swoon

The flopping Meadow Browns; here to the skies
Two single trees in turbaned grandeur rise,
High sovereigns, each recognising each,
Cool tulip-tree and dark-bright copper beech—
Pride of the village, set within whose frame
A *Warwick* landscape turns midsummer flame
To catlike drowsiness.
              And still between
The shaggy hayfield and the shaven green
Blinking in heat the gravel drive descends
Till shadow-chilled under tall trees it bends.
Trees overhang the highroad. Outward swing
Trees in a portly round enveloping
Garden and orchard trees that nod and talk
Above the path nicknamed *The Lovers' Walk*,
Where on a moonlit night behind you creep
The clammy-fingered ghosts that cannot sleep.
Yet there, when night and whisperings are gone,
In friendly daylight you may walk alone,
Or in the shine of dew, as bird-songs wake,
With feet unfollowed through the circle break
And cross by open fields to *Corley Wood*:
A name by some for foxes understood,
By some for bluebells, but much more by one.
For Orange Underwings that in the sun—
He droops his net, the chase not yet begun—
Fly among catkins high above the cool
Rim of a private, cloud-reflecting pool.

    But that was April morning; now 'tis June,
And after tea-time. Hark! the ringing tune;
Again, of Father's axe! And Mother stands
To watch him in his shirt-sleeves with gloved hands
Chop the low trailing boughs, to make a new
Tunnel through leaves, an open-window view
To *Coventry*. Ah! there, this very minute,
The thinning space falls clear and, sharpened in it,
Three pencil spires in the showering light
Salute us, rising level with our sight;[1]
While, strange to think, three hundred feet below
Invisible, but large as life, there go
Hiscock the chemist, Moore of the *King's Head*,

---

[1] The top of St Michael's spire was said to be on a level with the keyhole of the Rectory front-door.

Laxton and Blythe. Among the trams they tread,
Between the houses that lie safe and snug
As any rich man tucked up in a rug,
The centre round which all of England lies
And drinks in peace from wide, unpeopled skies.

G. ROSTREVOR HAMILTON, *Corley, 1902*

Coventry
A Hymne to his Ladies Birth-place

COVENTRY, that do'st adorne
The Countrey wherein I was borne,
Yet therein lyes not thy prayse,
Why I should crowne the Tow'rs with Bayes:
'Tis not thy Wall me to thee weds,
Thy Ports, nor thy proud Pyrameds,
Nor thy Trophies of the Bore;[1]
But that Shee which I adore,
Which scarce Goodnesse selfe can payre,
First there breathing blest thy Ayre.
   IDEA, in which Name I hide
Her, in my heart Deifi'd,
For what good, Man's mind can see,
Onely Her IDEAS be;
She, in whom the Vertues came
In Woman's shape, and tooke her Name,
She so farre past Imitation,
As (but Nature our Creation
Could not alter) she had aymed
More than Woman to have framed:
She whose truely written Story,
To thy poor Name shall adde more glory,
Then if it should have beene by Chance
T'have bred our Kings that Conquered *France*.
   Had She beene borne the former Age,
That house had beene a Pilgrimage,
And reputed more Divine
Than Walsingham or BECKET's Shrine.
   That Princesse,[2] to whom thou do'st owe

---

[1] The Shoulder-bone of a Bore of mighty bignesse.
[2] Godiva, duke Leofrick's wife, who obtained the Freedome of the City, of her husband, by riding thorow it naked.

Thy Freedome (whose Cleere blushing snow
The envious Sunne saw, when as she
Naked rode to make thee free)
Was but her Type, as to foretell
Thou should'st bring forth one should excell
Her Bounty; by whom thou should'st have·
More Honour than she Freedome gave.
And, that Great Queene,[1] which but of late
Rul'd this Land in Peace and State,
Had not beene, but Heaven had sworne
A Maide should raigne when She was borne.
    Of the Streets, which thou hold'st best,
And most frequent of the rest,
Happy *Mich-Parke*[2] ev'ry yeere,
On the fourth[3] of *August* there,
Let the Maides, from FLORA'S bowers,
With their Choyce and daintiest flowers
Decke Thee up, and from their store,
With brave Garlands crowne that dore!
    The old Man passing by that way
To his Sonne in Time shall say,
'There was that Lady borne, which long
To after-Ages shall be sung;'
Who, unawares being passed by,
Back to that House shall cast his Eye,
Speaking my Verses as he goes,
And with a Sigh shut ev'ry Close.
    Deare Citie, travelling by thee,
When thy rising Spyres I see,
Destined her place of Birth;
Yet me thinkes the very Earth
Hallowed is, so farre as I
Can thee possibly descry:
Then thou, dwelling in this place,
Hearing some rude Hinde disgrace
Thy Citie with some scurvy thing,
Which some jester forth did bring,
Speake these Lines where thou do'st come,
And strike the Slave for ever dumbe.

MICHAEL DRAYTON

[1] Queene Elizabeth.
[2] Noted Streete in Coventry.
[3] His Mistresse birth-day.

Aston & Edgbaston

Queen of the sounding Anvil![1] ASTON thee,
And EDGBASTON with hospitable Shade
And rural Pomp invest. O! warn thy Sons,
When, for a Time, their Labours they forget,
With no licentious Boldness to invade
These peaceful Solitudes.

RICHARD JAGO, *Edge-hill*

Expansion of Birmingham

While neighbouring cities waste the fleeting hours,
Careless of art and knowledge, and the smile
Of every Muse, expanding BIRMINGHAM,
Illum'd by intellect, as gay in wealth,
Commands her aye-accumulating walls,
From month to month, to climb the adjacent hills;
Creep on the circling plains, now here, now there,
Divergent—change the hedges, thickets, trees,
Upturn'd, disrooted, into mortar'd piles,
The street elongate, and the statelier square.

ANNA SEWARD, *Colebrook Dale*

Birmingham

Smoke from the train-gulf hid by hoardings blunders upward, the brakes
of cars
Pipe as the policeman pivoting round raises his flat hand, bars
With his figure of a monolith Pharaoh the queue of fidgety machines
(Chromium dogs on the bonnet, faces behind the triplex screens),
Behind him the streets run away between the proud glass of shops,
Cubical scent-bottles artificial legs arctic foxes and electric mops,
But beyond this centre the slumward vista thins like a diagram:
There, unvisited, are Vulcan's forges who doesn't care a tinker's damn.

[1] BREMICHAM, alias BIRMINGHAM.

Splayed outwards through the suburbs houses, houses for rest
Seducingly rigged by the builder, half-timbered houses with lips pressed
So tightly and eyes staring at the traffic through bleary haws
And only a six-inch grip of the racing earth in their concrete claws;
In these houses men as in a dream pursue the Platonic Forms
With wireless and cairn terriers and gadgets approximating to the fickle
    norms
And endeavour to find God and score one over the neighbour
By climbing tentatively upward on jerry-built beauty and sweated labour.

The lunch hour; the shops empty, shopgirls' faces relax
Diaphanous as green glass, empty as old almanacs
As incoherent with ticketed gewgaws tiered behind their heads
As the Burne-Jones windows in St Philip's broken by crawling leads
Insipid colour, patches of emotion, Saturdays thrills
(This theatre is sprayed with 'June')—the gutter take our old playbills,
Next week-end it is likely in the heart's funfair we shall pull
Strong enough on the handle to get back our money; or at any rate it is
    possible.
On shining lines the trams like vast sarcophagi move
Into the sky, plum after sunset, merging to duck's egg, barred with mauve
Zeppelin clouds, and Pentecost-like the cars' headlights bud
Out from sideroads and the traffic signals, crême-de-menthe or bulls'
    blood,
Tell one to stop, the engines gently breathing, or to go on
To where like black pipes or organs in the frayed and fading zone
Of the West the factory chimneys on sullen entry will all night wait
To call, in the harsh morning, sleep-stupid faces through the daily gate.

LOUIS MACNEICE

WORCESTERSHIRE
Hagley Park, With Prospect

These are the Sacred Feelings of thy Heart,
Thy Heart inform'd by Reason's purer Ray,
O LYTTLETON, the Friend! thy Passion thus
And Meditations vary, as at large,
Courting the Muse, thro' HAGLEY-PARK you stray,
Thy *British Temple*! There along the Dale,
With Woods o'er-hung, and shag'd with mossy Rocks,

Whence on each hand the gushing Waters play,
And down the rough Cascade white-dashing fall,
Or gleam in lengthen'd Vista thro' the Trees,
You silent steal; or sit beneath the Shade
Of solemn Oaks, that tuft the swelling Mounts
Thrown graceful round by Nature's careless Hand,
And pensive listen to the various Voice
Of rural Peace: the Herds, the Flocks, the Birds,
The hollow-whispering Breeze, the Plaint of Rills,
That, purling down amid the twisted Roots
Which creep around, their dewy Murmurs shake
On the sooth'd Ear. From these abstracted oft,
You wander thro' the Philosophic World;
Where in bright Train continual Wonders rise,
Or to the curious or the pious Eye.

* * *

Meantime you gain the Height, from whose fair Brow
The bursting Prospect spreads immense around;
And snatch'd o'er Hill and Dale, and Wood and Lawn,
And verdant Field, and darkening Heath between,
And Villages embosom'd soft in Trees,
And spiry Towns by surging Columns mark'd
Of household Smoak, your Eye excursive roams:
Wide-stretching from the *Hall*, in whose kind Haunt
The *Hospitable Genius* lingers still,
To where the broken Landskip, by Degrees,
Ascending, roughens into rigid Hills;
O'er which the *Cambrian* Mountains, like far Clouds
That skirt the blue Horizon, dusky, rise.

JAMES THOMSON, *The Seasons (Spring)*

Upon Eckington Bridge, River Avon

O Pastoral heart of England! Like a psalm
  Of green days telling with a quiet beat—
O wave into the sunset flowing calm!
  O tirèd lark descending on the wheat!
Lies it all peace beyond that western fold

Where now the lingering shepherd sees his star
Rise upon Malvern? Paints an Age of Gold
   Yon cloud with prophecies of linked ease—
   Lulling this land with hills drawn up like knees,
To drowse beside her implements of war?

Man shall outlast his battles. They have swept
  Avon from Naseby Field to Severn Ham;
And Evesham's dedicated stones have stepp'd
  Down to dust with Montfort's oriflamme.
Nor the red tear nor the reflected tower
  Abides; but yet these eloquent grooves remain,
Worn in the sandstone parapet hour by hour
   By labouring bargemen where they shifted ropes.
   E'en so shall man turn back from violent hopes
To Adam's cheer, and toil with spade again.

Ay, and his mother Nature, to whose lap
  Like a repentant child at length he hies,
Not in the whirlwind or the thunder-clap
  Proclaims her more tremendous mysteries:
But when in winter's grave, bereft of light,
  With still, small voice divinelier whispering—
  —Lifting the green head of the aconite,
   Feeding with sap of hope, the hazel-shoot—
   She feels God's finger active at the root,
Turns in her sleep and murmurs of the Spring.

SIR A. T. QUILLER-COUCH

In Flanders

I'm homesick for my hills again—
   My hills again!
To see above the Severn plain
Unscabbarded against the sky
The blue high blade of Cotswold lie,
The giant clouds go royally
By jagged Malvern with a train
Of shadows. Where the land is low

Like a huge imprisoning O
I hear a heart that's sound and high,
I hear the heart within me cry:
'I'm homesick for my hills again—
    My hills again!
Cotswold or Malvern, sun or rain!
    My hills again!'

F. W. HARVEY

Cricket at Worcester
(1938)

Dozing in deck-chair's gentle curve,
Through half-closed eyes I watched the cricket,
Knowing the sporting press would say
'Perks bowled well on a perfect wicket'.

Fierce mid-day sun upon the ground,
Through heat-haze came the hollow sound
Of wary bat on ball, to pound
The devil from it, quell its bound.

Sunburned fieldsmen, flannelled cream
Seemed, though urgent, scarce alive,
Swooped, like swallows of a dream
On skimming fly, the hard-hit drive.

Beyond the score-box, through the trees
Gleamed Severn, blue and wide,
Where oarsmen feathered with polished ease
And passed in gentle glide.

The back-cloth, setting off the setting,
Peter's Cathedral soared
Rich of shade and fine of fretting
Like cut and painted board.

To the cathedral, close for shelter
Huddled houses, bent and slim,
Some tall, some short, all helter-skelter,
Like a sky-line drawn for Grimm.

This the fanciful engraver might
In his creative dream have seen,
Here, framed by summer's glaring light,
Grey stone, majestic over green.

Closer, the bowler's arm swept down,
The ball swung, pitched and darted,
Stump and bail flashed and flew;
The batsman pensively departed.

Like rattle of dry seeds in pods,
The warm crowd faintly clapped,
The boys who came to watch their gods,
The tired old men who napped.

The members sat in their strong deck-chairs
And sometimes glanced at the play,
They smoked, and talked of stocks and shares,
And the bar stayed open all day.

JOHN ARLOTT

STAFFORDSHIRE

Tettenhall to Wellington
(1757)

Prepared to start about the noon of day,
I thro' delightful *Tet'nal* take my way;
Where, from the bank, the stranger first espies,
In ample prospect, *Wolverhampton* rise.
A thriving town, for arts *Vulcanian* fam'd,
And from its foundress, good *Walfrune*[1], nam'd.
Hence through the *Wergs* I pass, and view the seat,[2]
Whose master won new greatness from retreat:
Exchanging busy crowds and empty show
For the true joys that from religion flow.
Musing, alone, I travell'd slowly on,
And came to *Shiffnal* with the setting sun.
With morn's returning light my course renew'd,
Of *Briggs* and *Anstey* the fair seats I view'd.

[1] Wife to the Duke of Northampton, founded the town, anno, 996.
[2] Wrottesley, the seat of the Rev. Sir Richard Wrottesley, Bart.

But now the welkin sable clouds deform,
And driz'ling mists prognosticate a storm.
Among rude coal-mines in a miry way,
I feel the fury of a winter's day:
Howl the fierce winds, in floods descends the rain,
And sudden lakes o'erflow the dreary plain:
Devious to *Wellington* my steps I bent,
And o'er a glass th' inclement ev'ning spent.

WILLIAM VERNON, *A Journey into Wales*

The Angler's Wish
(Shallowford)

I in these flowry Meades wo'd be:
These Christal streams should solace me;
To whose harmonious bubling noise,
I with my Angle wo'd rejoice,
Sit here and see the *Turtle-dove*,
Court his chaste Mate to acts of love,
Or on that bank feel the West wind
Breathe health and plenty, please my mind
To see sweet dew-drops kisse these flowers,
And then washt off by *April*-showers:
Here hear my *Clora* sing a song,
There see a Black-bird feed her young,
Or a *Leverock* build her nest;
Here give my weary spirits rest,
And raise my low-pitcht thoughts above
Earth, or what poor mortals love:
    Thus free from *Law-suits*, and the noise
    Of Princes Courts I wo'd rejoice.

Or with my *Bryan*, and a book,
Loyter long dayes near *Shawford-brook*;
There sit by him, and eat my meat,
There see the sun both rise and set:
There bid good morning to next day,
There meditate my time away:
    And angle on, and beg to have
    A quiet passage to a welcome grave.

IZAAK WALTON

Adbaston

Dear, native ADBASTON!—remote from care,
Thy tranquil fields would mitigate despair;
In thy sweet vales a balsam I could find,
When nought on earth could calm my troubled mind.
Each wild, each trifling object that surrounds,
Each lonely stile in thy sequester'd grounds;—
The ancient elm that shades the cottage door
The distant grange, the dusky, rush-grown moor,
The echoing wood, that joins the neighb'ring farm,—
Each hath, by turns, the magic pow'r to charm.
And yet, while thus the landscape I pursue,
What sad sensations pierce my heart to view
Such change in ev'ry once frequented scene,
That many a trace is fled of what has been.
Remember'd trees, on which I've carv'd my name,
Or hung the trophy of some boyish fame,
Are seen no more;—the axe, with well-aimed blow,
Long since has laid their leafy honours low;
Whilst others rise upon the tufted lawn,
Which then were only in their sapling dawn.

C. B. ASH, *Adbaston*

The River Manifold

(Which takes an underground course between Wetton Mill and Ilam Hall in
Dovedale)

What found ye wanting here?
Ye languished, ebbing waters! Round you lies
Earth's beauty as it broke on Adam's eyes;
Music ye added fit for an angel's ear,
Yet as in thirsting sands ye waste, or desert drear.

As though in sick disdain
Of all that gave your strength and beauty birth,
And fed your song, ye plunge in caverned earth,
Threading the darkness like a molten vein,
Till, with a vast upheave, ye front the stars again.

Where Ilam rears her towers,
Ringed round and shadowed deep with ashen grove,
As when the courtly Congreve loved to rove,
And tune his wit where ye made bright his bowers,
Ere fashion's smooth deceits laid waste his youthful powers.

Thou dost but do as they,
Fair stream! who, shrinking from encounter rude,
Steep their embittered souls in solitude,
Till their forbidden music ebbs away,
And brows are swathed in gloom that might have borne the bay.

May these win back, as thou,
The light forsaken and the song forsworn,
That in their age, some grace youth might have sworn
May break like blossom on a sullen bough,
That long has idly hung, and seems all sapless now.

THOMAS THORNELY

DERBYSHIRE *Mining Places*

Beauty never visits mining places,
For the yellow smoke taints the summer air.
Despair graves lines on the dwellers' faces,
My fellows' faces, for my fellows live there.

There by the wayside dusty weed drowses,
The darnel and dock and starwort run rife;
Gaunt folk stare from the doors of the houses,
Folk with no share in the beauty of life.

There on slag-heaps, where no bird poises,
My fellows' wan children tumble and climb,
Playing in the dust, making shrill noises,
Sweet human flowers that will fade ere their time.

Playing in the slag with thin white faces,
Where headstocks loom by the railway lines—
Round-eyed children cheated of life's graces—
My fellows' children, born for the mines.

FREDERICK C. BODEN

The Valley of the Dove

How pleasant it is, wandered from all ways,
And strength decaying; at length, to look down,
On Doves fair-streaming Dale: to view from hence,
Beneath, lie her green pleasant meadows; where
These wayworn joints, the long day forth, may rest;
And be refreshed from aching weariness!
   There may I drink my fill, and lie in the Sun;
And listen to Doves waters' trickling sound,
Twixt his two banks, mongst his grey pebble-stones.
   This brow is steep, and the descending path
Painful and grievous, to the sore of foot;
Full all of rolling stones. Whilst I my breath
Withhold, and feeling sense; the worst is past:
I am come, from cliffy brink, to tufted grass.
   Stands one a-fishing yonder, in Doves stream,
(That shines thus shire and trembles in the Sun;)
He whips for trout, else I am overseen.
Nigher to look on, worthy man this seems.
I'll ask my way of him: Goodmorrow, Sir!
PISCATOR. The like to you again.

*   *   *

Your words have set me thinking, whilst we speak;
Of my dear Master Izaak Waltons friends.
   See, his *Cómpleat Angler*! bound in purple velvet;
Lies (so I esteem it precious) on my cloak.
I'd sooner lose some ruby, if I had it,
Than this small volume, which I con by heart;
And bear it always about with me. In it
Parfume of heaven is, and souls holy thought.
   I joy, whilst sometimes I, for Sun and weather,
Must sit and wait, therein to pore and look;
Still studying to conform my spirit to his;
Which was conformed to Christ and His first saints.
   With him, I joy to hear chant of all birds;
And this small teeming wavering infinite hum,
In the sheen air, and thymy web of grass;
Of silver-winged flies, and derne creeping things:
And children of Lifes Breath, on my Doves brinks.

And rustling gurgling never-ending song,
Of these shire sliding waters; wherein, like
Our fleeting lives, frail bubbles dance along.
And one day hope: if Heaven some ray of light
Will stream into my barren breast, to set,
To music. Oft methinks, in these fair meads;
My master Walton turned his thoughts to verse.
　　Now by this Sun; which is mine only clock,
When I go fishing, and our shadows cast
Upon the path; since Noonday, an hour is past.
And with good luck, I've filled my creel already,
With trouts enough. I'll prove but one more cast,
Of fishermans art: for know, that 't is an art;
(And meet for only very honest men,
As Father Walton says) . . . With this gnat-fly,
You've seen me make, the dubbing of bears dun,
The whiles we talked; although it fits not boast:
(A very killing fly, as Cotton saith).
　　Under this root, good graylings use to lie:
And you shall see me, I hope, take presently
A brace or leash; which you and I together
Will eat, on this fresh brink, in fellowship.

CHARLES DOUGHTY, *The Clouds*

Bolsover Castle

William Cavendish, the first Duke of Newcastle, entertained Charles I at Bolsover
Castle in 1634 with a performance of Ben Jonson's Masque of *Love's Welcome*, for
which Inigo Jones designed an elaborate stage setting.

Joining up the Castle with the Riding School
Along the other cliff face runs the Banquet Hall
With the long windowed chambers built to house the King
That day he rode from Welbeck here to see the play.
The lawn was pitched with palaces from overnight
With doors and windows focussed for the strongest light;
Out of those balconies toward the hall
Inigo leaned to get their angle right,
Calling out his orders as he came down the ladder,
While Ben Jonson stood among these walls and listened,
For his were the words that echoed out from every side:

294

That day the palaces were peopled by live shades
Called out from their myrtle groves to talk with Mosca,
For while they floated on a cloud or rolled in chariots,
Mosca and Corvino fixed their stratagems in shadow.
But night came and never were those windows lighted,
Those black and open doorways showed no life within,
Although the glittering mullions of the Banquet Hall
Glowed across the darkness like so many pools of fire
And loud out of the fire's heart did the music ring,
While the feasters, tired and blinded by the torches,
Looked out through the windows to the ghosts outside,
For the palaces, like figures made from smoke, were fading,
Fast did they die until by morning light
The lawns lay bare again but branded as by fire.

When the sun climbed high enough to see into the garden
The palaces were down and Charles had ridden far away,
The towers still were lived in, as the trees are full of doves,
But the Banquet Hall has never shone with lights again,
Empty are its windows of the glass that glowed like water
And long dead the torches that turned the glass to flame,
While the rooms stand roofless for the rain to spoil them
Each time those glancing armies rattle out from Heaven.
The long and weedgrown terrace cracks and falls on the hillside,
That once the steps led down to from the Banquet Hall
As though you left a cloud and climbed upon a steady ship,
But now is it wrecked among the gnarled trees
Soon to sink deep down to where its loose stones roll.
Through the windows of the Banquet Hall
You see the level lawns before you reach them walking round,
Down along the terrace past the riven walls,
And when you reach the corner you can see the Castle keep,
Soft is the grass without the print of horsehoofs
And empty the caves of shade below the deep leaved trees.
But Venus, down the alleys, still stands upon her shell,
She glitters through the hornbeams like those fruit boughs heaped with
    snow
And, higher than the apples, do the lofty trees stand back
To let her lover down and never tear his cloud with leaves;
Loud do the boughs ring, but not with lutes,
For a deep and rumbling murmur sounds among their very branches.

SACHEVERELL SITWELL, *Bolsover Castle*

Poole's Hole

At a high *Mountains* foot, whose lofty Crest
O're-looks the Marshy Prospect of the *West*;
Under its Base there is an *Overture*
Which Summer Weeds do render so Obscure,
The careless *Traveller* may pass, and ne're
Discover, or suspect an entry there:
But such a one there is, as we might well
Think it the *Crypto-porticus* of *Hell*,
Had we not been instructed that the Gate,
Which to Destruction leads is nothing straight.

Through a blind door (which some poor Woman there
Still keeps the Key of, that it may keep her)
Men bowing low take leave of days fair light,
To crowd themselves into the Womb of Night,
Through such a low and narrow pass, that it
For *Badgers, Wolves,* and *Foxes* seems more fit;
Or for the less sorts of Chaces, then
T'admit the Statures, and the Bulks of men,
Could it to reason any way appear
That men could find out any business there.
But having fifteen paces crept or more,
Through pointed stones and dirt upon all four,
The gloomy *Grotto* lets men upright rise
Although they were six times *Goliah's* size.
There, looking upward, your astonish'd sight
Beholds the glory of the sparkling light
Th' enamel'd *Roof* darts round about the place,
With so subduing but ingrateful Rays
As to put out the lights, by which alone
They receive lustre, that before had none,
And must to darkness be resign'd when they are gone.
But here a roaring *Torrent* bids you stand,
Forcing you to climb a Rock on the right hand,
Which hanging, pent-house-like, does overlook
The dreadful Channel of the rapid Brook,
So deep, and black, the very thought does make
My brains turn giddy, and my eye-balls ake.
Over this dangerous *Precipice* you crawl,
Lost if you slip, for if you slip you fall;

But whither, faith 'tis no great matter, when
Y'are sure ne'er to be seen alive agen.
Propt round with *Peasants*, on you trembling go,
Whilst, every step you take, your *Guides* do show
In the uneven Rock the uncouth shapes
Of *Men*, of *Lions, Horses, Dogs* and *Apes*:
But so resembling each the fancied shape,
The *Man* might be the *Horse*, the *Dog* the *Ape*.
And straight just in your way a Stone appears
Which the resemblance of a *Hay-cock* bears
Some four foot high, and beyond that a less
Of the same Figure; which do still increase
In height, and bulk, by a continual drop,
Which upon each distilling from the top,
And falling still exactly on the Crown,
There break themselves to mists, which trickling down
Crust into stone, and, (but with leasure) swell
The sides, and still advance the Miracle.
So that in time, they would be Tall enough,
If there were need, to prop the hanging roof,
Did not sometimes the curious Visitors,
To steal a Treasure is not justly theirs,
Break off much more at one injurious Blow
Than can again in many *Ages* grow.

CHARLES COTTON, *Wonders of the Peake*

NOTTINGHAMSHIRE

Nottingham

There wee crost *Trent*, and on the other side
Prayd to Saint *Andrew*: and up hill wee ride.
Where wee observ'd the cunning men, like moles,
Dwell not in howses, but were earth't in holes;
So they did not builde upwards, but digg thorough,
As *Hermitts* caves, or *Conyes* do their Borough:
Great Underminers sure as any where;
Tis thought the Powder-Traitors practis'd there.
Would you not thinke the men stood on their heads,
When Gardens cover Howses there, like Leades;

And on the Chimneyes-topp the Mayd may know
Whether her Pottage boyle or not, below;
There case in Hearbes, and Salt, or Bread: her Meate
Contented rather with the Smoake then Heate?
This was the Rocky-Parish; higher stood
Churches and Howses, Buildings stone and wood.

RICHARD CORBET, *Iter Boreale*

Approach to Newark

The ground wee tread is Meddow, fertile Land,
New trimm'd, and leveld by the Mowers hand,
Above it grew a Rocke, rude, steepe and high,
Which claimes a kind of Rev'rence from the Eye:
Betwixt them both there slides a lively Streame,
Not loud, but swift: *Meander* was a Theame
Crooked and rough, but had those Poets seene
Straight-even *Trent*, it had immortall beene;
This side the open Plaine admits the Sunne
To halfe the River which did open runne;
The other halfe ranne Clouds, where the curld wood
With his exalted head threatned the Flood.

RICHARD CORBET, *Iter Boreale*

Nottingham

Thence to Nottingham where rovers,
High-way riders, Sherwood drovers,
Like old Robin-Hood, and Scarlet,
Or like Little John, his varlet;
Here and there they show them doughty,
In Cells and Woods to get their booty.

RICHARD BRAITHWAIT, *Barnabees Journall,
His Northerne Journey, First Part*

Clifton Grove

And oh! how sweet this walk o'erhung with wood,
That winds the margin of the solemn flood!
What rural objects steal upon the sight!
What rising views prolong the calm delight!
The brooklet branching from the silver Trent,
The whispering birch by every zephyr bent,
The woody island, and the naked mead,
The lowly hut half hid in groves of reed,
The rural wicket, and the rural stile,
And frequent interspersed, the woodman's pile.
Above, below, where'er I turn my eyes,
Rocks, waters, woods, in grand succession rise.
High up the cliffs the varied groves ascend,
And mournful larches o'er the wave impend.

HENRY KIRKE WHITE, *Clifton Grove*

LEICESTERSHIRE

Husbandry and the Chase

Each in its turn: can any spot of ground,
Tho' we search Albion through, more rich be found
Than what Leicestria's fertile realms afford,
With cattle, corn, and herbage amply stor'd?

'Twere most ungenerous here, and most unfit,
Thy commendation, Bakewell, to omit,
Whose judgement, skill and well-digested thought
Our cattle's breed have to perfection brought.

Had Dyer at this later period liv'd,
What praises had our ample fleece receiv'd!
Whose worth let Halifax and Leeds proclaim,
And love the country whence the treasure came.

Ye sons of Nimrod, eager for the sport,
Here to your aged master pay your court;
The science of the Chase, by Meynell taught,
Its pleasures here enjoy, with health unbought.

W. P. TAYLOR, *Leicestershire*

Lutterworth

Our next dayes stage was *Lutterworth*, a Towne
Not willing to be noted or sett downe
By any Traveller; for, when w'had bin
Through at both ends, wee could not finde an Inne.

RICHARD CORBET, *Iter Boreale*

RUTLAND   *Rutland*

Love not thy selfe the lesse, although the least thou art,
What thou in greatnesse wantst, wise Nature doth impart
In goodnesse of thy soyle; and more delicious mould,
Survaying all this Isle, the Sunne did nere behold.
Bring forth that *British* Vale, and be it ne'er so rare,
But *Catmus* with that Vale, for richnesse shall compare:
What Forrest-Nymph is found, how brave so ere she be,
But *Lyfield* shewes her selfe as brave a Nymph as shee?
What River ever rose from Banke, or swelling Hill,
Then *Rutlands* wandring *Wash*, a delicater Rill?
Small Shire that can produce to thy proportion good,
One Vale of speciall name, one Forrest, and one Flood.
O *Catmus*, thou faire Vale, come on in Grasse and Corne,
That *Bever* ne'r be sayd thy sister-hood to scorne,
And let thy *Ocham* boast, to have no little grace,
That her the pleased Fates, did in thy bosome place,
And *Lyfield*, as thou art a Forrest, live so free,
That every Forrest-Nymph may praise the sports in thee.
And downe to *Wellands* course, O *Wash*, runne ever cleere,
To honour, and to be much honoured by this Shire.

MICHAEL DRAYTON, *Polyolbion*

ACKNOWLEDGEMENTS

The editor and publishers wish to thank all those who permitted the reproduction of the copyrighted poems herein. In particular:–

Sidgwick & Jackson Ltd for 'Walsham-le-Willows' by Claude Colleer Abbott from *Miss Bedell and Other Poems*

Anthony Sheil Associates Ltd for 'Return to Cardiff' by Dannie Abse

Dr David Bone for 'April in Holderness' and 'Humberside' by the late J. Redwood Anderson

John Arlott for his poems 'Brighton', 'Southampton' and 'Cricket at Worcester' and for 'Basingstoke' and 'Isle of Wight' by Leslie Thomas

Gerald Duckworth & Co Ltd for 'The South Country' by Hilaire Belloc from *Sonnets and Verse*

John Murray (Publishers) Ltd for 'May-Day Song for North Oxford', 'Tregardock', 'Trebetherick', 'Business Girls', 'Upper Lambourne', 'Croydon' and 'Blackfriars' by John Betjeman from his *Collected Poems*

Mrs Nicolete Gray and The Society of Authors on behalf of the Laurence Binyon Estate for 'Oxfordshire' and 'Narcissus' by Laurence Binyon

A. D. Peters & Co Ltd for 'Village Sketch' and 'At Rugmer' by Edmund Blunden

J. M. Dent & Sons Ltd for 'Mining Places' by F. C. Boden from *Out of the Coalfields*

A. D. Peters & Co Ltd for 'The Moorland Way' by Ivor Brown

Thomas Nelson & Sons Ltd for 'Hawarth in May' and 'Vale' (extract) by Wilfred Rowland Childe from his *Selected Poems* (1936)

The Estate of Richard Church for 'Archaeology' by Richard Church from his *Collected Poems*

Century Hutchinson Ltd for 'The Coast: Norfolk' from *Collected Poems* by Frances Cornford (Cresset Press)

R. N. Currey for his poem 'Reconquest' from *Tiresias and Other Poems* (OUP 1940)

Carcanet Press Ltd for 'Barnsley and District' by Donald Davie from *Collected Poems 1970–1983*

Jonathan Cape Ltd for 'The Sleepers' by W. H. Davies from his *Collected Poems*

Macmillan, London and Basingstoke, for 'Rugby to Peterborough' and

'Living in the Midlands' from *Mournful Numbers* by Colin Ellis

Pat Flower for 'The Forest of Dean' by Robin Flower from *Poems and Translations*

Macmillan, London and Basingstoke, for 'The Cheviot', 'Northumberland' and 'The Shepherd' from *Collected Poems 1905–1925* by W. W. Gibson

Patrick Hamilton for 'The Rectory Remembered' and the epigram 'On the Albert Memorial' by G. Rostrevor Hamilton

P. W. H. Harvey for 'In Flanders' by F. W. Harvey

Jonathan Cape Ltd for a poem 'Ground Defence' (here entitled 'Tilbury Docks'), from *SOS Ludlow* by Christopher Hassall

Unwin Hyman Ltd for 'Corfe Castle' from *Ha! Ha! Among the Trumpets* and 'The Rhondda' from *Raider's Dawn* by Alun Lewis

Sidgwick & Jackson Ltd for 'The Devourers' by Rose Macaulay

Faber & Faber Ltd for 'Birmingham' by Louis MacNeice from *Collected Poems* by Louis MacNeice

The Society of Authors as the literary representative of the Estate of John Masefield for 'Lollingdon Downs' (extract) from *Collected Poems of John Masefield*

Phoebe Hesketh for two poems by Herbert Palmer

Century Hutchinson Ltd for 'Romford Market' by Ruth Pitter from *Poems 1926–66* (Cresset Press)

Faber & Faber Ltd for 'Langdale: Nightfall January 4th' by Michael Roberts from *Collected Poems*

A. L. Rowse for 'April Landscape'

Curtis Brown Ltd, London on behalf of the author's estate for 'Beechwoods at Knole', 'Penn-y-Pass', 'Black Tarn' and lines from 'The Land' by Vita Sackville-West

Macmillan, London and Basingstoke, for 'In the Dim City' from *Collected Poems* by A. L. Salmon

George Sassoon for 'View of Old Exeter' and 'Sheldonian Soliloquy' by Siegfried Sassoon

Macmillan, London and Basingstoke, for 'On Holmbury Hill' from *Collected Poems 1912–32* by Edward Shanks

David Higham Associates Ltd for 'Bolsover Castle' and 'Brighton Pier' from *Collected Poems* by Sacheverell Sitwell (Gerald Duckworth & Co Ltd)

James MacGibbon, executor, for 'The River Humber' by Stevie Smith from *The Collected Poems of Stevie Smith* (Allen Lane)

Macmillan, London and Basingstoke, for 'Stonehenge' and 'Rivers' (an extract) from *Collected Poems* by Sir John Squire

ACKNOWLEDGEMENTS

David Higham Associates Ltd for 'Fern Hill' by Dylan Thomas from *Collected Poems* (J. M. Dent & Sons Ltd)

Grafton Books, a division of the Collins Publishing Group, for the poem 'Welsh Landscape' by R. S. Thomas from *Song at the Year's Turning*

Chatto & Windus and The Hogarth Press for 'Glaramara' by R. C. Trevelyan

Christopher Davies Publishers Ltd for 'Welcome to Wales' by John Tripp from *Province of Belief*

The Bodley Head for 'Chough' from *Poems* by Rex Warner

Ann Wolfe for 'The Tramps' from *Kensington Gardens* by Humbert Wolfe

Carcanet Press Ltd for 'Cockermouth' by David Wright from *To the Gods the Shades*

Martin Secker & Warburg Ltd for 'Beaulieu River', 'Wiltshire Downs', 'In Avebury Circle', 'The Thunderstorm' and 'Gloucestershire' from *The Poetical Works* by Andrew Young

INDEX

OF POETS WHOSE WORK IS INCLUDED IN THIS VOLUME

INDEX OF PRINCIPAL PLACES

No attempt has been made in this Index to include place-names incidentally mentioned in the text of the poems